Don—
Hope you enjoy
the book. It's
a sports fans treat.

Steve Prent

THE GREAT BOOK OF
LOS ANGELES SPORTS LISTS

THE GREAT BOOK OF LOS ANGELES SPORTS LISTS

STEVE HARTMAN AND
MATT "MONEY" SMITH

RUNNING PRESS
PHILADELPHIA · LONDON

9 8 7 6 5 4 3 2 1
Digit on the right indicates the number of this printing
Library of Congress Control Number: 2008926966

ISBN 978-0-7624-3520-3

Cover and Interior Designed by Matthew Goodman
Cover photograph by Varon Panganiban
Edited by Greg Jones

Running Press Book Publishers
2300 Chestnut Street
Philadelphia, PA 19103-4371

Visit us on the web!
www.runningpress.com

CONTENTS

Dedication

Steve Hartman dedicates this book to his family:
Denise, Garrett, Drake and Paris

Matt "Money" Smith, unlike Steve, doesn't need a book to show his family he loves them. Instead, he dedicates this to all the idiots (like himself) who wasted their employers' money arguing about sports during work hours.

Acknowledgements

Us. That's right, us. We did it all—with the help of Al Gore's invention (the Internet) and a few media guides.

Matt's friend Bob helped a little bit with the hockey, and Jim Hill had to put up with Hartman writing his portion of the book during his *Sports Central* TV appearances on the weekend.

We would also like to thank everyone who helped out with a "guest" list:

Jeanie Buss, Kobe Bryant, Luc Robitaille, James Worthy, Erik Karros, Eric Dickerson, Jim Hill, Jimmy Kimmel, and his Cousin Sal.

A big thank-you to Greg Jones at Running Press for asking us to put this book together; we certainly enjoyed the process.

"This f***ing job is not that f***ing easy!"

To borrow one of the more famous Tommy Lasorda quotes, we present to you *The Great Book of Los Angeles Sports Lists*. Some of the questions we answer have been kicked around for years, decades, hell, even lifetimes. Who are the 10 greatest Lakers? What were the worst trades in Dodgers history? How in the world did the Angels manage to win the 2002 World Series?

Other lists cover a breadth of topics you might have never considered, but will see you become better informed and a more complete person for now knowing: What college has the best mascot?; Which 10 YouTube videos do you have to see?; Where are the best places to watch your favorite team should the spouse or kids take over the remote for a night? And so on. . . .

It's not only a ranking system of sorts, but a guide to your Los Angeles sports life. We look back in history (remember the NFL?) and celebrate (and chastise) the great (and not so great) moments our favorite teams provided us over the years. College and professional, preps and over-the-hill players that had no business sticking around—they're all in the pages ahead.

You want to relive some of the best moments in your favorite teams' history because these guys nowadays just don't get it (we've got those too). And while one of us thinks he knows it all and can recite it from memory, the other was able to convince him that we actually have a few guys who like us and might have a better perspective on the topic than we do. And so we asked for and received generous contributions of original lists from the likes of Kobe Bryant, Luc Robitaille, James Worthy, Jimmy Kimmel, and more to provide some great stories and information you readers otherwise wouldn't have been privy to.

The ridiculous and sublime also make an appearance in the form of nicknames that should have been given, 10 songs we never need to hear again while trying to watch a game, 10 players Cousin Sal thinks he can beat up, and others.

Because this is Southern California, included are the 10 best skateboarders and 10 best local punk bands. Because this is a book that revolves around sports, we have our all-time best players who wore the numbers 1 through 10, and only one list relating to soccer—"Why the David Beckham Experiment Failed." We even took on the reasons why the rest of the nation insists we're bad fans, and why that's simply not the case.

And at the end of the book, we give you the *coup de grace*—the All-Time Top 100 Athletes in Los Angeles Sports history. Don't agree with us? Write your own book!

Depending on the level of your sports knowledge, you will either find this book a great source of information, a great trip down memory lane, or a great reason to insist "these guys don't know what the heck they're talking about."

Have at it.

—Steve Hartman & Matt "Money" Smith

If there's one thing that upsets those who love sports in Southern California, it's the tag of being bad fans. Showing up late, leaving early to beat traffic—we hear it all. As a person who's traveled up and down, back and forth across this great country, I'm here to say it's the same in every city. Still, some fans are better than others. Some are more apt to stick around through the lean years instead of just hanging out with the celebrities who get face time during winning streaks. Below are the best of the best, those who earned their spot by witnessing some bad play on the way to the good.

10. Clippers. Some might suggest they're the best fans considering there's never been any sense of hope when it comes to this franchise. I have a few issues with the so-called "Clippers Nation." First of all, give the Raiders back their nickname and come up with something original. Second, I get the sense some Clipper fans are fans just to be contrarians. They don't really like the Clippers, they simply want to rebel against the Lakers. Finally, the Clippers have no home. They play in an arena that showcases the Lakers' retired numbers and championship banners, and the seats are colored Lakers' purple. No self-respecting fan should have to put up with that.

9. Chargers. Since no professional football team exists in the greater Los Angeles area, the Chargers make the list thanks to Orange County having adopted them as one of their own. You have to credit these fans too, since it's great dedication to head 90 miles south to help sell out the Q and avoid the blackouts that used to be the norm before the Orange Curtain started. Plus, this new support has created a spirited rivalry with the more Raider-friendly Los Angeles County.

8. Ducks. A good 5,000 are diehard, but the rest are rich families that often skip games and don't really understand what's going on. The sad part is, Orange County is more of a hockey hotbed than L.A. County, but all the kids grew up on the Kings after their arrival in 1967, and loathed the creation of Disney's Mighty Ducks. With new ownership, the best general manager in the league, and the first West Coast Stanley Cup championship, they are making strides toward respectability.

7. Angels. Prior to the team's 2002 World Series win, very few people rolled out to the "Big A" to catch Angels games. A few seasons between 1979 and 1986 saw Anaheim become a good spot for baseball as Gene Autry's teams consistently made runs at the postseason and occasionally appeared to be World Series contenders, but a 15-year drought erased all the hope that had been built with the community. Enter Mike Scioscia and one magical run and the rest is history. Since their 2002 title, the team's attendance typically ranks among the best in the league and their fans have developed a reputation for showing a good understanding of the game. All of it adds up to making the Angels the official squad of Orange County.

6. UCLA. The Bruins got knocked down a bit thanks to the lack of support for their basketball team the past couple seasons. Despite being arguably the most successful program that's not the University of Florida the last three years, their regular season contests remain sparsely attended. The Rose Bowl will start to fill up with the arrival of Rick Neuheisal, but as of press time there's a considerable gap between the support this public university gets compared to the private school about 15 miles east on the Santa Monica Freeway.

5. USC. While they may look like the top team in town thanks to Pete Carroll putting together quite possibly the most dominating stretch of college football in the television era, it wasn't always there. No question the alumni are dedicated followers of their beloved Trojans. But I've been in this town long enough to see the Coliseum in the early 1990s, when USC's Pac 10 contests were no better than half full. That said, you have to acknowledge what Mike Garrett has done as athletic director to help make the Trojans the city's premier football team in the absence of an NFL franchise.

4. Raiders. If they weren't so intolerable I just might have made them No. 1. The Raiders may have left Los Angeles 14 years ago, but driving behind one Chevy pickup after another with a Raiders logo in the back window, and walking through all of the Tim Brown jerseys at the L.A. County Fair every September, you'd swear they were still playing at the Coliseum on Sundays. "The Raider Nation" is undoubtedly alive and well here in Southern California, and if the team returned tomorrow it's likely home games would be just as well attended—and just as dangerous—as they were in 1994.

3. Dodgers. Every season Dodgers Stadium hosts nearly four million fans, and that's without having won a playoff series since 1988. The team's fans are almost loyal to a fault—players like Alex Cora and Todd Hollandsworth are hailed as gods around town just because they wear Dodger Blue. Tommy Lasorda still remains one of the most popular Angelinos around town. Anyone that dares do harm to the franchise—say, Paul DePodesta—better make sure to avoid Southern California at all costs. And there's no denying that with all those "Doyers" shirts, the Latino community has also embraced this as their team. I'm guessing "Fernando Mania" played just a small part in that.

2. Lakers. It's unquestionably the most popular franchise in Southern California. When the Lakers are going well the city stops, and it's been that way from the start. Jerry West and Elgin Baylor were followed closely by the arrival of Wilt Chamberlain, which led to Kareem Abdul-Jabbar's return to the place where he experienced college glory, followed by the Showtime Lakers of the 1980s, when nary a seat was to be found to any game—be it the playoffs, regular season, or an exhibition. The Lakers currently feature one of the game's greatest attractions in Kobe Bryant, and have become bigger than just Southern California. The Lakers now play to sold-out exhibition crowds from San Diego to Fresno, Bakersfield to Las Vegas. Fans are more knowledgeable than any local following, a credit to legendary announcer Chick Hearn, who educated fans prior to his passing earlier this decade.

1. Kings. Really? A hockey franchise in Southern California has the best fans? When Jack Kent Cooke (who owned both the Lakers and Kings) asked why television ratings were so dismal, rumor has it Chick Hearn answered, "Because they're all here at the game." Sellouts are the norm for this mostly average NHL franchise. I would put their knowledge of the Kings, the team's history and the league as a whole up against any fan base in town. The Kings are an attraction no matter their record, and even though they've been pretty bad lately, once they get rolling, they create emotion in the city that's hard to match. Nobody lives and dies by their franchise like this loyal group.

As a man who once made a living on the road, I found myself in countless conversations with people about the makeup of a "SoCal Fan." Listed below are the reasons most people cited for why we "stink" in comparison to other fans. A lot of these criticisms exist in every major market that hosts a professional sports franchise, but we just happen to be everyone's favorite example.

10. Transplants. Everyone wants to live here. The only people who don't are those who tried to get out here and couldn't, or took a crack at it and failed. Yes, there are plenty of transplants who still hold some reverence for their hometown team, and show up when they roll into town to play the local squad, but in a metro area that's home to 13 million people, I think it's safe to say plenty of them are natives and true to their home teams.

9. Too Cool for School. I must admit, we're not nearly as vociferous as some other cities when it comes to our teams. Some high-rolling fans think it makes them look ridiculous and, with ticket prices being so high and them being the closest to the action, it makes local crowds look subdued. But again, as a man who's been in every arena and stadium in this fine nation, that's pretty much par for the course. Except in Utah—them peoples be crazy.

8. The Bandwagon Effect. True, the Angels had issues getting people to come to the park prior to their 2002 World Series run, but that's never been the case with the Lakers or Dodgers. Those franchises are typically at the top of their respective leagues in attendance every season. Besides, if fans refuse to go to games and pay good money for an inferior product, doesn't that make them a good fan for forcing management to adhere to their wishes to get better?

7. People Trying to Act Relevant. Yes, attractive women will often get a pair of tickets to the game and proceed to do laps around the lower bowl every 10 minutes or so, making sure all the rich dudes in the stands know they're available for some post-game conversation. And you think this is a bad thing?

6. Leaving Early. You got us here. People do leave early to "beat traffic," but if you had an average commute of an hour a day just to go 20 miles, you might also take a few opportunities to avoid the rush.

5. Fashion Show. I guess good fans are the ones who show up in team colors, with their face painted and a giant foam finger on one hand. That's not us. Lakers games might as well be a Sunset Boulevard Club considering how people dress in the lower bowl. But that's a single franchise. Dodgers and USC games aren't that way.

4. The Celebrity Factor. They're celebrities, they can't be fans. Actually, turns out *Us Weekly* or *People* or whatever rag it is that puts out a "Just like us" section shows that, in fact, Jack and Penny Marshall and some other famous people in town are not only fans, but freaks when it comes to their favorite teams.

3. We Lost Two NFL Teams. Great sports towns don't lose franchises, do they? Of course they do. Baltimore lost the Colts, Cleveland lost the Browns, Houston lost the Oilers, and freaking Chicago and St. Louis the Cardinals. So this argument doesn't fly.

2. Arriving Late. You know why people are always late to games? It's because even if they left their house two hours before tip off/first pitch/kickoff, they're still not going to make it on time. Traffic here blows. When Firestone, General Motors, Standard Oil and a grip of other big businesses conspired to squash the Pacific Electric Railway, or the "Red Car" system, we were out of luck and destined to have brutal traffic problems. Thanks guys, thanks a lot.

1. Jealousy. This is pretty simple. We have the best weather, the most beautiful women, and it's god-awful expensive to live here so we must all be rich. People hate us for this. If we have all that going for us then clearly we must be poor supporters of our local teams.

Top 10 Lakers Celebrity Fans

You might hate it, but this is what Dr. Jerry Buss wanted all along: entertainment so compelling that the entertainers must show up. When you watch a Lakers game on television you always get the gratuitous pan of the crowd for glimpses of celebrities. While some are surely there just for camera time, you may not know that others are true fans. Below are 10 celebs that put forth the effort to earn those floor seats come playoff time.

Honorable Mention. Denzel Washington. While Denzel attends a number of games throughout the season and deserves to be placed on this list, why does he have to wear that stupid Yankees cap to every single game? I'm not saying he has to wear a Dodgers lid, but rock a Phillipe's or Fatburger or something—anything but the Yankees.

10. Toby Maguire. I get the sense that since he earned a grip of cash from the *Spiderman* franchise he's spending the money on things he really enjoys. He's always playing poker around town, and in the last two or three seasons has become a fixture on the northeast corner of the court. And to his credit, he's not texting away or talking on the phone, but instead fully invested in the game.

9. Jeffrey Katzenberg. I think he likes the power. I'm guessing if you want a role in a Dreamworks animation film, you best be getting to a Lakers game to kiss Katzenberg's ring. He's at center court, probably the best seats of any celebrity—even Jack—so it's a pretty sweet deal. The one thing that's a bit of a turnoff is the amount of ball washing that goes down with him. Every celeb in the house has to make a pit stop at some point during the game to say "Hello."

8. Glenn Frey. While he may be the most talented name on the list, sadly Frey is the least recognized person when they do the regular celebrity pan shot. Considering I'm at every game every season, I'm thinking they might just want to leave him out of the rotation. I mean it makes you want to punch someone in the face that a guy who sings lead vocal on some of the best Eagles tunes of all time can't get the same enthusiasm as freaking Soulja Boy.

7. Ice Cube. Cube is legit. He's at games against Memphis and Charlotte, as well as the high-profile Western Conference Finals, and don't try to step to Ice Cube's Lakers knowledge because he knows his history. He also typically shows up with family, instead of friends and other celebs, which is an extra bonus.

6. David Arquette. While he might not be the biggest name on the list, he might be one of the biggest fans. Arquette attends nearly every single game and rocks Lakers gear while doing it. He's even part of the cult group, the Bynum Brigade.

5. B Real. The Cypress Hill MC gets bonus points for sitting about five rows behind the south basket and keeping a low profile. No laps around the court to make sure everyone knows he's in attendance, and no elaborate wardrobe to stand out in the crowd. Just mellow, kicking it with his section watching the game.

4. Andy Garcia. As much as I hate his parade through the arena two minutes into the first quarter, while everyone else is already in their seats, I have seen him engaged with the fans and getting fired up about the Lakers. While I may bitch and moan about Denzel's Yankees cap, Garcia's stupid beret looks way worse.

3. The Red Hot Chili Peppers. They get a slot as a group. I mean, they did write a song called "Magic Johnson." But if I had to pick one of the four, I'm going with Flea as the dude who best represents them. He is a Lakers freak—just read his blog at nba.com—and a regular on my post-game call-in show. He's also visibly affected by the way the game is playing out and yells at people in his section to be more vocal. Finally, Flea may be the fans' second favorite when he's shown on the Jumbotron.

2. Dianne Cannon. Cannon sits next to Magic Johnson for every game, and is considered to be part of the "Lakers Family." She was even allowed to party with the players after the 1988 championship. Cannon claims she fell in love with the Lakers when attending a game in the 1970s and Jerry West fell into her lap while chasing a loose ball.

1. Jack. The best way to characterize his fandom is that he reportedly schedules his movie shoots around the team's schedule. At the games, he heckles the opposing players and coaches, referees and anyone not rooting for the Lakers. Remember he and friend Lou Adler didn't just show up and get floor seats—they started at the top of the Fabulous Forum and worked their way down over the years.

With my co-author Steve apt to focus on the negatives, that leaves me with the job to find some uplifting moments in Lakers general manager history. After all, they employed the best front office executive in the game's history, Jerry West, for nearly three decades. Speaking of Mr. Clutch, remember West was drafted by the Minneapolis Lakers, as was Elgin Baylor. Hall of Famer Gail Goodrich was obtained with a territorial pick, allowing teams to forfeit their first round pick to select a player within 50 miles of where the franchise was located. They're not included in this list.

12. 1990: Elden Campbell. Perhaps no player frustrated fans over seven-plus seasons more than Elden Campbell. He'd manage to trip over his own feet in the open court at least once every three games and could follow up a 30-point, 15-rebound night with a six-point, one-board effort. But considering he and Vlade Divac formed a pretty solid 4–5 combo up front and he averaged 13 points, seven rebounds and nearly two blocked shots from 1993 to 1998, you'd have to say he was a decent find at the end of the first round (27th overall), especially since the Pistons took Lance Banks with the pick directly in front of him.

11. 2007: Javaris Crittenton and Marc Gasol. This draft won't be remembered for what the players selected gave the Lakers on the court, rather for what they provided off it. Crittenton and Gasol, chosen 19th and 48th overall, respectively, were traded along with Kwame Brown to bring Marc's older brother, All-Star Pau Gasol, to the Lakers from the Memphis Grizzlies in 2008. Led by a Bryant-Gasol combination, the team went all the way to the NBA Finals that very season.

10. 1994: Eddie Jones. In what became a rather down decade for the Lakers with only one NBA Finals appearance (1991), Eddie Jones, chosen 10th overall, was a cause for excitement. Chants of "ED-eeee" can still be heard from the Forum rafters after a big steal and coast-to-coast finish. This selection was the Lakers' highest in nearly 10 years, and considering Jones went after Eric Montross, Lamond Murray and Sharone Wright, and one pick before Carlos Rogers, this has to be considered another example of Jerry West out-drafting his counterparts.

9. 2005: Andrew Bynum and Ronny Turiaf. Prior to Bynum's recent knee injury, he would have been considered the third best player from this draft, behind Chris Paul and Deron Williams. The Lakers selected him with the 10th overall pick and the three players selected before Bynum—Ike Diogu, Channing Frye and Charlie Villanueva—are no longer on the teams that drafted them. Adding a solid contributor like Ronny Turiaf in the second round (37th overall) was a bonus.

8. 1993: Nick Van Exel. Nick the Quick. Nick Van Excellent. The University of Cincinnati product scared off a number of teams with his "character issues," but West was quick to grab him in the second round (37th overall) and create a flashy backcourt with Eddie Jones. While George Lynch was a pedestrian choice at 12th overall, Nick made the 1993 draft a great one for the Lakers—at least up until his "1–2–3 Cancun!" chant before the Lakers lost the last game of a four-game sweep to Utah in the 1998 playoffs got him shipped out of town.

7. 1989: Vlade Divac. The first-ever foreign player selected by the Lakers, Divac played center unlike anyone else in the NBA at the time. He possessed deft passing skills and wasn't afraid to shoot from long range to stretch defenses. Divac, selected 26th overall, opened the door to the Balkans for many NBA scouts and future draft picks. He also factored into another major draft, which you'll see in a few spots.

6. 1985: A.C. Green. Taken 20 picks after the Clippers selected Benoit Benjamin third overall, Green's a perfect example of West's keen eye for talent. The NBA's "Iron Man" sported the league's best Jheri curl—a close competition with Michael Cage—and led the Lakers in rebounding in six of his eight seasons with the team. In just his second and third seasons, Green was a vital part of the team's back-to-back championships in 1987 and 1988, averaging 11 points and eight rebounds in the playoffs. And don't discount his presence on the first of the Shaq-Kobe title teams in 2000, when he averaged four points and four boards in 18 minutes of action during the playoffs.

5. 1977: Norm Nixon. Nixon, selected with the last pick of the first round, paid immediate dividends for the Lakers. The former Duquesne star averaged 16.3 points and eight assists per game over six seasons with the Lakers, winning two NBA titles. He was known for raising his level of play in the playoffs, including an average of 20 points per game in the 1982 championship run. Adding to Norm's value was the fact he was traded to the Clippers in return for Byron Scott, who went on to help the Lakers to three more titles in the 1980s.

4. 1978: Michael Cooper. Coops is the only Laker not named Magic Johnson or Kareem Abdul-Jabbar to be part of all five of the team's 1980s titles. Coop-a-loop, drafted 60th overall, was a five-time All-Defensive first-team selection, including the Defensive Player of the Year award in 1987. Ask any member of those five title teams and they'll say that without Coops locking up the opposing team's top perimeter scoring threat, the Lakers don't win those championships.

3. 1982: James Worthy. In exchange for trading Don Ford to the Cavs, the Lakers received Cleveland's first pick—which turned out to be first overall—in the 1982 draft. So, just weeks after winning the 1982 title, West had to the choice between adding Dominique Wilkins, Terry Cummings or James Worthy to his championship club. While Wilkins, "The Human Highlight Reel," could have done some serious damage with the Showtime Lakers, it's hard to argue with what James did over his 12-year Hall of Fame career.

2. 1996: Kobe Bryant and Derek Fisher. We'll start with Fisher, the scrappy do-everything point guard who was part of the team's three-peat in the early 2000s. Fisher was selected 24th, one pick after someone named Efthimios Rentzias. As for Bryant, he won three titles alongside Shaquille O'Neal, earned multiple scoring titles, numerous All-NBA first-team selections, numerous All-Defensive first-team selections, and a league Most Valuable Player trophy. Some argue he's the best player of his generation. And to think, the Cavs could have had him at 12 instead of Vitaly Potopenko.

1. 1979: Earvin "Magic" Johnson. This pick was conveyed to the Lakers as compensation for the Jazz signing free agent Gail Goodrich, but the team had to win a coin flip with the Chicago Bulls for the right to draft first overall. That pick turned out to be Earvin "Magic" Johnson, who went on to be the greatest Laker ever. The Bulls, meanwhile, landed David Greenwood out of UCLA, who, let's just say, wasn't as good as Magic. The unconventional point guard—Magic was six-foot-nine and could play any position on the court—won five NBA championships and named finals' MVP three times, won three season MVP trophies, was a 12-time All-Star, and was elected to the Hall of Fame in 2002. But even if it all ended after his first season, Magic would still have a place in every basketball fan's heart. He was awarded the NBA Finals' MVP as a 20-year-old rookie, and his performance in the sixth game of the series, playing center in place of the injured Kareem Abdul-Jabbar, might be the greatest finals moment ever: 42 points, 15 rebounds, seven assists, three steals and a blocked shot.

Note: Perhaps no player in NBA history increased the level of his play in the biggest games quite like "Big Game" James Worthy. That may sound strange for a seven-time All-Star, but Worthy's numbers were always best when the games were the biggest. In fact, his best game ever occurred in the seventh game of the 1988 NBA Finals when his Lakers held off the Pistons for the championship. That day Worthy scored 36 points, grabbed 16 rebounds and added 10 assists. No wonder he is a member of the Hall of Fame and was chosen as one of the 50 greatest players in NBA history. Here is his personal list of the 10 best "big game" players that he either played with or against.

10. Gerald Henderson. I was playing in my first NBA Finals in 1984 against the Celtics and we were about to go up two games to none in Boston when I got my first taste of a "Big Game" play. We had a two-point lead with 18 seconds left when Gerald Henderson stole a pass I made and he scored the tying basket. We lost the game in overtime and lost the series in seven. That one play taught me what it takes to make a big play in a big game.

9. Joe Dumars. He was very much like me—a third wheel on a team with great stars. Like me, he earned a place in the Hall of Fame by playing big when it counted the most. He was the MVP when the Pistons beat us in the 1989 Finals. I hated to guard him because he was such a smart player. As much as I hated some of those Pistons you couldn't hate Dumars because he was a truly nice guy.

8. Dennis Johnson. Believe me, D.J. was the only likeable player on the Celtics at that time. He was so cool when the pressure was on. He won a title in Seattle before he came to Boston and he won two more with the Celtics. Magic Johnson hated playing against him because his defense was relentless. There's no question he belongs in the Hall of Fame. It's a shame he passed away before that day will come.

7. Michael Cooper. "Coop" was my reliever and he was my cushion. He was the most versatile defensive player in the league. Coop could shut down any guard or forward in the league. I know Larry Bird hated when Coop got in the game. When you think of the Lakers in the 1980s you think of Kareem and Magic, but Coop was the only other player to be on all five championships during that run.

6. Kevin McHale. We matched up against each other in three NBA Finals and he actually changed my game for the best. McHale had these long arms and I realized that scoring inside on him would be difficult. He forced me to become a better outside shooter. McHale was also tough to guard because he had so many different shots. That front line of Bird, McHale, and Parish has to be one of the best in the history of the NBA.

5. Larry Bird. Understand this about Bird—he had very little athleticism. He became a great player by outworking everyone else on the court. Sometimes he got away with things because he was a star, but he used that to his advantage. Bird was also one of the underrated trash-talkers in the league. He would whisper things on the court just to get under your skin. There was nothing better than beating a player like Larry Bird.

4. Michael Jordan. I played with Michael at North Carolina and it was his shot that clinched the 1982 national championship. From day one you could tell that he had a certain attitude. You could even say he was arrogant. But he was the one player who could intimidate another team just by his presence on the court. When we lost to the Bulls in the 1991 Finals, Jordan could sense when we lost our confidence after I suffered an injury in the fourth game. No one went for the jugular like Michael Jordan.

3. Dennis Rodman. Some people may be surprised that I have Rodman ahead of players like Jordan and Bird, but I can tell you that there was never a tougher defensive player for me than Rodman. Even when he was a young player with the Pistons his relentless pressure gave me fits. We played Detroit in three straight finals and every time he was on the court I knew I had my work cut out for me. In my opinion, Rodman is one of the most underrated players in NBA history. The guy won five rings and several rebounding titles while being the best defensive player in the league. That's big time.

2. Kareem Abdul-Jabbar. "Cap" was poetry on the court. When I joined the Lakers he had already been a legend for 20 years and he never lost his desire to win championships. That skyhook was the single most unstoppable shot in the NBA. Even when he got older, we still looked to him first when we needed a shot to be made in the clutch. More often than not he delivered.

1. Magic Johnson. What made Magic so great was his refusal to lose. Nobody knew how to win like Magic. Everyone thinks about the great passes and the unforgettable shots but what made Magic the best was his ability to raise everyone's game. I knew I had to be at my best at all times when I shared the floor with Magic. He was tough on all of us and if we failed to measure up he would let us know to no uncertain terms. If I could start a team from scratch and pick one player there's no question I would start that team with Magic Johnson.

When a franchise has nine titles, countless appearances in the NBA finals, and a host of Hall of Fame players, it's safe to say picking out the 10 greatest moments isn't easy. We could have gone with coin flips that led to Magic Johnson or the relocation to Los Angeles, but that makes things more convoluted. So consider this top 10 the greatest moments on the court in Lakers History.

10. April 29, 1970. The Lakers found themselves down two with just seconds left in Game 3 of the NBA finals after Dave DeBusschere hit a jumper to seemingly give the Knicks the victory. But Jerry West took the ensuing inbounds pass and, with Walt Frazier alongside him step-for-step, West connected on a 60-footer like it was a 15-footer from the elbow, sending the game into overtime. The Lakers went on to lose the game and West missed all of his shots in the extra period, but that doesn't take away one of the greatest buzzer-beaters in NBA history.

9. May 13, 2004. It looked to be curtains for the Lakers—not only in this game, but for the team's 2003–2004 season. The defending champion San Antonio Spurs had just watched their MVP, Tim Duncan, connect on an improbable 20-foot fade-away jumper over the outstretched hand of Shaquille O'Neal to take the lead. Only four-tenths of a second remained on the clock, barely enough for an allowed shot attempt. With four sure-fire Hall of Famers on the court—O'Neal, Kobe Bryant, Gary Payton and Karl Malone—the final shot belonged to a role player, scrappy Derek Fisher. Payton in-bounded the ball to Fisher, who caught it midway through his shooting motion and released the ball just before the buzzer sounded. The shot dropped, giving the Lakers a 74–73 victory, and sent the team back to Staples Center with a 3–2 lead in the series.

8. April 22, 2001–June 15, 2001. The Lakers post a 15–1 playoff record on their way to the 2001 NBA championship. In the first round the Lakers faced the same Portland team that extended them to seven games in the Western Conference final the previous season, but had little trouble winning all three games by an average of 14.6 points. Their most bitter rival at the time, the Sacramento Kings, went quietly in the next round, losing the two games they hosted in hostile Arco Arena by a combined 28 points. In the Western Conference finals, the team won the first two games in San Antonio, came back to Staples Center and won Game 3 by 39, and then took Game 4 by 29. It looked like they would go undefeated throughout the playoffs after the team jumped out to a 21–9 lead over Philadelphia in Game 1 of the finals, but the Sixers came back to win in overtime, 107–101. The Lakers went on to win four straight to capture their second consecutive title.

7. January 22, 2006. Few could have imagined a Sunday evening game against the Toronto Raptors at Staples Center as being historic. Lakers television broadcaster Joel Meyers thought so little of the contest he was off calling the Seattle Seahawks and Carolina Panthers NFC championship on Westwood One Radio. But Kobe Bryant played 41:56 of the game's 48 minutes, made 28 of his 46 shots from the field, seven of his 13 3-point attempts, and converted 18 of his 20 free throws to score 81 points. He also had to lead his team to victory as the Lakers were down 14 at half. Kobe outscored the entire Toronto team in the second half, 55–41, a feat Jalen Rose said was unparalleled.

6. November 5, 1971–January 9, 1972. The streak started with a 110–106 win over the Baltimore Bullets, and two months and four days later it finally came to an end with a 120–104 loss to the Milwaukee Bucks. Bill Sharman's team won 33 consecutive games after starting the season 6–3. Some other remarkable numbers from that season: The Lakers finished with a 69–13 record, which stood as the NBA's best until the 1995–1996 Chicago Bulls won 72. The Lakers led the league in scoring (121 points per game), rebounding (56.4 per game), assists (27.2 per game), and point differential (plus 12.3). And the team's 31–7 road record, an .816 winning percentage, still stands as the best in NBA history.

5. April 14, 1962. Elgin Baylor makes history by hanging 61 on the Boston Celtics in Game 5 of the 1962 NBA finals, leading the Lakers to a 126–121 victory. Did I mention he also grabbed 22 rebounds in the game? And remember who he had to deal with to get those numbers—Bill Russell manned the paint for the Celtics and Tom "Satch" Sanders guarded Baylor on the perimeter. After the game Satch was famously quoted saying, "Elgin was just a machine." Baylor's 61 points was surpassed by Michael Jordan's 63 as a postseason record against the Celtics, but it took Jordan two overtimes to hit that number, and it was in the first round of the playoffs, not Game 5 of the finals.

4. June 4, 2000. The largest fourth quarter comeback in NBA playoff history occurred with the Lakers on the brink of losing three consecutive games for the first time all season, and being eliminated from the playoffs. But L.A. went on a 15–0 run to erase the Blazers fourth quarter lead and, with 40 seconds left, Kobe Bryant fed an alley-oop to Shaq for the exclamation point everyone remembers. Kobe finished with 25 points, 11 rebounds, seven assists, and four blocked shots in the 89–84 victory, and the team advanced to the finals in the first season with Phil Jackson at the helm.

3. May 26, 2002. With Sacramento winning two of the first three games in the Western Conference finals, the Lakers found themselves down 20 at the end of the first quarter in Game 4. They cut that lead to 14 going into the half, and then trailed by seven at the start of the fourth quarter. With the exception of being up 2–0 early, the Lakers had never led in the game. But in the fourth quarter, Shaq managed to connect on all six of his free throw attempts, and with just 11 seconds left, Kings center Vlade Divac could only convert one of two from the charity stripe, putting the Lakers down just two. After the in-bounds pass exchanging hands between a couple players, Kobe Bryant found the ball and attacked the rim with 7 seconds left, but missed his floater. Shaq grabbed the offensive board, but missed a bunny with two seconds left. Instead of grabbing the rebound, Divac tapped the ball away from the basket and right into the hands of Robert Horry, who was in position to take—and make—a 3-pointer as time expired for the 100–99 win. The Lakers went on to win Games 6 and 7 and win their third consecutive title.

2. May 16, 1980. It's one thing to lose the NBA's regular season MVP for Game 6 of the NBA Finals in hostile Philadelphia. It's another when that player is Kareem Abdul-Jabbar, who up to that point was dominating the series against the Sixers by averaging nearly 35 points per game. Heading into Game 6 without the services of "Cap," most supposed the series would shift back to Los Angeles for a seventh and deciding game. But coach Paul Westhead chose to start Magic Johnson at center in Kareem's absence, and the precocious rookie did led his team to a 123–107 win, clinching the series and starting a dynasty that would last all decade. Magic's numbers on the night: 42 points, 15 rebounds, seven assists, three steals and one block.

1. June 9, 1987. Our top moment had to be the best of the historic Lakers–Celtics rivalry. In the closing minutes of Game 4 of the NBA Finals, the Boston Garden was rocking after the Celtics took a two-point lead on Larry Bird's 3-pointer from the left corner. On the ensuing possession, Kareem Abdul-Jabbar is fouled, makes his first free throw, but misses the second. Thinking he has the rebound secured, Kevin McHale hears the crowd cheering what appears to be a series-tying victory, only to have Mychal Thompson knock the ball loose and out of bounds off McHale. On the inbounds pass, Michael Cooper finds Magic Johnson, who faces up on McHale, dribbles to the middle of the lane, and, with everyone expecting him to take a jump shot, steals a page out of Kareem's book and puts up what he calls "a junior, junior sky-hook." The ball sails just past McHale's fingertips and in, giving the Lakers a 107–106 victory and a 3–1 series lead. The Lakers eventually won in six games.

When up to 500,000 people in a city as diverse as Los Angeles turn out for a celebration of athletic achievement, there's bound to be plenty of unintentional comedy—or intentional comedy that's so god awful it comes full circle. Following three consecutive NBA championships in the summers of 2000, 2001, and 2002, we were treated to countless examples of exactly that.

10. Slava Medvedenko Steps to the Microphone. We didn't know much about Slava at the start of his career, but over the years fans got used to hearing his name. That didn't work out for Slava in 2001 when he was asked to say something to the crowd instead of just casually soaking in the scene in his black wraparound sunglasses. All he could come up with was about three seconds of a speech that included "Hello Ukraine" in his native language followed by an "I love L.A." To his credit, he put together a good 15 seconds of generic thank you phrases in 2002.

9. Contrived, Pun-Filled Political Comedy. It's a rite of passage. Team wins championship, parade is scheduled, and every city official lines up to speak. In 2001, police chief Bernard Parks took the award for corniest contribution by a politician with his police-themed message. If asked to guess how much time he put into it, I'd go with about nine hours. "Shaquille O'Neal is being charged with assault and battery for countless acts against NBA centers," he said. "Kobe Bryant is being charged for flying without a permit, and the other Lakers, who carry the alias 'The Super Friends,' are accused of breaking and entering—breaking records and entering the new championship era." Whooooo, ding ding ding ding . . . we have a winner.

8. Shaq and Shakespeare. I appreciate the big man quoting *Twelfth Night, or What You Will*, but he failed to build on it. I love that he avoided an overused *Hamlet* or *Romeo and Juliet* quote, and went with, "Some men are born great, some achieve greatness, some have greatness thrust upon them." Had he stuck with a literary theme over the course of his career I might have appreciated it more. For instance, after being traded the summer of 2004, he could have used, "All the world's a stage, and all the men and women merely players. They have their exits and their entrances; And one man in his time plays many parts," but instead he just insulted a couple people and promised a championship.

7. "Have Sex with Me A.C. Green" Signs. Nothing like being mocked for promoting a worthy cause. The NBA's "Iron Man" let it be known that he had never tasted the forbidden fruit of pre-marital sex. On a campaign from campus to campus, high school to high school, A.C. preached the virtues of abstinence. Instead of being celebrated for his maturity and dedication, he was roundly mocked by most in the league and in the media (behind his back, of course). I have to believe the 10–15 people holding the signs thought they were brilliant before leaving the house, only to realize it was an obvious play, replicated by quite a few meretricious females.

6. Mark Madsen's 2001 Speech. Mark Madsen's performance in 2001 was so memorable, it deserves two spots on this list. Although his speech ranks as the lower of the two, you could make the case that Mad Dog's words were just as goofy as his dance. He screamed, "Who let the dogs out? WHO? WHO? WHO? WHO?" and then addressed the large Chicano portion of the crowd with a message in Spanish that essentially translated to "For all our fans, we thank you and tell you next year we'll do it again."

5. Sportscasters Jogging Alongside the Players' Bus. If this reads like I'm taking great pleasure in the misery of local television personalities, it's because I am. You want an interview with a Laker at the parade you're going to have to go above and beyond to lock it up. Much like the cable news field reporter in the middle of a hurricane, these guys were looking to one up each other, and that meant jogging—and occasionally even sprinting—next to a flatbed truck carrying Shaq and Kobe in an effort to keep the microphone in front of the player.

4. Shaq's "Can You Dig It." It's one thing to quote a movie, but it's another to quote one as cool as the 1979 classic, *The Warriors*. When Shaq busted out the quintessential moment from Cyrus' speech to the collection of New York City gangs— "Caaaaaaan yooooooou diiiiiig iiiiiiiiit?" few in the audience had the slightest idea where it came from, but those who did surely appreciated the reference.

3. Mark Madsen Dancing. "The Dance" became a topic on Southern California sports radio—and national shows—for a good week. It's nearly beyond description, but I'm going with part white guy wedding dance floor disco, part jogging in place, and part Stevie Wonder head bobbing. Making the moment all the better was the camera panning from Mad Dog to his teammates, who couldn't contain their laughter. To this day I think it might be Madsen's greatest contribution to the game.

2. Chick's Final Lakers Moment in 2002. After 42 years of calling games and a remarkable streak of 3,338 consecutive broadcasts, not to mention countless "Chickisms" (see page 43), we lost Hearn less than two months after his final official Lakers appearance—presiding over the team's championship parade festivities. As he addressed the crowd at the end he said, "I was thinking during the parade, 'Three-peat is not a bore, but let's go for four.'"

1. Christopher Nance. It's not even close. The former KNBC weatherman was put in the field for parade coverage. When you have 500,000 people crowded into the streets and parking lots of Los Angeles, and 50 different politicians and city officials that want their five minutes of fame, chances are broadcasters are going to have to stretch more than you might like. Luckily for the viewers, that meant a moment on the streets with Nance, who asked in his distinct high-pitched voice, "Where are my peeps at?" followed by a rail-thin, six-foot-five (at least) dude dancing to music that could not be heard by the viewer. Cabbage patch, running man, you name it—he busted out everything in his repertoire, and we're all the better for it.

The 10 Greatest Lakers

It's arguably the most storied franchise in basketball. While the Celtics may have more championships, they were dormant for nearly all of the 1970s, all the 1990s and, until last season, nearly all of this decade. When the Lakers weren't winning titles, at least they had talent, including some of the names below. When deciding the order for this list, I gave extra credit for players who are best defined as Lakers and had their biggest impact here. That means a slight demotion of Wilt, Shaq, and, depending on who you thought should be at the top, Kareem.

10. Chick Hearn. I agonized over Byron Scott, Michael Cooper, Jerry Buss, and a host of other names for this spot and kept coming back to one name: Francis Dale "Chick" Hearn. He called 3,338 consecutive games, and did so in a style that made him the best in the business. You'll see in our 10 greatest "Chickisms" (see page 43) that Chick's contributions to basketball vernacular—from "alley-oop" to "this game is in the refrigerator"—were historic. He made the Lakers as much of a must-listen event as the players made it a must-watch game.

9. Gail Goodrich. He was the leading scorer on the 1971–1972 championship team that won 33 games in a row. The Lakers didn't realize what they had in Goodrich until he left the team and made an impact playing for the Phoenix Suns. After two seasons in the desert, owner Jack Kent Cooke orchestrated Goodrich's return to Los Angeles and coach Bill Sharman allowed his new addition to focus on what he did best—scoring. Goodrich averaged 23 points per game in his second stint with the club, leading the team in scoring four consecutive years.

8. James Worthy. There's a reason his nickname was "Big Game." Worthy's regular season averages of 17.6 points and 5.1 rebounds per game rose to 21 points and 5.2 rebounds per game in the playoffs. He shot above 53 percent from the floor over the course of his first eight seasons in the league, and was a seven-time All-Star. He was named the MVP of the 1988 NBA Finals, an honor he secured with a triple double in the deciding Game 7: 36 points, 16 rebounds, and 10 assists. Magic Johnson called him, "One of the top five players in playoff history."

7. Shaquille O'Neal. His tenure has become one of the most polarizing of any Lakers superstar considering the terms of his departure. Some sided with the Diesel when he expressed the need to leave Los Angeles, others sided with Kobe Bryant and the team's management. No matter how you view Shaq's exit, his impact over the course of eight seasons in L.A. was undeniable. He averaged 27 points and 12 rebounds per game over the regular season, won a regular season MVP in 1999–2000, three NBA titles and three MVP awards in the NBA Finals. He spent the peak of his playing career in a Lakers uniform and became one of the most difficult players to guard in the history of the NBA.

6. Wilt Chamberlain. While they weren't quite as dominant as his tenure in Philadelphia, Chamberlain's five seasons in L.A. were a significant end to his distinguished NBA career. While Wilt's 1969–1970 season was cut short, he averaged 18 points and 20 rebounds over the course of the other four regular seasons and led the NBA in boards each year. He also lifted his game in the playoffs, helping the Lakers to the NBA Finals in his four complete seasons, and to the 1972 title, in which he was named the series' MVP.

5. Elgin Baylor. He is quite possibly the most underrated player in league history, despite being included on the NBA's 50th anniversary team. Baylor started early in Minneapolis, posting ridiculous rookie averages of 25 points and 15 rebounds per game, winning the All-Star game MVP award, and taking Rookie of the Year honors. That was just the start—over the next 11 seasons he posted a 71-point game, a 55-point game, and, in what's considered one of the NBA's greatest playoff performances, he dropped 61 against Boston in Game 5 of the 1962 NBA Finals. He averaged more than 30 points per game in three separate seasons, including in 1961–1962, when he averaged 38 points, 19 rebounds, and five assists. You could say he was like Kobe and Michael Jordan before those guys came around.

4. Kobe Bryant. Until Kobe wins that elusive fourth NBA title he will always be connected to Shaquille O'Neal. But thanks to Shaq now playing on his fourth NBA team and Kobe having spent his entire career in Los Angeles, I give Bryant the nod. Kobe delivered two of the greatest single game performances in the history of the league, with some even suggesting his 81 point game against the Raptors in 2006 was more impressive than Wilt's 100. One of the best perimeter defenders of his generation, he has been the league's single best defensive player for the last five years. Kobe will also likely be remembered as the greatest player of his generation.

3. Kareem Abdul-Jabbar. You know your franchise has quite the history when you win six NBA MVP awards—the most by any player in NBA history—and can't crack the top two. It's difficult to characterize the legacy of "Cap." He is the NBA's all-time career scoring leader with 38,387 points, a seemingly unbreakable record. He's also fourth in career rebounds and third in career blocked shots. The best measure of his success is helping to lead the Lakers to five NBA championships.

2. Earvin "Magic" Johnson. Dominant centers have come and gone, and great swing men, traditional power forwards, and lightning quick point guards have all made appearances in the purple and gold over the years. But a six-foot-nine, 255-pound force with court vision and a handle made Magic a one of a kind playmaker, and one of the greatest players in league history. The numbers are staggering: 20 points, 7 rebounds, and 11 assists per game, and he shot a remarkable 52 percent from the field. He won three regular season MVP awards and was named NBA Finals' MVP three times. He was a 12-time All-Star, two-time All-Star Game MVP, and arguably the toughest match-up in NBA history.

1. Jerry West. He deserves to be ranked first on this list considering he placed second four times in regular season MVP voting and never won. He did, however, play so well in the 1969 NBA Finals against Boston that he took the series' MVP award despite being on the losing team. Over his 14-year career, West carried the Lakers to nine NBA Finals appearances, winning just once in 1972. He averaged 27 points, six rebounds, seven assists, and more than two steals per contest over that stretch. He earns the top spot on this list thanks to his work beyond the court, working in the front office to build the Showtime Lakers of the 1980s and the three-peat Lakers of the 2000s. By my total he's contributed to nine titles with the Lakers, making Mr. Clutch, or "The Logo," the greatest Laker of all time.

Thanks to the Lakers being the greatest franchise in the history of the NBA, it makes sense to do a list of all-time greats based on uniform numbers. It's the only Los Angeles franchise for which this exercise makes any sense. Outside of the first listing—which I admit I chose for personal reasons—all of these players were at least respectable Lakers, and, in some cases, major contributors to championship teams.

1. Wes Matthews. I realize Caron Butler did more statistically in his single season with the Lakers than any other player who wore No. 1, but it wasn't enough to warrant his supplanting Wes Matthews. Why? Because despite his modest stats over the two seasons he spent here, Matthews is part of the greatest photo in the history of basketball. You know the one: He's on his back and Xavier McDaniel has both hands wrapped around his throat. No doubt, the best ever.

2. Derek Fisher. One of the greatest role players, emotional leaders, contributors to the community, and clutch dudes in franchise history. It's not worth looking at the stats—eight points and three assists per game—because D-Fish gave the team more than just numbers night-in and night-out. Plus, .4 seconds, anyone?

3. Sedale Threatt. He'll always be known as the man who replaced Magic Johnson at the point, but I'll remember him as a pleasant surprise when I expected the worst. For the 1991–1992 season he stepped in and posted some of the best numbers in the league at the position: 15 points on 49 percent shooting, two steals, and seven assists with only two turnovers per game. He didn't make us forget about Magic—that's simply not possible—but we did think, "Hey, this guy's pretty good."

4. Byron Scott. You'll read about the player Los Angeles had to give up to get Scott, a local kid out of Morningside High in Inglewood. But considering all he did for the Lakers during their dominating mid-1980s run, it worked out better than anyone could have imagined. Scott contributed to three titles, and led the 1987–1988 team in scoring and steals.

5. Jim McMillan. He's another player on this list that had to replace a legend. In just his second season, McMillan replaced Elgin Baylor and helped lead the Lakers to a championship. I'm not suggesting he was better than Baylor, but his insertion to the starting lineup coincided with the longest winning streak in league history. That season, 1971–1972, he averaged 18.8 points and 6.5 rebounds, then got better in the playoffs by averaging 19.1 points per game.

6. Eddie Jones. After a disappointing 1993 season the Lakers found themselves in the draft lottery for the first time since the order was decided by a coin toss. With the 10th overall pick, Jerry West grabbed a spindly shooting guard out of Temple who the fans immediately embraced. While he was jettisoned just before the team's 2000 title, Jones made the worst decade for the Lakers tolerable with his aggressive offense and tenacious defense.

7. Lamar Odom. While he may best be explained as an enigma, Odom doesn't have much competition when it comes to Lakers who have worn No. 7. He's posted impressive numbers—15 points, 10 rebounds per game—since his arrival. Factor in those half-dozen games a year when he goes for more than 20 points and nearly 20 rebounds, and Odom is the most talented No. 7 the team's ever had.

8. Kobe Bryant. Even if you were to take just the years he played with an "8" on his uniform—as opposed to the "24" he wears now—you'd still have a better career than all the other No. 8s combined. Kobe won three championships while wearing this number, including an average of 29 points, seven rebounds and six assists per game in the 2001 playoffs.

9. Nick Van Exel. His exit from Los Angeles wasn't the greatest—he led a "1–2–3 Cancun!" cheer before losing the last playoff game to San Antonio in 1998—but during Nick's time here he was as exciting as any point guard in the NBA. Flashy ball handling skills and a penchant for hitting big shots were his best attributes on the court.

10. Norm Nixon. Nixon averaged 16.4 points and 7.9 assists per game over six seasons with the Lakers. He was in the top five in assists per game in five of his six seasons with L.A., and made one All-Star appearance. Most importantly, he helped the Lakers win two titles as the team's primary scorer off the bench in 1980, and the starting shooting guard in 1982.

Note: Jeanie Buss is the Vice President of the Los Angeles Lakers and daughter of the Lakers' owner, Dr. Jerry Buss.

10. Connie Hawkins. As a college freshman at Iowa he was unjustly associated with a point shaving scandal even though he was never arrested or directly implicated. This incident led to Hawkins being blackballed by the NBA. After 10 long years a *Life* magazine article strongly argued his claim of innocence, and the ban was finally lifted. At age 27 Hawkins had his opportunity. He harbored no bitterness, and instead chose to relish his time in the league. Maybe not worthy by statistical measures, but thanks to his peers recognizing his talent, he was voted him into the Basketball Hall of Fame in 1992.

9. Vlade Divac. Having been the first non-American drafted by the Lakers, Vlade triggered a movement for not only the Lakers, but the entire league to think globally. While his success on the court caused many teams to be more open to the drafting and signing of foreign players, Divac's greatest contribution came off the court. Using his charisma to raise funds for the humanitarian assistance of children and refugees in his native Serbia, in his post-playing career Vlade now oversees Humanitarian Organization Divac and is a Goodwill Ambassador for UNICEF.

8. Kermit Washington. Over 30 years ago while playing for the Lakers in a contest against the Houston Rockets, a skirmish broke out and a punch thrown by Washington nearly killed Rudy Tomjonovich. He received the longest suspension in league history at the time, and once he returned to the court his career was never the same. The negative perception associated with the simple mention of his name would have sent many into hiding, but Washington funneled his energy into Project Contact Africa, an organization with the goal of ending hunger in Africa and providing medical attention to those in need.

7. Kareem Abdul-Jabbar. Most players who earned the recognition Kareem had in the game of basketball would be content with their "one of the best to have ever played the game" label. Instead, one of the most intelligent men I've ever crossed paths with continued what he started as a child and remained a student of life. He is an accomplished actor, a best-selling author and a devoted historian of his beloved jazz music.

6. Jerry West. "The Logo" exemplified the idea that being from a small town doesn't inhibit true talent and desire. West dominated at the amateur level, both during his high school days and while a student at West Virginia University. "Mr. Clutch" then graduated to the NBA and became one of the all-time greats on the court and off it. While he faced a tremendous amount of adversity on the court, winning just one championship as a player despite numerous appearances in the NBA Finals, he would exact his revenge on his playing day peers by dominating in the front office. West was the architect of arguably all eight Lakers titles during my father's time as owner of the team. West epitomizes the idea it's not where you start, but instead where you finish.

5. George Mikan. I strongly believe without George Mikan there's a chance professional basketball wouldn't exist in its current capacity. He was a star in college thanks to DePaul coach Ray Meyer teaching the clumsy near-seven-footer to dominate the game, thereby debunking the philosophy big men were too awkward to play basketball. Mikan was such a draw for ticket sales that a famous photo from a 1949 Madison Square Garden marquee read: "WED BASKETBALL: GEO MIKAN VS KNICKS." Mr. Basketball was a one-man show and put professional basketball on the map.

4. Chick Hearn. Chick created a lexicon that forever changed the way fans spoke about the game of basketball. While not an actual player for the Lakers, his contributions to the team surpass any one person to have ever played for the team. He connected with the fans and had the instinctive ability to create a "words eye view" for millions of listeners. There will never be another "Chickie Baby."

3. Derek Fisher. Fisher repeatedly displays grace under enormous pressure. With .4 seconds remaining on the clock in the 2004 Western Conference Finals, he drained the game winning shot—almost a physical impossibility. In 2007 as a member of the Utah Jazz, Fisher sacrificed a playoff game in order to be by his daughter's side during her surgery due to complications from retinoblastoma, a form of eye cancer. On the same day, once assured by doctors she was stable following the procedure, he flew directly to Utah to join his team mid-game. Walking out of the runner to a standing ovation in the third quarter and almost immediately inserted into the game, his defensive play led the Jazz to an overtime victory with him, once again, hitting the game-winning shot. Fisher truly is a man with his priorities in order and the leadership to achieve those priorities.

2. Elgin Baylor. After three phenomenal seasons in the NBA (including earning Rookie of the Year in 1959), Elgin was, thanks to the draft, required to report for military service. He requested a station close to Los Angeles and was assigned to Fort Lewis, in the state of Washington. When Baylor was granted a weekend pass he would fly down and play for the Lakers. Never once did Elgin complain, instead he honorably served his country and stayed loyal to his team without complaint.

1. Earvin "Magic" Johnson. I'll never forget the day he bravely stood in front of the world admitting he was HIV Positive, making it his mission to bring awareness to a misunderstood, growing, and dangerous epidemic. Now everyone has a friend with HIV, helping to eliminate ignorance and discrimination. Almost 20 years later Magic remains at the forefront of what is now a pandemic and a seemingly never-ending battle. Seeing him as mayor of Los Angeles, the governor of California, or president of the United States would not be a surprise.

Top 10 Reasons Why Shaq and Kobe Couldn't Work It Out

It's a debate that will rage on for generations of Lakers fans. Talk to someone over the age of 40 and you hear "selfish and arrogant" when referring to Kobe. People under the age of 30 bring up "he's a rat" or "he's too fat" when talking about Shaq. Whichever side you're on, when it comes to the breakup of the NBA's best one–two punch at the time, the reality is that it was an inevitable split. Below are the ten rather disheartening reasons why.

10. How can I be the man if you're the man? Shaq, rightfully so, considered the Lakers his team. He was the elder statesman, the player with the MVP trophy, and the player with three NBA Finals' MVP trophies. But he handled the responsibility that goes along with being the elder statesman poorly. When asked about Kobe, you would hear things like, "He's my Robin" or "That's my little brother." Never once did Shaq, until it was far too late, deflect to Bryant. I'm not saying he had to, but as the team leader you have to recognize personalities, and play to them. He did a poor job of it with Bryant.

9. Pocketbooks were opened for Kobe, pre-game cheers were the loudest for Kobe, and All-Star voting favored Kobe. Fans embrace explosive two-guards that fly above the rim more so than powerful, back-to-the-basket big men, and if you think Kobe was the only player in this struggle for power and acknowledgment you'd be wrong. Shaq had the respect of the players around the league; Kobe had the undying love of the fans and their monetary support.

8. Phil Jackson's hands-off approach. There could not have been a worse coach to deal with this sort of situation than Phil Jackson. He likely considered the back and forth between his two star players as childish, selfish, and not worthy of his attention. Problem being, he was the only person who could have had an impact on his players. Instead, we read about the issues he had with Kobe in one of his books, and a couple years later Shaq took shots at him through the media.

7. Infidelity on the record and off the record. When a hotel worker in Eagle, Colorado, accused Kobe of sexual assault it was just the tip of the iceberg in the Shaq-Kobe relationship. We later learned about Kobe's conversation with the police, where on the record he alleged Shaq pays off his mistresses to keep quiet. In the meantime, Shaq made light of the situation back at training camp with new friends Gary Payton and Karl Malone, suggesting the team didn't need Kobe around to win games, and that with the new weapons and Kobe coming off injury, maybe Kobe should look to be more of a pass first player.

6. "I got hurt on company time, so I'll heal on company time." Shaq's comment was one of the dumbest positions ever taken in the history of sport. He had injured his toe late in the 2002 season as the Lakers won their third straight title. Healing on company time meant Shaq missed all of training camp and the first 15 games of the regular season. The Lakers struggled to a 5–10 start, which didn't help the Diesel's relationship with Kobe.

5. Kobe can't take the "You'd have zero rings without Shaq" criticism. I mentioned Shaq had the respect of players around the league. This drove Kobe mad. He worked his butt off to get into and stay in shape all year round, while Shaq reported to camp fat and out of shape. Every season Kobe added something to his repertoire, unlike Shaq. Yet Kobe was the one being called out by other players in the league. He heard the whispers of critics saying, "He's only got rings because he played with Shaq." When you're the guy chipping in more than 29 points, seven rebounds and six assists per game over a 16-game stretch in the playoffs where your team went 15–1, I'm guessing you want just a tiny bit of respect. Kobe's not wired to be cool with that.

4. Kobe and the Clippers. The moment the Detroit Pistons eliminated the Lakers in five games in the NBA Finals, the Lakers were on the clock. It was an awful year off the court between Shaq and Kobe, and no doubt many thought there would be a "him or me" showdown with Kobe an unrestricted free agent. Depending on whom you ask, a deal for Kobe to join the Clippers was done, agreed to, and final, and only required his signature. Others say he simply used the Clippers as a pawn to get more out of the Lakers. Whatever it was, he did agree to re-sign with the Lakers immediately after Shaq was traded to Miami.

3. Statistical history was not on Shaq's side. Among the current generation of players there's a pattern of decline around the age of 33. Shaq was 33 when his deal with the Lakers was up. Giving him an extension of three years was a risky proposition at best for the Lakers, but Dr. Buss was willing to do it. Shaq, however, wanted five years, which never had a chance of happening in Los Angeles. No question this played as big a part as anything in the acrimonious departure of one of the Lakers' greatest players ever.

2. The disappointing finish to the 2004 post season. After Derek Fisher's remarkable shot with just .4 second remaining in San Antonio, and making easy work of the Timberwolves, everyone suspected the Lakers would be the favorite to win the title—and secure the first rings for veteran additions Gary Payton and Karl Malone. Instead, the Pistons humiliated the Lakers by taking four of five games. Having missed out on their goal, the team suddenly looked old. Payton, Malone, Rick Fox, Horace Grant, Bryon Russell—I mean, dudes were old. So, the old man blew it to pieces. Had they won the title, no doubt everyone would have been back to make another run at it.

1. August 7, 2000. After his seventh title with the Lakers, Jerry West decided he'd had enough. Enough of the feuding between Shaq and Kobe, enough of the power struggle between Dr. Buss' kids, Phil Jackson and himself regarding player personnel, and enough of the media circus that ensued at the start of every Lakers season. He was a father figure to Kobe, a mentor to Shaq, and demanded the utmost respect from both of them. Once he left there was nobody to keep the two in check. Mitch Kupchack couldn't command the players' attention, and Phil Jackson wasn't interested in playing disciplinarian. It was just a matter of time before it all fell apart, and Lakers fans should be happy they got four more seasons from the duo before it was all blown apart.

I'm a fan of the game, have been for as long as I can remember. Watching as a kid there was Dr. J or Charles Barkley in my hometown at the Spectrum, Michael turning Chicago into a basketball city at Chicago Stadium, or Larry, DJ, McHale and the Chief making the Celtics that team I loved to hate in Boston Garden. I'm a little upset I barely missed out on playing in the places that were in my dreams growing up. By the time I got to the NBA in 1998, they were gone, replaced by nice looking and comfortable, but not historically significant arenas. So no doubt some of my favorite places are the old ones that were or are still around. The Palestra in Philadelphia is on top, with the Forum and Staples Center right behind it. And I guess you could say the rest are pretty much even.

Beijing Olympic Basketball Gymnasium. It probably didn't matter where the games were played since it was the Olympics. You lose sight of the arena itself because it's all about the people playing and the countries represented. You get caught up in it truly being a world competition and remember you're playing for a World Championship. The building itself was strange because from the outside it looked pretty ordinary, but once you got inside you found, under the floor you were playing on, there were another 3 or 4 more levels. And at the Olympics there were always other events happening at the same time. Really hit home how big the games are when it's all around you like that.

PalaEUR. Roma, Italy. It's now called the PalaLottomatica, and home to Virtus Roma in the Italian league. When I was living in Italy while my dad was playing with Pistoia, he made the All-Star team and played the game in that Arena. It only seats about 12,000 but because of the architecture, and especially the Dome style ceiling while I was sitting under the basket (I was a ball boy for the game), it seemed like one of the biggest places I'd ever been in. I was only 10 at the time, and I remember very clearly looking up into the rafters, seeing thousands of people screaming and yelling, and thinking "These people are nuts."

The Barn/Arco Arena. Crazy fans, I mean crazy. Cow Bells, Mohawks, 6-year-old kids saying things you'd be offended by if an adult yelled them. That rivalry, back when we were in the middle of our three titles, was unreal. The fans are so close to the floor you feel like they're on the court with you. It's almost like an old college arena instead of something in the NBA.

Alamo Dome. Just like Arco a lot of meaningful games were played there during our first two titles, with the Spurs moving to their new arena in 2002. We swept them in the 2001 conference finals, winning the first two games on that floor to finish a perfect 11-0 in the Western Conference playoffs before dropping just one to Philly in the finals. In 2002 we lost our first game at Staples Center before winning both at the Alamo Dome on the way to the three-peat title. It was a weird venue to play in since it was a football stadium that was curtained off, and had all kinds of temporary seating brought in for basketball games.

Madison Square Garden. It's the only old school arena on the East Coast that was still around when I finally made it to the NBA. For that reason alone I appreciate every game I play on that floor. The New York fans are part of it, and of course it's New York, which is a great basketball town. There's a lot of history there—you're talking about Willis Reed, Bill Bradley, Walt Frazier, and in the '80s the Pat Ewing teams that always went up against the Bulls. Every one of my games played at MSG felt like an event.

The Forum. It was great for me to come into the league and not only join the Lakers, a team with just as much or more history than any other in league history, but to play home games at the Forum. I remember seeing champagne sprayed all over the place with Magic, Kareem and Worthy in the middle of the celebration and telling myself one day I'd get there. When I walked in for the first time, even though it was old, smelly and had a tiny locker room, I got chills. You could feel the history just walking through the tunnels underneath the seats. Elgin, Wilt, Jerry, Coops, Magic, I'm happy I got to be part of it before we moved to Staples Center.

Staples Center. Obviously Staples Center is a very special place for me. It was part of 3 NBA Championships and the bulk of my NBA career has been played in that building. While it's a new arena, it's kind of cool to think I've been part of all the Lakers history in that building. The 2000 Game 7 Western Conference Final comeback against Portland, and we won the title at home against the Pacers in Game 6 for the first championship of my career. There was the Horry game-winning 3 in Game 4 of the 2002 Western Conference Finals, and both the 81-point game and 62 points in 3 quarters game were played on that floor, so you could say I'm pretty comfortable with the setting.

The Palestra. Philadelphia, PA. If you're from Philly, before you even think about playing at MSG or any other NBA arena you dream about playing for a title at the Palestra. To this day I still say it's the craziest crowed I've ever seen. It seemed inevitable that there would be a Lower Merion v. Coatesville game somewhere on the way to the title every season. Remember Coatesville had Rip Hamilton, and if you ask anyone that was there in '96, they'll tell you it was a Philly classic. Sold out, not standing room only, but *no* standing room, I mean you couldn't get into the place. I heard they were scalping tickets for something like $500 apiece. The Palestra *is* Philly. An 80-year-old building that used to be home to the Philadelphia Big 5 (Penn, St. Joe's, Temple, La Salle, Nova) and countless PIAA Championships. I'd bet it's had more meaningful games played on its floor than any other arena in the country.

In the course of history, some names are forever linked. In Hollywood, there are duos like Laurel and Hardy and Fred Astaire and Ginger Rogers, and triumvirates like the Three Stooges. The world of sports is no different. Here are some names that will forever be linked in local sports history.

10. Mike Haynes and Lester Hayes. Haynes and Hayes were the NFL's best cornerbacks when the Los Angeles Raiders took the field in Super Bowl XVIII against the favored Washington Redskins. The Skins had set an all-time NFL scoring record that season, but they were no match for the blanket man-on-man coverage of the Raiders' duo. L.A. won 38–9, and Haynes and Hayes both secured their place in pro football lore.

9. Reggie Bush and LenDale White. Is it possible to win the Heisman Trophy as a part-time running back? Bush proved it was when he took home the hardware in 2005. For three seasons, this dynamic duo shared ball-carrying duties for USC with remarkable results. The Trojans won 34 straight games and two national championships during the duo's three-year run and, while Bush won the Heisman, White became the team's all-time leading touchdown scorer.

8. Marcel Dionne, Charlie Simmer, and Dave Taylor. The Los Angeles Kings' "Triple Crown" line is still one of the greatest ever assembled. These three were the perfect blend of speed, size, and a relentless assault on the goal. Dionne still ranks as the fifth-leading scorer in league history. Simmer had back-to-back 56 goal seasons. Taylor topped 90 points in four straight seasons. Before Gretzky ever arrived there was the "Triple Crown" line—still the best days in team history.

7. Shaquille O'Neal and Kobe Bryant. Shaq and Kobe would rank even higher on this list had they just learned to get along. The Lakers won three straight NBA titles and could have won at least three more if egos could have been put in check.

6. Venus and Serena Williams. The girls from Compton rewrote tennis history when they exploded on the scene in the late 1990s. Venus, the oldest, first served notice by reaching the finals of the U.S. Open in 1997. Two years later, Serena stunned the tennis world by winning the same tournament. All told, the sisters have won 15 grand slam titles and, amazingly, faced off in five grand slam finals, including four consecutively in 2002 and 2003. Their showdown in the 2008 Wimbledon final proved they have even more records to set.

5. The Fearsome Foursome. The Rams were not a good team in the mid-1960s, but they had the best defensive front in NFL history. Hall of Famers Deacon Jones and Merlin Olsen teamed with Rosey Grier and Lamar Lundy to form an imposing quartet. Jones was the biggest star, posting three seasons with more the 20 sacks, although official records were not kept for another 15 years. Olsen played in 14 straight Pro Bowls while drawing double-teams that opened the floodgates for his teammates. By 1966, this "Fearsome Foursome" had turned one of the NFL's worst teams into one of the best.

4. Garvey, Lopes, Russell, and Cey. The infield consisting of Steve Garvey at first, Davey Lopes at second, Bill Russell at shortstop, and Ron Cey at third played together longer for the Dodgers than any infield in MLB history. Their nine-season run produced four National League titles and a World Series win in 1981. They also combined for 21 All-Star appearances. In this era of free agency, there is no question the solidity of this quartet will remain unique in baseball history.

3. Elgin Baylor and Jerry West. Perhaps the most prolific scoring duo in NBA history, Baylor and West were also the most snake-bitten. In their 10 full seasons together, they set all kinds of scoring records while leading the Lakers to seven NBA Finals. They won none of those series. Bill Russell and the Celtics beat them six times and Willis Reed's Knicks got them in 1970. Still, anyone who saw these two on the court together will tell you they had no peers.

2. Sandy Koufax and Don Drysdale. Koufax and Drysdale were the perfect lefty-righty combination, dominating baseball from 1959 through 1966. In those eight seasons, the two Hall of Famers won four Cy Young awards and seven strikeout titles while leading the Dodgers to four National League pennants and three World Series titles. They also staged the most famous tandem holdout in baseball history after winning a combined 49 games in 1965. They eventually received a combined $230,000 for the 1966 season. Imagine what they would get these days?

1. Magic Johnson and Kareem Abdul-Jabbar. When Earvin "Magic" Johnson joined the Lakers in 1979, Kareem had already established himself as the NBA's most dominant player. The next decade, however, would be even more satisfying for the big guy as he blended his talents with the most potent point guard in NBA history. Together, Magic and Kareem led the Lakers to eight NBA Finals and five championships. The Showtime Lakers are still the most electric team in Los Angeles' sports history. The supporting cast was great, but the Magic Man and the Captain were the pillars that held up the most successful franchise in city history.

Top 10 "Chickisms"

When it comes to ranking the most famous signature phrases of the greatest play-by-play man in the history of sport—Frances Dale "Chick" Hearn—there's bound to be plenty of second-guessing. I decided on a combination of the two major categories of "chickisms": Phrases that can be linked to only Chick and will forever be considered his and his alone, and those he coined that are now part of standard basketball vernacular. Limiting this list to 10 entries wasn't easy, considering that over his 42-year career there are literally hundreds to choose from. Here are my ten favorite.

10. Not Phi-Beta-Kappa. Is there any better way to say someone is dumb as a box of rocks? If Chick really got upset at a particular player, this would show up. Hearn wasn't interested in making a fool out of the players on the court, but from time to time his frustration would seep through the broadcast and phrases like this, or the many that incorporated his grandmother being able to play better than the current group on the floor, started to work themselves in regularly by the end of the contest.

9. Frozen Rope. This was one of the many phrases that made its way from the Lakers broadcast booth to other NBA broadcasts—and other sports. While Chick used the "frozen rope" to describe a shot with little arc, in baseball it's a line drive with tremendous speed, and in football it's a zinger of a pass from the quarterback.

8. They couldn't beat the Sisters of Mercy. When the team was playing particularly bad, Chick who was never one to hold his tongue. Of all his insulting phrases—"They couldn't throw a pea in the ocean," "They couldn't guard his suitcase at the train station"—his "They couldn't beat the Sisters of Mercy" is especially interesting. What was he insinuating? That a collection of nuns dedicated to benevolent acts for those less fortunate could lace 'em up and beat the Lakers? Every time he said it, I always got the best visual image.

7. Put him in the popcorn machine. Said to describe a defender getting fooled so badly by the offensive player that he landed in the popcorn machine hundreds of feet from the playing floor. He'd sometimes add "salt and butter" if the move was especially humiliating. Chick was the master of insulting someone, but making it go down somewhat easy.

6. Call that one with Braille. It was an easy call for the official to make, but there was a little more to it than that. Home team announcers are particularly annoying when their team is losing and they start to join in the players' insistence that calls are unfairly going against them. When a player would complain about a call after an obvious foul Chick would throw out the Braille comment. Or if he wasn't happy, he might direct it at the officials.

5. He did the bunny hop in the pea patch. Traveling in the lane/paint. The remarkable thing about saying something like "Bunny hop in the pea patch" or "Caught with his hand in the cookie jar" is that any other announcer would probably sound corny or outdated. But Chick's cadence and delivery made us wonder why everyone didn't use such phrases.

4. Coop-a-loop. Simply put, an alley-oop pass to Michael Cooper. The Coop-a-loop is special to fans of the Lakers because Coop meant so much to team. Along with Magic Johnson and Kareem Abdul-Jabbar, he was part of all five championship teams in the 1980s.

3. The mustard came off the hot dog. When a player got a little too fancy and missed what should have been a guaranteed basket, Chick would throw this out there. While I understand it's all about entertainment, there are few things more frustrating than a player showing off and costing his team points. Chick was all too happy to point that out with this signature phrase.

2. Slam Dunk. What can you say about "slam dunk"? People across the world know it refers to a player getting his hands and the ball over the rim and flushing it through, but likely have no idea the term came from Chick. By far, it's his most famous saying, and arguably the most famous term in basketball. Along with "slam dunk," Chick also originated "finger roll" and "dribble drive."

1. It's in the refrigerator. "This game is in the refrigerator. The door's closed. The light's out. The eggs are cooling. The butter's getting hard, and the Jello's jiggling." Meaning, despite the game not being over, a victory was in hand for the Lakers. When it comes to Chick's defining phrase, one of the more popular sayings might be considered tops to a national audience. But to those who grew up with Chick calling games, the number one spot was in the refrigerator all along.

Despite all the East Coast bias littering the sports world, there should be no question that Los Angeles has had the greatest collection of team announcers and sports anchors in broadcast history. Compare this list to any other in the country.

10. Jaime Jarrin. Everyone knows about Vin Scully, the longtime voice of the Dodgers. But Jarrin has had just as big an impact on the Big Blue as the Spanish-language voice of the team since 1959. This Ecuador native earned a spot in Baseball's Hall of Fame in 1998.

9. Ralph Lawler. When the lowly Clippers moved up the coast to L.A. in 1984, nobody took notice. They still don't. But the work of Lawler is one shining light. Nobody has had to endure more losses as a broadcaster, yet his game has been true for more than 20 years. He was even deemed the best NBA play-by-play guy by *Sports Illustrated*.

8. Jim Hill. How many local television sports anchors have a star on the Hollywood Walk of Fame? Count local legend Jim Hill among that exclusive fraternity. For more than 30 years, he has been the most trusted voice of sports in town. I've worked with him the past 10 years and still marvel at his ageless appearance. He's also a throwback—a television anchor that actually *goes* to the games.

7. Bill King. He was only in Los Angeles for a short time, but the late great voice of the Raiders was unmatched in his eloquence and style. "Holy Toledo!" He went back to the Bay Area even before the Silver and Black left town, but what a treat while he was around.

6. Stu Nahan. The other local sports anchor with a star on the Hollywood Walk of Fame. Nahan passed away earlier this year but his legacy will last well beyond the local scene. As the fight announcer for the Rocky Balboa movies and the man who interviewed Jeff Spicoli in *Fast Times at Ridgemont High*, all we can say is "Hey Bud, let's party."

5. Bob Kelley. He was *the* voice of L.A. sports, beginning with the Rams arrival from Cleveland in 1946. Kelley was known for his deep baritone voice and his ability to make every play sound important. He was also the voice of the Los Angeles Angels in the Pacific Coast League before the Dodgers arrived west in 1958. His only flaw was poor health. A massive heart attack claimed his life as the 1966 Rams season got under way. He was just 49 years old.

4. Dick Enberg. "Oh my!" Enberg was actually working at Cal State Northridge as a professor and baseball coach when the Angels tabbed him as one of their new announcers in 1965. He also took over the Rams play-by-play when Bob Kelley died. I can recall the 1967 comeback win over the Packers when Tony Guillory blocked a Donny Anderson punt setting up the winning touchdown. Enberg was also the voice of UCLA and made his first national splash calling the infamous Astrodome game when Elvin Hayes and Houston stunned Lew Alcindor and the Bruins. Enberg went national in 1975, but I still think his best work came in Los Angeles.

3. Bob Miller. Hockey may not be King in Los Angeles, but everyone recognizes Miller as one of the greatest announcers in his sport's history. He's been with the Kings since 1973 and actually has a star on the Hollywood Walk of Fame. Take that Jack Nicholson. He says his greatest fear of retiring is watching the Kings win the Stanley Cup after he leaves. That may never happen, but the longer he sticks around, the better for all L.A. sports fans.

2. Chick Hearn. If there is any question about the magnitude of the late great Chick Hearn, keep one thing in mind: He is the only announcer to have a place in the Basketball Hall of Fame as a contributor. Sorry Johnny Most fans, but Chick *was* the NBA. Ever heard of the term "slam dunk"? That was Chick. How about "air-ball"? That was Chick. "No harm, no foul"? Chick. I could go on all day with Chickisms but why embarrass all other NBA announcers. Best ever. Case closed.

1. Vin Scully. Just having the nine aforementioned sports broadcasters would lap the field of any other city's announcers, but now I throw in the voice of the Dodgers for the past 59 years. Mr. Scully was named the greatest announcer of the 20th century by a national poll. He also one of the greatest gentlemen you will ever meet. Poll after poll has proclaimed Scully as the most popular sports personality in L.A. history. The master has no peer.

Top 10 Reasons the Dodgers Have Not Been to the World Series in 20 years

It's been two decades since Kirk Gibson limped around the bases after his Game 1 home run against Dennis Eckersley and the Oakland A's in the World Series. Since 1941, the Dodgers had never gone more than eight years without a World Series appearance, but we're at 20 years and counting after the 2008 season.

10. The manager carousel. From 1954 through 1996, the Dodgers had exactly two managers: Hall of Famers Walter Alston and Tommy Lasorda. Joe Torre is the Dodgers sixth manager since Lasorda's forced retirement. The Dodgers have also had seven general managers over that period of time. Stability has given way to impatience.

9. Dumping Mike Scioscia. In 1999, the Dodgers inexplicably shoved Scioscia out the door after nearly 20 years with the organization as a player, coach, and minor league manager. Kevin "The Sheriff" Malone, the Dodgers' general manager, allegedly thought Scioscia was short on the tools to become a major league manager. Three years later, Scioscia led the cross-town Angels to their first Worlds Series title. Oops.

8. Disastrous draft picks. From 1986 through 1992 the Dodgers had eight first round draft picks who played a combined 29 major league games. The all-time dog was Bill Bene, the fifth overall choice in the 1988 draft. His career college ERA was 5.62, but he had a blur of a fastball. The only problem was getting the ball over the plate. He never got past the minors leagues.

7. Signing Darren Dreifort and Kevin Brown to monster contracts. The Dodgers gave Dreifort, a pitcher with a history of arm trouble, a five-year, $55 million contract despite the fact that his career record was 39–45. He blew out his elbow that first year and won just nine games for that stack of cash. Brown's seven-year, $105 million deal was ridiculous at best. By the fourth year of that signing, Brown was 3–4 with a 4.81 ERA.

6. Steroid abuse. No less than 10 Dodgers were named in the Mitchell report, including Kevin Brown, Paul LoDuca, and Eric Gagne. The Gagne mention was no surprise to those who wondered how a journeyman starting pitcher could overnight become the greatest closer the game has ever seen. His record of 84 straight saves may stand the test of time—unlike his arm, which unraveled after three spectacular seasons.

5. The Pedro Martinez trade. On November 19, 1993, the Dodgers pulled off one of the worst trades in major league history. They traded the 22-year-old Martinez to Montreal for second baseman Delino DeShields. Martinez has since gone 199–86 with three Cy Young awards. DeShields never hit above .256 in three years with the Dodgers. You think Martinez could have helped the Dodgers get to a World Series or two?

4. Signing Darryl Strawberry. In 1990, the Dodgers signed the top free agent on the market that off-season. It was supposed to be the ultimate homecoming for the L.A. product, but Strawberry gave the Dodgers just one good season. In fact, he only stayed for three of the five years of the deal. Personal problems have plagued Strawberry ever since and he will always be remembered as one of baseball's all-time enigmas.

3. Selling the franchise to Fox. Rupert Murdoch had no intention of making the Dodgers a winner. He was only protecting his Fox broadcast rights to Major League Baseball. The O'Malley family kept the Dodgers in the World Series hunt for nearly 50 years, but the best Fox could do was make excuses. At least the current ownership seems to give a damn.

2. Passing on Vladimir Guerrero twice. That's right. The Dodgers had two chances to sign the future Hall of Famer. When he was a kid in the Dominican, the Dodgers got the first look, but would not give him the $500 necessary to secure his services. Instead, they signed his brother Wilton, who has long since left the game. They had another shot at Vladimir in 2004 but let him get away to the Angels. Guerrero has led the Halos to three division titles in four years, during which he has never placed out of the top 10 in MVP voting.

1. Trading Mike Piazza. Fox ownership had just taken over when they were faced with their first crisis. Mike Piazza, the greatest hitting catcher in MLB history, wanted more money. Their answer was to trade him without the knowledge of general manager Fred Claire. When Claire publicly denounced the deal, he found himself in the unemployment line. The fans have never forgiven the Dodgers for this disaster.

The 10 Worst Draft Picks in Lakers History

Even though the Lakers have enjoyed amazing success over the years in the NBA draft, the team could have been even more productive had they made a few better choices. Here are some of their most glaring missed opportunities, all from the draft's first round.

10. Ken Barlow, 1986. The Lakers drafted Ken Barlow out of Notre Dame with the 23rd overall pick and than traded him immediately for another bust, Billy Thompson. At least Thompson played in the league. Barlow did not. The Lakers also passed on Dennis Rodman who went on to become the league's most dominate rebounder and cross-dresser.

9. Mark Madsen, 2000. Mark Madsen was the Lakers' first pick in 2000 and, while he provided plenty of laughs with his victory parade dances, the team may have been better served if they had drafted Michael Redd, an All-Star who has become one of the NBA's great scorers.

8. Kenny Carr, 1977. The Lakers had three first round picks in 1977 and the third one turned out to be a great choice in Norm Nixon. Unfortunately, the Lakers made a huge mistake with their first pick. Kenny Carr was selected sixth overall and went on to be a career journeyman. The Nets selected Bernard King with the next pick. Enough said.

7. Earl Jones, 1984. Earl Jones was one of the most celebrated high school players in history. In fact, he joined Lew Alcindor as the only players selected as *Parade* high school All-Americans three straight years. The Lakers ignored the fact that Jones played his college ball at lowly District of Columbia and they selected him 23rd overall. His career with the Lakers lasted exactly two games. Jerome Kersey and Jeff Hornacek, meanwhile, were there for the taking.

6. Devean George, 1999. Devean George is one of those players who continues to collect fat paychecks without doing anything to earn them. In nine NBA seasons, he has a career shooting percentage below 40 percent while averaging six points and three rebounds. Blame the Lakers. They made this stiff a first-round pick while passing on Andrei Kirilenko and Manu Ginobli. I guess the Lakers were set against drafting a foreign player.

5. Brian Cook, 2003. Mitch Kupchak got off to the slow start as a general manager thanks in part to lousy first round picks like Brian Cook. Soft does not begin to describe his game. He's a so-called shooter who seems to miss way more shots than he makes. What made his selection even more glaring were the players selected right behind him in the draft: Leandro Barbosa has become one of the league's best sixth men and Josh Howard is an all-star.

4. Sam Jacobson, 1998. Yes, Jerry West made some mistakes as general manager of the Lakers. "The Logo" can take credit for much of the team's success over the years, but not with his selection of Sam Jacobson in the 1998 draft. Jacobson played five games for the Lakers. Total. It's safe to say that the team would have been better off drafting Rashard Lewis or even Cuttino Mobley. Thankfully, this was one of West's few mistakes.

3. Leroy Ellis, 1962. The NBA draft hasn't always been the spectacle it is today. Looking back on drafts from yesteryear, it seems as though general managers made their picks by throwing darts on a board. This appeared to be the case in 1962 when the Lakers picked Leroy Ellis with the seventh overall pick. They were looking for someone to counter the Celtics' Bill Russell. Ellis was not that guy. But the Celtics were grateful for the Lakers' gaffe because they selected John Havlicek with the very next pick.

2. Chris Jefferies, 2002. You always blame just the Lakers for missing an opportunity to draft a great player. In 2002, the whole league passed on Carlos Boozer, now a perennial all-star in Utah. The Lakers that year drafted the immortal Chris Jefferies who was immediately traded for the equally forgettable Kareem Rush. Imagine Boozer with this current Lakers lineup. Yikes!

1. Roger Strickland, 1963. I had to go way back to find the worst player ever drafted by the Lakers in the first round. His name was Roger Strickland, a six-foot-five guard out of Jacksonville. I'm not sure how they heard of this guy, but they made him the seventh overall pick in the 1963 draft. Apparently he was so bad the Lakers released him before the season began. Strickland signed with the Baltimore Bullets and played just one game before calling it a career. The Lakers could have had Gus Johnson, the dominant power forward of his day. I think Elgin Baylor and Jerry West would like that pick back.

Jim Hill's All-Time Favorite Interviews :: Jim Hill

Note: Jim Hill is a true sports icon in Los Angeles. For more than 30 years this former NFL standout has been the city's most respected television sports anchor—beloved by viewers and athletes alike. Hill received his greatest honor by earning a star on the Hollywood Walk of Fame. He has interviewed most of the world's great sports figures and here's a short list of his all-time favorites with his thoughts on each. They are listed in alphabetical order.

Muhammad Ali. "The Greatest" is just that. He is the most important athlete of my generation.

Lyle Alzado. I have a picture of Lyle in a silver frame above my toilet. It reminds me that Lyle flushed his life away with steroids just to please Al Davis. It reminds me everyday to do the right things in life.

Roy Campanella. He never complained about the misfortune of his life. He was the most inspirational athlete I ever met.

Pete Carroll. He restored the glory of football to USC and he did it the right way. His practices are tougher than the games and he gets away with that kind of discipline because of his personality. His enthusiasm is contagious. I also admire his work with inner city gangs that few people know about.

Wayne Gretzky. I have never met a superstar athlete more humble than Wayne Gretzky. He brought an interest in hockey to Los Angeles never seen before or since and he did it with total class.

Reggie Jackson. The stir in the drink no matter where he played. He brought a bravado when he came to the Angels from the Yankees and he helped the team achieve great success. He is one of the smartest people I know and he should be running a baseball franchise somewhere.

Magic Johnson. He was "Showtime." I told him as a rookie that he could own the city if he helped the team win championships. Magic has been a beloved figure ever since that first title. He has also done more than any other athlete to give back to the community.

Deacon Jones. We were almost teammates in San Diego when he came from the Rams, but I was traded to Green Bay the same season. I wish I could have played with him because he played the game the way it is supposed to be played. He also cheats in gold, but that's an entirely different story.

Shaquille O'Neal. The "Big Aristotle" is the biggest baby I've ever known in sports. You can't help but to like the big guy. I loved his Shaq-isms. Every interview I did with him brought a smile to my face.

Vin Scully. Vin is the best thing that ever happened to the Dodgers. He's like a walking dictionary with his ability to always say the right words whether he's calling a game or just talking to you privately. There is no one I would rather listen to.

Jerry West. He is the most brutally honest person I have ever met in sports. When he tells you something, he means it. Too many people will say things just to avoid the truth or they'll say things you want to hear. Jerry just tells the truth and as someone that must share information with the people in LA, that makes my job a whole lot easier.

John Wooden. Of all the people on this list and the hundreds of others who thought they should be on this list, no one has taught more about life than Coach Wooden. If everyone lived his or her lives with the grace and conviction of this man the world would be a much better place.

The Best Los Angeles Sports Blogs

While newspapers continue to re-structure and trim their newsrooms—a trend that causes many of us who love the format to sink deeper and deeper into depression—there's a pleasant silver lining in the rise of the blog. In Southern California, we have quite a few, and listed below are what I deem to be the best of the best. Some are more for entertainment, others for information, and still others for straightforward opinion.

10. sportsbybrooks.com. Since it's more of a national blog than a local one, I put it in this spot. But I included it on the list because Brooks does so well with the site. When it comes to the local angle, he will reference local radio, newspaper, and television dudes and ladies. I think it's even on whether people hit his spot up for the sports or for the pictures.

9. halosheaven.com. A hardcore Angels blog that's run by hardcore Angels fans. Updated daily, you get all the current news along with features like the all-time top 100 Angels. I guess my real reason for picking this site above the others covering the team is their use of the Panther, a term awarded to great Angels accomplishments. It's an homage of sorts to the writings of Darby Crash from The Germs, who you can find in our list of best So Cal punk bands.

8. aqueenamongkings.blogspot.com. There are plenty of Kings blogs to choose from, but I'm going with Connie's as my favorite. She knows her hockey, and her being—well, a her, gives it a unique angle. She hooks up with other bloggers that talk Kings for podcasts, and is all over breaking news every Kings fan should be aware of.

7. Bruinsnation.com. It's the best Bruins blog in town. Plenty of video separates it from the others, especially considering how much access one can be granted these days. For instance, instead of summarizing what happened in interviews or press conferences, you get the actual raw footage. There's so much to digest, often times after spending an hour there, I throw up my arms and say, "They have too much."

6. 6-4-2.blogspot.com. A great source of general information for all things baseball in and around Los Angeles. The subtitle is "an angels/dodgers double play blog" and every link to every story is available every day. From the big league clubs to every level of the minor leagues to updates on former players we managed to grow a little attached to—if you want to keep up with the Angels and/or Dodgers, this has to be in your daily rotation.

5. sportshubla.com. From the brothers Kamenetzky, who also run the *L.A. Times'* Lakers and Dodgers blogs. But this site is better than the work they do for the *Times*, so hit this first. It covers everything in town and even a little bit out of town. Andy and Brian are smart dudes with a sharp wit and great sense of humor.

4. forumblueandgold.com. Not a Bruins blog, but a Lakers one. Kurt does a great job with the site as his observations and opinions are sound, articulate, and interesting. He even gets the award for blog title that creates the most questions. "Forum Blue" is what former Lakers owner Jack Kent Cooke wanted the Lakers uniform color to be called instead of purple.

3. insidesocal.com/tomhoffarth. This gets ranked separately because it's Tom's personal blog, open to anything he feels like writing about. Be it ranking the town's media sports personalities, doing an all-time numerical roster from 00–99, or creating some of the most compelling stories that seemingly come from nowhere, it's a can't miss of sports entertainment. And no, I'm not sucking up to Tom in the hopes it will affect my ranking in future lists.

2. dodgerblues.com. I find it to be the most humorous of the irreverent "everything sucks" blogs. Some of the features welcoming you to the site include the upper right hand corner clock counting the time since the "Last Meaningful Dodger Moment," the "Random Dodger" of the day, and "The Useless Poll," which features questions like, "If you could punch anyone in the nuts, how many times would you punch Ned Colletti?"

1. insidesocal.com/_____. This is the blog home for *The Daily News*. While we have plenty of capable journalists here in Southern California, the beat writers for this paper come out on top across the board. Scott Wolf, who runs insidesocal.com/usc, is the best of the bunch, but Tony Jackson isn't far behind him covering the Dodgers.

The 10 Biggest Lottery Pick Busts in L.A. Clippers History

The timing could not have been more perfect: The same season the NBA adopted the draft "lottery" was the same season the Clippers moved their sorry franchise to Los Angeles. From that day on, the Clippers and the lottery were as inseparable as peanut butter and jelly. Unfortunately, most of the Clippers' choices over the years have varied from bad to worse, so it comes as no surprise that a bottom 10 list of the team's lottery picks is a must for this book. Here are the worst of the worst.

10. Danny Ferry, 1989. Ferry was considered a "can't miss" player after his four-year run at Duke. His father was a solid NBA player before becoming one of the most respected executives in the league. The Clippers never had a chance to see Ferry play because he had no intention of becoming a Clipper. After being drafted second overall, he signed a deal in Europe and his draft rights were eventually traded to Cleveland. He became a career journeyman.

9. Darius Miles, 2000. Miles was the first high school player drafted by the Clippers in the lottery—third overall—and he showed why it's not smart business to draft prep players. Miles displayed great athletic ability, but he was overmatched against more mature players. The Clippers passed on that year's top rookie, Mike Miller, and then they passed on Miles after just two seasons. His career was cut short by a knee injury.

8. Antonio McDyess, 1995. McDyess never played for the Clippers because, after drafting him second overall, they traded him before his rookie season for mediocre Rodney Rogers and forgettable Brent Barry. McDyess has been a solid if unspectacular player for 13 seasons, but the real crime in the Clippers drafting him were the guys who were passed up. How would Kevin Garnett have helped the Clippers? Or Rasheed Wallace? Yikes.

7. Shaun Livingston, 2004. Sometimes you just get unlucky. Livingston was picked by everyone to be a future NBA star after he decided to forego a free ride at Duke to enter the NBA draft right out of high school. The Clippers picked him fourth overall and he showed promise until one play ended it all. His leg collapsed on a routine layup and the dream was over—at least in a Clippers uniform. The team dumped him after the 2007–2008 season.

6. Reggie Williams, 1987. Who knew? Williams was a four-year star at Georgetown and a sure bet for NBA stardom—until the Clippers drafted him fourth overall. He shot just 35.6 percent as a rookie and two years later—along with fellow bust Danny Ferry—was shipped to Cleveland. The player selected right after Williams went on to join the Dream Team at the 1992 Olympics: Scottie Pippen. They also passed on future Hall of Famers Kevin Johnson and Reggie Miller.

5. Chris Wilcox, 2002. Everyone said Wilcox had the greatest pro potential from the Maryland team that won the 2001 national championship, but that potential has yet to surface in six NBA seasons. After being drafted eighth overall, Wilcox never really got off the bench during his three years with the Clippers because coach Mike Dunleavy had zero-tolerance for a player who played no "D." The guy picked ninth overall in 2002 has had a "slightly" more productive career. Anyone heard of Amare Stoudemire?

4. Bo Kimble, 1990. This was the "feel good" pick when the Clippers drafted the local legend eighth overall in 1990. Kimble had led Loyola Marymount to the Elite Eight in the 1990 NCAA Tournament after his teammate and friend, Hank Gathers, died suddenly during a game. It was a great story except for one problem—Kimble was not good enough to play in the NBA. His career lasted just three seasons—including one with the Knicks—with a scoring average of 5.5. That's 30 points less per game than his senior season in college.

3. Lorenzen Wright, 1996. Another career journeyman the Clippers misfired on, this time with the seventh pick of the draft. He lasted just three seasons with the team before being exiled to Atlanta. Wright was a "big man" who could not rebound or block shots. His ineptness was further amplified by the players the Clippers passed over in that draft. Jermaine O'Neal could have been a Clipper. Steve Nash could have been a Clipper. Oh, and some guy named Kobe Bryant could have played for L.A.'s "other" team. You think that may have changed NBA history?

2. Benoit Benjamin, 1985. Forget that the Clippers passed on players like Karl Malone, Chris Mullin, and Joe Dumars with the third overall pick. Forget that Benjamin's 15-year NBA career was a case study in mediocrity. What makes Benoit stand out on this list is the fact that he was the *first* lottery bust in team history. The Clippers may have drafted much worse players, but Benoit will always be synonymous with disastrous draft picks. Plus, how many players are named Benoit?

1. Michael Olowokandi, 1998. The 2008 NBA Finals were a cruel reminder for Clippers fans of what could have been. Paul Pierce, the series' MVP and a Los Angeles native, was passed over by the hometown team. So were Dirk Nowitzki, Vince Carter, Antawn Jamison, and Mike Bibby. No, the Clippers sought fit to take an unknown center out of Pacific with the first overall pick, hoping he would exceed all expectations. He has—for all the wrong reasons. Wasting a first-round pick is bad enough, but the first overall pick? Only the Clippers.

The 10 Worst Coaches in Clippers History

When *Sports Illustrated* called the Clippers the "worst" franchise in American sports there was not a whisper of controversy. The Clippers have earned that tag with a relentless pursuit of failure. Some of it has come by accident. Most of that failure, however, has come by design—a very bad design. One problem has been the hiring of coaches who had no clue how to overcome the obstacles. Here's a list of those who failed the worst.

10. Alvin Gentry. It's almost unfair to put Gentry on this list because he never really wanted to be a head coach. The Clippers lost 67 games the year before he took over and improved 16 games that first season. However, two seasons later Gentry was fired after a 19–39 start. He has since become a fixture as a NBA assistant coach, which he says is the best job in the world. Yeah, especially after being the head guy for the Clippers!

9. Don Casey. Unlike Gentry, Casey fashions himself as perfect head coaching material despite his failed run with the Clippers. He took the helm of a team that was 10–28 in 1989 and they went 11–33 the rest of the season. Not exactly an upgrade. The next season was all his and the team "improved" to 30–52. Casey was outraged when he was fired, but the Clippers probably made a good decision. It would be 10 years before Casey got another NBA head gig and he failed once again in New Jersey.

8. Jim Lynam. Quick now, who was the first coach in Los Angeles Clippers history? That would be the same guy who was the first coach fired by the Clippers. Lynam had coached the Clippers in their last season in San Diego, but his move up north would not last long. They fired him during his first season in L.A. with a 22–39 record. It turns out that was not the right move. Lynam would later get the top job in Philadelphia and he guided the 76ers to three straight playoff seasons.

7. Mike Schuler. Talk about a fading star. Schuler was named the NBA's Coach of the Year in Portland as a first-year head coach in 1987. Two years later he was fired. A year later, the Clippers signed him on to right a sinking ship. Perhaps the Clippers failed to read the stories of how the players in Portland revolted over Schuler's coaching style. His final Clipper ledger read 52–74 and a quick boot after a season-and-a-half.

6. Bill Fitch. Only two coaches in Los Angeles Clippers history have lasted four or more full seasons. One is current coach Mike Dunleavy. The other is one of only three coaches to lead the Clippers to the playoffs—Bill Fitch. By the way, Dunleavy and Larry Brown are the only other coaches on that short list. Fitch coached a remarkable 25 seasons in the NBA with five different teams. He even won a championship in 1981 with Boston. But Fitch provided no titles in L.A., finishing with two 17–65 seasons during his four-year run.

5. Gene Shue. Like Fitch, Shue coached many years in the NBA. He also shared another distinction with Fitch—an overall losing record. Of course, it doesn't help when you're a two-time coach of the NBA's worst franchise. Shue coached the Clippers for two seasons when they were based in San Diego with mixed results, but his return in Los Angeles can only be termed a disaster. A 27–93 record would ruin anyone's resume and it came as no surprise that a former two-time NBA Coach of the Year would never get another head coaching job in the NBA.

4. Chris Ford. Ford was one of those reclamation projects that never panned out. He had been the Celtics coach for five years and had seen a once proud franchise collapse around him. It doesn't help when Larry Bird's career ends under your watch. Ford then spent two seasons as the head coach in Milwaukee, where he guided the Bucks to back-to-back last place finishes. No problem. The Clippers thought he was the perfect guy for the job. They were right. He fit in quite nicely with a 20–75 run that lasted less than two seasons. Ford would never get another full-time run as a head coach.

3. Bob Weiss. Some say bald is beautiful, but not when you're the head coach of the Clippers. Weiss has the distinction of being the only one-and-done coach in franchise history. His 27–55 record was actually better than most of his Clipper coaching cohorts, but he had the misfortune of following the most successful coach in team history in Larry Brown. Amazingly, Brown led the Clippers to successive playoff seasons and an overall winning record. No wonder he's in the Hall of Fame!

2. Don Chaney. The architect of the worst season in team history, Chaney proved you can resurrect your coaching career after a stint with the Clippers. Chaney took over as an interim coach in 1985 and won a respectable 32 games the following season. Then came the freefall. The Clippers lost a near-record 70 games, led by legendary stiff Benoit Benjamin. Chaney was fired, but it turned out to be for his own good. He would later be hired by Houston, Detroit, and the Knicks. He was even once named the NBA Coach of the Year. Not bad for a Clipper castoff.

1. Jim Todd. Who is the worst coach in NBA history? If you go by pure record few could match the ineptness of a poor interim coach who happened to be in the wrong place at the wrong time. Todd was a respected assistant and he remains as much to this day. But his one run as a head coach was beyond a nightmare. Chris Ford was fired after an 11–34 start for the 2000 season and the team had pretty much thrown in the towel. They took that wretched play to a whole new level when Todd took over. His final record was 4–33 for a "winning" percentage of .105. That also included a 17-game losing streak. The only positive news was the season's final game when the Clippers ended that 17-game slide with a win over Seattle. Hey, it's not often a Clippers coach ends his run on a winning note.

Top 10 Skateboarders of All Time

There's a reason why the X Games have found a permanent home here in Southern California—alternative sports are pretty much our deal. From *Dogtown and Z-Boys* to *The Search for Animal Chin* any movement in the world of skateboarding has originated from Southern California. Millions around the world have watched the Del Mar Skate Ranch, the Mega Ramp in the Staples Center parking lot, and even countless dudes in schoolyard parking lots riding rails and curbs in front of their buddy's handicam. For your educational pleasure, here are 10 dudes who contributed to all those kids in the neighborhood making that loud cracking sound on the sidewalk at all hours of the day.

10. Matt Vallely. One of the most influential skaters of the late 1980s thanks to his aggressive style, reckless approach, and the ability to inject personality to a crew of rather soft-spoken technicians, Vallely is also credited with getting kids more interested in street riding than focusing simply on vert. To this day he still reaches out and tries to expose as many as possible to the sport and what it has to offer by taking his board to some pretty impoverished spots around the world. That said, he's on this list for his ability; he's one hell of a skater.

9. Christian Hosoi. The perfect foil to Tony Hawk. You were in one of two camps during the 1980s—you either backed Hosoi or you backed Hawk, and there really was nobody else at the height of vert ramp popularity. Hawk was more of a technician and Hosoi more balls out, constantly pushing how fast he could go, how high he could get. Few things were more awe inspiring than his "Christ Air," which indeed had him looking like a deity soaring above the ramp and the crowd. His popularity reached the marketplace as well, as he launched the "Hosoi Hammerhead" skateboard as a legitimate alternative for kids to Powell Peralta's "Tony Hawk."

8. Eric Koston. He's the best out there right now. His s-k-a-t-e version of H-O-R-S-E has become a bit of a phenomenon. He's capable of executing nearly every street trick ever imagined, and he does it with a sickly aggressive style. He's maintained his best in the world status for nearly a decade thanks to his fearlessness and willingness to keep trying new tricks. Did I mention he skates hard?

7. Bucky Lasek. How sick is a list when Bucky Lasek ranks seventh? Lasek is one of the most accomplished vert riders in the world. He's won 10 medals at the X Games medals, including six gold, and, like Bob Burnquist below, he's one of the best switch riders in the business (equally good going backward as forward). He consistently performs tricks others could never dream up let alone pull off.

6. Mark Gonzales. Pioneer. No other way to put it. While Rodney Mullen invented the "ollie," Gonz took it to the next level as the first rider to guide his skateboard through the air over large gaps without using his hands. It had a profound effect on the sport—kids spent all day trying to replicate the "Gonz Gap." He'd eventually take street skating where it had never been, incorporating kick flips over gaps, riding handrails, getting giant air off launch ramps—pretty much every kid wanted to be Gonz if they were skating in the 1980s. Without him, I'm not sure the sport is where it's at today.

5. Danny Way. Most know Way from his work on the Mega Ramp, one of the most popular events at the X Games. But before that, Way was considered one of the world's best vert riders. He was known for going bigger and higher than anyone, and, once he grew tired of the half-pipe's limitations, he came up with the Mega Ramp. When people talk about staring into the eyes of some giant linebacker as "intimidating" and write off skating as a kid's "game" I submit Way. You tell me what you would rather do—get suited up in pads and take a huge shot from a strong safety, or stand on top of an 80-foot high platform and roll toward the 50 or 70-foot gap you have to glide over while some 30 feet in the air?

4. Rodney Mullen. Back in the days of Bones Brigade's *Searching For Animal Chin*, impressionable young men were a bit confused as to how they were supposed to feel about Mullen. The guy's tricks were beyond remarkable, but his freestyle was more graceful than full of power. It's a testament to how good Rodney was that during a period where it was all about how big could you go, or how hard could you grind, he made a name for himself. But I guess it's not that hard to believe considering the guy invented the "ollie" (popping your board into the air without using your hands).

3. Bob Burnquist. Were it not for the groundwork set by Tony Hawk, and the style created and perfected by Tony Alva, Bob would be in the top spot. The fact he skates switch (backward) better than most people do regular speaks volumes to how good he is. If you want to see some pretty remarkable moves, check out his work in "the loop." Skating backward and doing a full rotation is plain ridiculous.

2. Tony Alva. There are two types of videos you see when looking into the archives of how and when skateboarding started. One set features dudes slaloming through cones in a populated parking lot or cruising down hills in a graceful manner. The other type stars Tony Alva. He's the angry looking guy in an empty pool who looks like his style is actually doing damage to things. The legend goes Tony skated so fast and so hard that when he hit the lip of the pool he would get airborne, thereby creating the aerial.

1. Tony Hawk. When he was just a kid and part of the Bones Brigade Hawk was all legs and arms, his spindly body spinning in every direction imaginable when gliding above the vert ramp. Back then it was back-to-back McTwists (one and a half rotations) and the occasional 720 (two rotations), but in 1999 he took it to another level with a 900 (two and a half rotations in the air) at X Games 10. Add in the popularity of his signature board and his "Tony Hawk's Pro Skater" video game, and he's the dude who took skateboarding to the next level, positioning it to enjoy the success it does today.

We're Hollywood. We're Warner Brothers and Capitol, but also SST and Epitaph. Music and movies are an essential part of the everyday fabric here in Southern California. I could have easily put together a list of the most popular bands here, but that would be received as too arbitrary and create more argument than acceptance. So instead, much like Chicago has the blues, Detroit has Motown, and Nashville has country, we here in Southern California have one hell of a punk rock history. And many of these bands, although you may not recognize them, are regulars at Kings, Lakers, Dodgers, Ducks and Angels games. Pennywise even played the Honda Center before games during the Ducks' Stanley Cup run. Full disclosure: I worked at Slash Records for a period of about two years, and The Germs have a soft spot in my heart that could have influenced their inclusion. I also went with 11 instead of 10—and I didn't rank them—since it's punk rock and supposed to be different.

True Sounds of Liberty (TSOL). More hardcore than punk in my opinion, but ask someone else and they'll say more thrash metal than hardcore. It was an evolving sound, that's for sure. Fronted by now political activist Jack Grisham, you'll get the whole death punk vibe, which was rare at the time on their CD, *Dance With Me*.

The Adolescents. The band was affected by multiple lineups that prevented them from ever having any real mainstream success. Just about every So Cal punk rock band that followed lists The Adolescents as a major influence. Get their eponymous debut and check out the song "Amoeba."

Circle Jerks. Probably best known for their connection to Black Flag. Circle Jerks frontman Keith Morris was the original lead vocalist for Black Flag before quitting to start his own group and get away from Greg Ginn. *Group Sex* is the release you're looking for—14 songs, 15 minutes long. I'd say that's pretty punk rock. Guitarist Greg Heston is still currently playing in the group Bad Religion.

The Vandals. This Huntington Beach band is still going strong with only Joe Escalante as the remaining original member. Still, the lineup is solid and it's pretty hard to top their live show. No political or heavy overtones, this is goof-off punk rock at its finest. Two beat releases would be their first, *Peace through Valdalism*, with the original line up, and the best of the current group, *Fear of a Punk Planet*, with an unreal cover of "Kokomo."

Minutemen. From "The Roar of the Masses Could Be Farts" to "Bob Dylan Wrote Propaganda Songs," it's pretty clear the Minutemen didn't take themselves too seriously. San Pedro-based and comprised of D. Boon, Mike Watt, and George Hurley, maybe 10 percent of the songs in their catalog clock in over 90 seconds. Get *Double Nickels on the Dime* and you're gold.

Bad Religion. "PhD punk," as it's often called, thanks to the education of frontman Greg Graffin. Bad Religion is one of the only bands on this list that is still going, and has 14 studio releases to show for their long history. *Stranger than Fiction* was their most popular, but I'm going with *Recipe for Hate* as the one your collection needs. A little more raw, and "Struck a Nerve" might be the best song they've ever written.

The Germs. Their 1977 single, "Forming/Sexboy," is typically considered the first-ever L.A. punk/hardcore release. A history that at some point included members Pat Smear and Belinda Carlisle, the band is probably best known for pulling the ultimate punk rock move—killing themselves right as their star was starting to shine brightest. After playing arguably their finest gig, frontman and the band's heart and soul, Darby Crash, decided to call it a life and intentionally overdosed on heroin. Probably would have been more of a story had John Lennon not been murdered the very next day. Only one full-length release to consider: *(GI)*.

Suicidal Tendencies. Another original, formed in 1981 in Venice. Mike Muir is the only remaining original member. They were definitely punk rock, but mixed in metal, funk, and some hip hop influences. While Cyco Miko is the face of the band, the best-known member is most likely current Metallica bassist Rob Trujillo, who played with the band for six years. Their eponymous debut is one of the best-selling hardcore albums of all time, and includes the classic "Institutionalized."

X. Exene Cervenka and John Doe were the driving forces behind this L.A. staple. Their debut release, *Los Angeles*, features the song by the same name, and is easily their most popular, but *Wild Gift* is their finest work. John Doe's lyrics and songwriting are a bit smarter than your average punk band's, which separated X from others, as well as the whole female lead singer thing.

Descendents. In my opinion, Milo Aukerman-fronted Descendents has to be one of the major influences on what kids today know as pop punk rock. Without them, there is no Green Day. *Milo Goes to College* was both juvenile and intelligent, catchy and straight-up punk rock. The dichotomy of sound, lyrics, and personality is what separated them from the pack. How many bands that sing about Wienerschnitzel have a frontman who's got a doctorate in biochemistry? Pick up *All* and you'll realize *Dookie* wasn't all that groundbreaking after all.

Black Flag. A band that you could say started it all. Hardcore pioneers, do it yourselfers with their SST record label, and relentless touring were all calling cards of Black Flag, and especially the band's founder, Greg Ginn. Unique album artwork, intelligent lyrics, and blistering live shows all come to mind too. While you may not know Ginn, you surely know the frontman who landed the gig after asking, as a fan, to fill in on vocals for one song at a live show: Henry Rollins. *Damaged* is your album of choice.

The 10 Songs I'd Prefer to Never Hear Again at a Sporting Event

We are at your mercy Mr. Music Director. While taking in a game at one of the fine stadiums or arenas in town, tens of thousands of fans are waiting to hear what you choose to pump through those giant PA speakers. Considering the choices usually included on your play list, that's unfortunate. Here's to hoping this could be the start of a fan revolt to get these 10 songs permanently removed from the rotation.

10. Blur, "Song 2." I actually don't mind this song despite having heard it at least 5,000 times. Problem is, since not a single person in the arena knows the words following "WAH HOO" are "When I feel heavy metal" you get a different five words from everyone in the place. So it sounds something like, "WAH HOO, when I feel this bleem and kong." If we could pass out lyrics before every game in which the song was played, it would be cool. But since we can't, lose it.

9. Chumbawumba, "Tubthumping." Yes, I know, they say "I get knocked down, but I get up again, you ain't ever gonna keep me down," and that's pretty appropriate for a team to hear after they just came back from sure defeat. But since the song is so terrible, why not play something else so they don't become trained to just pack up and quit the next time so they don't have to hear "Tubthumping" again?

8. Offspring, "The Kids Aren't Alright." This rests solely on the USC band, and especially the scaled down version that plays at Staples Center for every Lakers home game. First off, KROQ has probably played that freaking song more than 4,000 times—and I should know, I used to be the music director there. Second, it's damn depressing. A song about the dudes you grew up with killing themselves and overdosing? Wheeeeeeee, let's go Lakers!

7. Gary Glitter, "Rock & Roll Pt. II." Used to like it, but now the only thing I think of when it comes on instead of, "Here comes the part where I'm supposed to say, 'Hey!'" is, "Was that guy convicted of child sex abuse in Cambodia or Vietnam, or both?"

6. 3 Doors Down, "Kryptonite." Maybe I'm being a little harsh here, but these might be the most ridiculous lyrics of all time. When you combine them with a beat that makes white dudes purse their lips and aggressively bob their head, it's one heck of a mess to have to watch.

5. Reel 2 Real, "I Like to Move It." Biggest culprit of causing Old Dude who has no idea how to dance to dance and thereby make an ass of himself in front of his terrified teenage son/daughter. Still, that's not as bad as the guy who's not moving to the beat one bit, but pumps his fist in the air and screams "Move it!" when the time comes.

4. Disturbed, "Down with the Sickness." Made popular in Anaheim during the 2002 World Series run as the Rally Monkey's theme song. While it's a bad—but not terrible— song, the way it's edited for use at Angels Stadium makes it brutal. It's just some dude screaming, "Ohhhhh, WAH WAH WAH WAH" followed by some giant six-note guitar riff, followed by another "Ohhhhh, WAH WAH WAH WAH."

3. Rednex, "Cotton Eye Joe." Nothing says, "Let's party!" like a Swedish techno interpretation of a classic American folk song that predates the Civil War and was made popular in minstrel shows. But hey, despite all that, at least the song might be one of the most annoying in the history of music.

2. Sixpence None the Richer, "Kiss Me." Please understand, I'm not some crusty sports dork that doesn't want there to be any fun in the stands during the games. But do we really need to O.D. on the "Kiss Me Cam"? How about busting it out on Mondays or Saturdays instead of every single game, in every single sport, every single night? And Guy Who Thinks He's Clever Guy? We've already seen it. Whatever you're thinking might be funny, it's been done. So just get on with it already.

1. DJ Casper, "Cha Cha Slide." You play this and everyone in the place should get one free punch to your junk. Worst . . . song . . . ever! Since it's number one on our list, let's go through the first verse real quick: "To the left, take it back now y'all. One hop this time, right foot lets stomp. Left foot let's stomp, Cha Cha real smooth." How about an amended version that goes a little something like this: "In the concourse, up the stairs now y'all. To the booth this time, kick the door in right. Now grab the DJ, and strangle real hard."

The most common surname in America is Johnson, and Los Angeles has had no shortage of legendary Johnsons. Here are the best of the best with apologies to Johnnie, one of our favorite Rams from the 1980s.

10. Kermit Johnson. Along with his former high school teammate, James McAllister, Kermit Johnson came to UCLA with huge expectations and delivered in a big way. The lightning quick running back averaged more than seven yards per carry as a senior in 1973, earning All-American honors and among the top 10 in Heisman voting. He was the guy who made the Bruins' wishbone attack nearly unstoppable.

9. "Sweet" Lou Johnson. When Tommy Davis broke his ankle early in the 1965 season, the Dodgers needed help in the outfield and they found a gem in "Sweet" Lou. That season, the former Negro Leaguer tied for the team lead in home runs and hit a round-tripper that decided Game 7 of the World Series. He's still a fixture in the organization as a beloved goodwill ambassador.

8. Dennis Johnson. No one ever heard of D.J. when he came out of Compton High School. That's because he barely got off the bench as a basketball reserve. His luck would change when he attended local Harbor College, where he did enough to earn a scholarship at Pepperdine. Three years later, he was the MVP of the NBA Finals. His recent passing came too soon and sadly before what we believe will be his eventual election to the Hall of Fame.

7. Jimmy Johnson. He was a two-way player during his college days at UCLA before being drafted in the first round of the 1961 NFL draft by the San Francisco 49ers. At first they were convinced he would be a great receiver, but eventually the team figured out his true calling at cornerback. Sixteen years later, Jimmy retired with 47 career interceptions and five Pro Bowl appearances. He was elected to the Pro Football Hall of Fame in 1994.

6. Alex Johnson. He may have been a surly character, but Alex Johnson could hit. In fact, he remains the only Angels player ever to win the batting title. With two hits in the final game of the 1970 season, Johnson edged Hall of Famer Carl Yastrzemski for the American League title. Johnson finished the season with a .329 batting average but he would never come close to that mark again. The Angels dumped him for being "lazy" after the 1971 season.

5. Keyshawn Johnson. *Throw Me the Damn Ball* was the book Keyshawn wrote early in his NFL career and it typified his brash nature and constant need for attention. He burst on the scene during a two-year stint at USC, where he earned All-American honors as a senior. The Jets made him the first overall pick in 1996 and he went on to play 11 seasons with four different teams. His 814 career receptions and Super Bowl title in Tampa Bay justified his hype and bravado.

4. Marques Johnson. Marques is the Jay Berwanger of college basketball. He earned that distinction by becoming the first-ever winner of the Wooden Award, college basketball's equivalent of the Heisman Trophy. In winning the award, Johnson concluded a great four-year career at UCLA, where he played on Wooden's last championship team. He went on to an outstanding NBA career, averaging more than 20 points over an 11-year career.

3. Randy Johnson. The "Big Unit" is arguably the most dominant left-handed pitcher in baseball history. He's second all-time to Nolan Ryan in strikeouts and has won five Cy Young awards, including four straight from 1999 through 2002. His dominance first drew notice during his college days at USC, where he teamed with another decent player, Mark McGwire. His three wins in the 2001 World Series earned him MVP honors and helped lead the Arizona Diamondbacks over the New York Yankees.

2. Rafer Johnson. The greatest athlete of his day, Rafer Johnson won the Olympic gold medal in the decathlon during the 1960 Games in Rome. His legendary battle with former UCLA teammate C.K. Yang is still a part of Olympic lore. Johnson also happened to be the older brother of the aforementioned Jimmy, the Hall of Fame cornerback. Today, Rafer is best known for his tireless work with the Special Olympics, which he helped start in 1969.

1. Earvin "Magic" Johnson. No athlete has meant more to the city of Los Angeles than Earvin "Magic" Johnson. His supreme talent on the court resulted in five NBA championships for the Lakers, but his work away from the game has cemented his legacy. His business ventures helped rebuild sections of the city that were once deemed condemned. He has also proven there's hope in living with HIV. His surname may be common but the man is extraordinary.

Since this is a book primarily consisting of top 10 lists, I figured why not in fact go 1-10 and figure out who the best of the best were or are, by uniform number. Some numbers were easier than others—Pee Wee only spent a season in L.A., and I'm guessing he couldn't have topped my selection regardless. Number 4 was the toughest—my love of the puck nearly led me down a path that would include a King, but the little swoll dude that could got the nod instead.

1. Rod Dedeaux. Arguably the greatest baseball head coach in the history of the sport. Dedeaux guided USC to 28 conference titles and 11 College World Series championships. He has a lifetime record of 1,332–571–11, a .699 winning percentage. The legend goes he worked for just $1 a year as coach of the baseball Trojans, thanks to his having founded the successful Dart Transportation Inc.

2. Tommy Lasorda. Appropriate he comes right after his dear friend Dedeaux. Not much debate here. Not only is Tommy one of the most beloved Dodgers in team history, but he's also one of the most celebrated sports fixtures in the history of Los Angeles. I think its safe to say he beats out Derek Fisher.

3. Carson Palmer. Were it not for the arrival of Pete Carroll and Norm Chow he doesn't get a sniff of this list. But Palmer turned in one of the greatest seasons ever by a college quarterback. He won the Heisman in 2002 after completing 63 percent of his passes for 3,942 yards and 33 touchdowns. He also led a USC team that crushed Iowa in the Orange Bowl, leading many to say they were the best team in football by the end of the season.

4. Byron Scott. I love Rob Blake. He's one of the greatest Kings ever. He's got one of the most devastating hip checks the NHL has ever seen. But last time I checked he didn't win jack here in Southern California. Without Byron Scott the Lakers might not have won the three titles he was a part of in 1985, 1987 and 1988. Scott led the team in scoring in 1987 and 1988, and the latter is in the conversation of the best teams of all time. In the playoffs he didn't have a drop either, averaging 17 points per game in 1985 and 20 per game for the 1987 and 1988 teams. He also shot above 49 percent in eight of his 10 seasons with the Lakers.

5. Kenny Easley. Go ahead and hate on me, USC fans, but I'll take Easley over Reggie Bush any day. Dude was one of the best safeties ever to have played the game. All he did at UCLA was amass 324 tackles and 19 interceptions. Think about that number—19 interceptions. He was also a four-time All-Pac 10 selection and three-time consensus All-American. In the NFL, he was named Defensive Rookie of the Year and won both the 1983 AFC Defensive Player of the Year and 1984 NFL Defensive Player of the Year honors while with the Seahawks.

6. Steve Garvey. Should be in the Hall of Fame, if for no other reason than those beautifully hairy forearms. Garvey was a man to be feared come playoff time, and god help you if you were the American League in the All-Star Game. In 11 post-season series all Garvey did was hit .338 with 11 home runs and 31 RBI. The NL's MVP in 1974, he had a career batting average of .294 with 1,308 RBI in 19 seasons.

7. Bob Waterfield. I was going to roll with Marc Carrier on this one, but it would have been an egregious oversight. Waterfield was a stud. The 1942 Rose Bowl team at UCLA starred Waterfield in the backfield, where he led the team in total offense with 1,177 yards. He split quarterback duties with Norm Van Brocklin when he joined the Rams, winning the championship in 1951. Not only did he play both ways, tossing nearly 100 touchdowns and grabbing more than 20 interceptions, but he was also a punter with a career average of 42.4 yards and a place kicker who connected on 60 field goals.

8. Kobe Bryant. He's number 8 and not 24 as far as I'm concerned. One of the greatest players to ever lace them up, and before it's all said and done Kobe will be in the conversation for best scoring guard in league history. While helping the Lakers to three straight titles beginning in 2000, consider his post-season numbers: In the 2001 playoffs he *averaged* 29.4 points, 7.3 rebounds, and 6.1 assists. The only reason he didn't get the MVP award for that series was Matt Geiger was responsible for guarding Shaq.

9. Paul Kariya. Without Kariya and Teemu Selane the Mighty Ducks might not have been long for Anaheim. Not only were they the faces of the newly minted franchise, but one of the most effective duos in the NHL. Kariya topped 100 points twice during his stay with the Ducks—and had 99 in 1996–1997—and no doubt is responsible for one of the greatest Southern California hockey moments: In the 2003 NHL Stanley Cup Finals he was knocked out by Scott Stevens and left laying on the ice for an extended period of time before eventually retreating to the locker room. He returned to the ice minutes later to score a goal and give the Ducks a 4–1 lead in the game.

10. Ron Cey. People who look at Cey's .261 lifetime batting average might initially dismiss his baseball prowess. But there's no denying "The Penguin" was one of the best players at his position in his era. A six-time all-star, Cey hit more than 20 home runs in 10 seasons—including a career best 30 in 1977—and was co-MVP of the 1981 World Series after hitting .350 with 6 RBI. Plus he had one super cool moustache.

Top 6 Things I Love About Going to the Ballpark

Few things in sports can trump opening day of the baseball season. Especially when your team is at home, and especially when it's a rivalry series. Why wouldn't you have the Dodgers and Giants open up against each other every single season? Just rotate which park they do it in. Opening night with the Kings or Lakers is cool, but it's not like the first day of baseball. There's something very American about it, so the following six things reflect, I guess, things I love about America.

6. The Beer Garden. You have to love a spot where, for at least 200–500 people a night, the fact that professional athletes are on display doesn't mean a thing. These people would rather sit in a patio section of the park where you can barely see the game, and get absolutely plowed on gigantic $15 beers. Sure, you could do it on your patio and save about a grand, but what fun would that be? At one point it used to be the spot to smoke, but with that now gone, it's simply a few four-tops with chrome chairs to kick back and drink at while enjoying the sounds of the game.

5. The Chapped Boyfriend. Baseball is a slow sport. Unless you appreciate pitching, it can be excruciating. Over the course of three hours, you get an awful lot of down time. If you're a guy who rolls to the park with a hot piece of ass in a halter top, you have to accept that she'll garner more attention than the game. Walking up and down the aisle holding her hand, giving hard looks to every guy who's blitzed by the seventh inning and staring at her chest isn't going to do any good. They're completely oblivious to your existence. So, let it go, accept that you got a pretty good deal by having her with you, and own it.

4. Ditching school, work, marriage counseling, etc., for the "Nooners." Playing hooky or ditching—whatever you want to call getting out of the office or school when you're not supposed to—in order to catch the game is a hell of a lot cooler when there are 30,000 to 50,000 others doing it with you. It's like the biggest inside joke in the city at one given moment. Every guy in a suit has an ear-to-ear grin because they got over on the man.

3. The Onion Wheel. Best condiment invention ever. Before this giant chrome feeder showed up at the ballpark, I remember the line for onions. It sucked. There was that stupid plastic spoon that I'm sure had a good 40 coats of Hep C on it, hit the ground, and had been in some kid's mouth. And then there was the fingernail dirt sprinkled in the tub o' white onions. All of it made me eat my dogs with just ketchup for a while. But thanks to the crank-operated onions contraption, I'm back eating my grilled dog with mustard and onions like every great American should.

2. The Trough. I've said it before and I'll say it again. It might be environmentally insensitive to have a 90-foot-long half-cylinder of stainless steel running water for five hours, but the Falcon waterless urinals just don't have the same sense of camaraderie fans feel when standing elbow-to-elbow in the eighth inning of a close game, when every single inch of urinal space is considered useable. If you have any question about the magic of the trough, just go ahead and hit up youtube.com and enter "Wrigley trough" into the search bar, and check out the magical five seconds.

1. The Organ. It's basically gone from the NBA and NHL games, which is a damn shame considering it's been replaced by techno and the 69 Boyz. But, thankfully the organ's still alive and well at the ballpark, and there's nobody better at tickling the plastic crafted simulated ivory than Nancy Bea at Chavez Ravine. From "Take Me Out to the Ballgame," to "Six Underground," it's a hell of a lot better than some hip hop beat or classic rock guitar riff.

The 10 Best Individual Seasons in Angels History

The Angels have experienced plenty of highs and lows as a team since their birth in 1961, but there has never been a shortage of individual talent. Here are the best seasons ever posted by an Angels' player.

10. Garret Anderson, 2002. In a season that saw the Angels win a World Series for the first time, Anderson stood out from the rest. He finished fourth in the MVP voting after hitting .306 with 29 home runs and a team-high 123 RBIs. He led the American League with 56 doubles and was second in the league with 88 extra-base hits. Anderson was named to his first All-Star team and he won a Silver Slugger award. He has gone on to break almost all of the team's career offensive records.

9. Frankie Rodriguez, 2006. "K-Rod" blew away hitters during a spectacular 2006 season that saw him earn the Rolaids Relief Award as the American League's top closer. His 47 saves set a team record while leading the league by a large margin. He struck out 98 batters in just 73 innings and posted a 1.73 ERA. Even more impressive was his record over the final three months of the season: In 33 appearances after July 1, he recorded 28 saves with a microscopic 0.46 ERA. In September, he struck out 29 batters in 17 innings.

8. Leon Wagner, 1962. One of the most memorable seasons in Angels' history occurred in 1962. In just their second season in existence, the Halos finished third in the American League with an 86–76 record. It would be 16 years before they would win more games in a season. The star of that team was Leon "Daddy Wags" Wagner. Wagner was rescued from the minor leagues in 1961 and he immediately brought some much-needed power to the lineup. In 1962 he hit 37 home runs with 107 RBIs to finish fourth in the league MVP voting. He was also named the MVP of the All-Star Game that season with three hits, including a home run.

7. Nolan Ryan, 1973. The "Ryan Express" was never more devastating than during the 1973 season. Although the Angels had a losing record that year, Ryan won 21 games to finish second in the Cy Young voting. His most memorable accomplishments that season included 383 strikeouts (still MLB's all-time record) and two no-hitters. He struck out 10 or more batters in 22 of his 39 starts that season. The durability of his arm still staggers the mind. They did not keep official pitch counts in those days, but Ryan pitched in 326 innings while throwing 26 complete games. Keep in mind he walked 162 batters that season. We'll never see his likes again.

6. Alex Johnson, 1970. The only Angels player to win the American League batting title was Johnson in 1970. He edged out Hall of Famer Carl Yastrzemski on the final day of the season, posting a .329 average. Johnson set a team record (since broken) with 202 hits while making his one and only All-Star team. The Angels were contenders for their first division title that season before faltering down the stretch. Johnson was hardly to blame for the collapse as he hit .381 in September and October. The rest of his career never matched that 1970 season, but he still holds a unique place in Angels' history.

5. Doug DeCinces, 1982. The Angels acquired the former Baltimore Orioles third baseman before the 1982 season and he exceeded all expectations. DeCinces set career highs in every major offensive category, including 30 home runs, 42 doubles, and 97 RBIs. He finished third in the MVP voting not only for his glowing numbers, but also his inspirational leadership as the Halos won their second division title. In August of 1982, DeCinces had one of the greatest months ever by an Angels player. In just 24 games that month he hit .392 with 11 home runs and 28 RBIs. DeCinces would help the Angels win another division title in 1986.

4. Darrin Erstad, 2000. If anyone ever defined "career" year it was Erstad in 2000. The former first overall pick of the 1995 draft, Erstad finally lived up to the hype with this monster season. His .355 average was 102 points higher than the season before and his 240 hits are the third most by a player since 1930. Erstad also had career highs with 25 home runs, 100 RBIs, and 28 stolen bases. He also won both a Gold Glove and a Silver Slugger award. Unfortunately, Erstad has never come close to those numbers since. In fact, the 2000 season remains the only year Erstad batted above .300.

3. Vladimir Guerrero, 2004. Everyone knew Guerrero was a great player when the Angels signed him to a free agent contract before the 2004 season, but he was still better than advertised. Guerrero became just the second Angels player to win MVP honors thanks to 39 home runs, 126 RBIs, and a .337 average. He finished with a flourish, hitting .363 in September and October with 11 home runs and 25 RBIs. To cap off his campaign, Guerrero helped lead the Angels to their first division title in 18 years. He has not placed outside the top 10 in MVP voting since that magical 2004 campiagn.

2. Don Baylor, 1979. Baylor had an outstanding major league career with 338 home runs and 10 post-season appearances. His career peaked in 1979 when he led the Angels to their first-ever division title with a MVP performance unmatched in team history. As the first Angels player to be so honored, Baylor accomplished a rare feat leading the league in both runs scored and RBIs. His 139 RBIs that season still stand alone in team history. Baylor did his biggest damage during a red hot July, knocking in 34 runs in 28 games. Amazingly, 1979 would be the only All-Star season of Baylor's 19-year career.

1. Dean Chance, 1964. The numbers still boggle the mind: a 1.65 ERA and 11 shutouts in just 35 starts. Those were the statistics for this 23-year-old right-hander in 1964. He earned that season's Cy Young award, which was presented at the time to the best pitcher in *all* of baseball. In fact, his numbers that year were better than Sandy Koufax's. Here's another number to inhale: a 1.07 ERA in 23 home appearances. How about two shutouts in two games at Yankee Stadium against the American League champions? Oh, did we mention that five of his shutouts were in 1–0 games? Chance's 1964 season stands as one of the best ever in major league history.

While the Dodgers were a model of consistency with just two mangers over a 43-year period—Hall of Famers Walter Alston and Tommy Lasorda—the Angels ran managers in and out like a line at a drive-thru restaurant. Their first hire, Bill Rigney, lasted more than eight seasons and proved to be a good hire. Their latest hire, Mike Scioscia, has lasted nine seasons, winning three division titles and the 2002 World Series. The problem was all the managers in between. Here are the worst of the worst.

10. Gene Mauch. It may not seem fair to include a manager who led the team to two division titles, but Mauch definitely belongs. His butchering of the pitching staff during the 1982 and 1986 ALCS has become part of pop legend. "The Little General" was a control freak that did everything by the book and it cost him dearly. He concluded his run with the Angels in 1987 posting a last-place finish after being one pitch away from the World Series. He managed more games than any manager in history without a single World Series appearance.

9. Doug Rader. Rader was one of those managers who thought he knew everything about the game. He also had total distain for the media. If you asked him a question he didn't like, you would get the death stare. Rader was cocky without reason. A five-time Gold Glove third baseman with the Houston Astros, Rader had already failed with Texas as a manager before the Angels hired him in 1989. His first season was a good one, but less than two years later he was fired. No one could stand the guy and he never got another MLB managerial job.

8. Cookie Rojas. Rojas was one of those guys that everyone seemed to like when he took over for Gene Mauch in 1988. But that love affair didn't even last one full season as Rojas was fired with eight games left. A five-time All-Star with the Phillies and Royals, Rojas was one of the most versatile players in baseball history, appearing in at least one game at every position—including catcher and pitcher—during his career. As a manager, he changed lineups frequently, even though he had nine solid starters who should have been left alone. Eight years later, Rojas managed his only other major league game with the Florida Marlins.

7. Lefty Phillips. Phillips was a well-respected baseball man who had coached with the Dodgers before succeeding Bill Rigney in 1969. The following season, the Angels had their most successful year since 1962. Everything seemed to be going fine until the curse of Alex Johnson reared its ugly head. The 1970 American League batting champion was hated by teammates for his surly demeanor. One of those teammates, Chico Ruiz, was so incensed by Johnson that he brought a gun into the dugout and threatened to use it. Phillips never regained control of his team and he was fired at season's end. He would never manage another major league team.

6. John McNamara. McNamara managed six different teams, including the Angels twice. He took over for Gene Mauch in 1983 and led a team that had won the division title the year before with a 93–69 record to a 70–92 team. He was fired following the next season and somehow got the Boston Red Sox job. It was those Red Sox that beat the Angels in the infamous 1986 ALCS featuring the ill-fated Donnie Moore. McNamara's last run as a major league manager came in 1996, again with the Angels, as he lost 18 of 28 games. In 20 seasons as a big league skipper, McNamara lost 70 more games than he won. Talk about the good-old-boy network.

5. Del Rice. Rice was one of the original Angels back in 1961 when he played his last season as a 17-year backup catcher. There's been a longtime belief that catchers make the best managers because they know how to handle a pitching staff. In 1972, Rice proved he could handle a pitching staff that included the recently acquired Nolan Ryan. The problem was an offense that posted a .297 on-base percentage. Rice was one of a rare breed of managers in the sense that he managed one full season with the Angels and then never managed another game in any other season with any other team.

4. Marcel Lachemann. Lachemann oversaw the worst collapse in team history and one of the worst in major league history. The 1995 Angels led the American League West by 11 games on August 9 only to lose 31 of their last 49 games to blow the division title to Seattle. Amazingly, the team won its last five games to force a one-game playoff only to get bombed 9–1. A nine-game losing streak in mid-September was particularly ghastly. Lachemann returned the following year, but would last just 111 games. Like others on this list he would never get another major league managerial job.

3. Buck Rodgers. Rodgers was one of the Angels' first homegrown stars as a catcher in the early 1960s. He went on to great success as a manager with both the Milwaukee Brewers—he beat the Angels in the 1982 ALCS to go to the World Series—and the Montreal Expos. It seemed like a coup when the Angels brought him "home" in 1991, but things went from bad to worse when Rodgers was injured in the team's 1992 bus crash incident on the New Jersey Turnpike. Rodgers suffered a broken rib, elbow, and knee. He sat out the rest of the season and returned the following year only to post a poor 71–91 record. The next season he was fired after just 40 games. His winning percentage with Milwaukee and Montreal was .517. It was just .447 with the Angels.

2. Bobby Winkles. Winkles was one of the most successful college baseball coaches of all time, leading Arizona State to three College World Series titles. That success would not follow him with the Angels. Winkles took over from the one-and-done Del Rice and showed some improvement the first year, but his follow-up season proved to be the second worst in team history. "Nice Guy" Bobby wasn't around by the end of the season—he was fired after just 74 games. He would get one last chance as a big league manager with Oakland in 1977, but his 37–71 mark as an interim skipper was too ugly to warrant a third chance to run a team.

1. Dick Williams. In 2008, Williams finally earned a place in baseball's Hall of Fame and for good reason. He led the 1967 Red Sox to its first World Series appearance in 21 years. In 1972 and 1973 he guided the Oakland A's to consecutive World Series championships. In 1979 and 1980 he had back-to-back 90-win seasons with the lowly Montreal Expos. In 1984 he led the San Diego Padres to their first National League pennant. And then there were his years with the Angels. Perhaps the Hall of Fame can erase those seasons from his Cooperstown plaque. Coming off his tremendous Oakland success, the Angels hired Williams in 1974 to turn the team into a winner. He accomplished just the opposite, finishing dead last in 1975, his only full season as the Angels' manager. After a 39–57 start in 1976, Williams was fired. His subsequent success in Montreal and San Diego only amplified his failures with the Angels.

The 10 Most Remarkable Numbers Associated with Nolan Ryan

The "Ryan Express" came roaring into Southern California in 1972 when the Angels engineered one of the biggest robberies in baseball history. The Halos acquired Ryan and three other players from the Mets for aging shortstop Jim Fregosi. Ryan was supposed to be nothing more than a project, but he turned out to be an instant star with 19 wins and a league-high 329 strikeouts. The rest of his career became a book of matchless numbers, some of which will never be seen again. Here is just a sampling of his most mind-numbing achievements—both good and bad.

10. 277 Career Wild Pitches. It only makes sense that a wild fastball pitcher would have a lot of wild pitches, but Ryan's total of 277 is remarkable for its sheer magnitude. Consider that Phil Niekro, baseball's most enduring knuckleball pitcher, had 226 wild pitches during his career. That total puts Niekro fourth on the all-time list, but still a whopping 51 short of Ryan's record. No active pitcher is even close to 200 career wild pitches.

9. 6.56 Hits Allowed Per Nine Innings. This relatively obscure statistic illustrates just how difficult it was to get a hit off of Ryan. Second on the all-time list is none other than Sandy Koufax with a mark of 6.792 hits per nine innings. Ryan also holds the single-season record of 5.26 set in 1972 and the third-best mark of 5.31 posted in 1991—accomplished at the age of 44!

8. 27 Seasons. One of Ryan's most remarkable achievements is playing a record 27 seasons in the major leagues. His career started with LBJ in the White House and ended with Bill Clinton as President. What makes this record even more amazing is the fact that Ryan was a power pitcher for the entire duration. There is no exact record of the number of pitches he threw, but it's safe to say no other arm could withstand such a strain.

7. The 1987 Season. Of all the seasons in Ryan's career none was quite like his 1987 campaign for the Houston Astros. That year Ryan led the majors with 270 strikeouts—his most in 10 seasons. He also walked "just" 87 batters, giving him his best strikeout-to-walk ratio of his career. In addition, Ryan led the National League with a 2.76 ERA. All that added up to a shocking 8–16 record, the worst of his Hall of Fame career. During one stretch, Ryan lost eight straight starts; the Astros scored just 13 runs in those games. No pitcher who led the league in ERA and strikeouts has ever posted a poorer record.

6. 215 Games with 10 or More Strikeouts. This record appeared to be safe until Randy Johnson came on the scene. Johnson entered the 2008 season with 209 games with 10-plus strikeouts, but it's unlikely that he will top Ryan's mark. In 1973 alone, Ryan had 23 games with 10 or more strikeouts. He also had 26 games with 15 or more strikeouts.

5. 383 Strikeouts in One Season. This record was set in 1973 and may withstand the test of time. First off, few contemporary pitchers will throw enough innings to come close to 383 strikeouts. Ryan threw 326 innings in 1973, a mark unlikely to be reached again considering the proliferation of multi-level relief pitching. Ryan's record is even more amazing when you consider he accomplished the feat in a league with a designated hitter. In other words, he had no easy strikeouts against opposing pitchers.

4. 2,795 Career Walks. This may be Ryan's most unbeatable record. Second on the all-time list is Steve Carlton with 1,833. Ryan reached a peak with 204 walks in 1977. He also had 202 walks in 1974. All told, Ryan led the league in free passes eight times while walking 100 or more batters in 11 different seasons. Let's face it: If any other pitcher was that wild today, he wouldn't last very long in the major leagues.

3. 5,714 Career Strikeouts. What more can you say about Ryan's strikeout numbers? No other pitcher has even reached 5,000 career strikeouts and only Randy Johnson, Roger Clemens, and Steve Carlton have passed 4,000 strikeouts. Ryan led the league in strikeouts 11 times. He had 15 seasons with 200 or more strikeouts and six years when he passed 300 Ks. His 301 strikeouts in 1989 were stunning when you consider he was 42 years old that season.

2. Zero Cy Young Awards. How does a pitcher who gathered more Hall of Fame votes than any other in history not win a single Cy Young award? In retrospect, Ryan could have won as many as three Cy Young's, but apparently the writers who voted were not paying attention. Ryan's 1973 season included his record 383 strikeouts, two no-hitters and 21 wins for a team with a losing record. He also should have been honored in 1977 and 1981. Without question Ryan is the greatest pitcher never to win the award since it was first issued in 1956.

1. Seven No-Hitters. Think about that: seven career no-hitters. The first came in 1973 and the last in 1991. That final no-hitter occurred when Ryan was 44, and he struck out 16 batters. He is one of just four pitchers to throw two no-hitters in the same season and he threw no-hitters for three different teams. In addition, Ryan had 12 one-hitters and 19 two-hitters. He also lost five no-hitters in the ninth inning. Koufax is second with four no-hitters, but only two other pitchers in the last 25 years—Randy Johnson and Hideo Nomo—have thrown more than one. Don't expect anyone to ever pitch eight. Ryan's record is safe.

Top 10 Reasons Why the Angels Won the 2002 World Series

Was the Angels' 2002 World Series victory a fluke? Some have suggested as much. A staff led by Jarrod Washburn, Kevin Appier, and Ramon Ortiz? A lineup that hit just 152 home runs on the season, fourth lowest in the AL? And a losing record during the regular-season against the other teams in the AL post-season, including just 3–4 against the Yankees, 4–5 against the Twins and 9–11 against the A's? But take a closer look and you'll see that they were actually the best team in the playoffs that year.

10. Mark the Date. After shelling out $80 million for Mo Vaughn in 1998, making him the highest-paid player in baseball, Mo missed the entire 2001 season with a biceps injury. Somehow, some way, Bill Stoneman was able to send the malcontent—and the $48 million left on his deal—to the Mets in a trade made on December 27, 2001. And the Angels received a pretty darn good starting pitcher in Kevin Appier. In 13 big league seasons Appier compiled a 147–115 record with a career ERA of 3.63. Just the previous season he worked over 200 innings and had a sub-3.75 ERA for the Mets. In the playoffs, Appier pitched his best in the ALCS, posting a 3.42 ERA in two starts, and was credited for bringing a veteran presence to the pitching staff.

9. The Road Not Taken. While that trade went through, there was an equally important one that didn't. The club was kicking around the idea of sending Darin Erstad to the White Sox for pitcher Jon Garland and centerfielder Chris Singleton. Some reports suggest the deal was done, only to be nixed by the Disney Ownership group because Erstad was a fan favorite and a marketable commodity. Ersty hit .421 in the Yankees series, .364 in the ALCS and .300 in the World Series, and appropriately caught the fly ball that clinched the World Series for the Angels.

8. Patience, Patience. Despite a 6–14 start, and in those 14 losses being outscored by almost 4 runs per game, management didn't panic and fire Mike Scioscia. Remember, he had a combined record of 157–167 in his two previous seasons finishing no better than third in the division. He'd go on to win manager of the year with his 99–63 record.

7. The Rally Monkey. Even though you don't want to admit it, that damn Rally Monkey worked. There's something to be said for getting a home crowd worked up. I went to a number of Angels games that season, and there were maybe 20,000 in the stands early on. But after they starting ripping off wins, the big A—or "Ed" at the time—was the place to be, and when Disturbed's "Down With the Sickness" started blaring and that random monkey showed up, people freaked the hell out.

6. Streaking. The A's posted a 20-game win streak that started August 13; the Angels answered with a 16–1 tear that started 16 days later. In the middle of that Halos run they took three out of four against the A's.

5. The Definition of "Team." Garrett Anderson had a big statistical year, but he was the only offensive player that showed up regularly in the top five of any major offensive category. Outside of Troy Percival's 40 saves, which ranked him third in the league, no individual statistics stood out among the pitching staff. Yet as a team, the Angels were first in hits and fourth in runs scored per game, and tops in the league with 8.3 hits and 3.98 runs allowed per contest.

4. Mashed the Yankees. In the four-game divisional series victory, Troy Glaus hit three home runs, Garret Anderson hit .389, Erstad hit .421, Tim Salmon hit two homers and knocked in seven RBIs, and Scott Spezio hit .400 with six RBIs. The Yankees starting pitching, meanwhile—well, Roger Clemens lasted 5.2 innings and gave up four runs, David Wells just 4.2 and gave up eight, and Andy Pettite went just three innings and allowed four earned runs.

3. K Freaking Rod. Again, a nod to Mike Scioscia. In his first post-season appearance Francisco Rodriguez threw two innings and gave up two runs. He would throw another 16.2 innings and allow just two more earned runs total. He struck out 28 batters issued just five walks, and his record was 5-1. He was so dominant some insisted his call-up was almost unfair.

2. ALCS Success. Torii, Big Papi, and Jacque who? Think about what David Ortiz has done to Angels pitching since he's been on the Red Sox. Don't forget he was on the Minnesota squad that faced the Angels in the ALCS, as was Torii Hunter and Jacque Jones. Ortiz did hit above .300, but had no power numbers and just one extra-base hit. Hunter hit .167 with zero homers. Jones was two for 20 with zero RBIs. During the regular season the three combined to hit 76 home runs. Angels' second baseman Adam Kennedy, meanwhile, hit just seven bombs in the regular season, but had three in the series.

1. Game 6. After three one-run games—including two in favor of the Giants—Game 6 pitted Russ Ortiz against Kevin Appier. In Game 2 Apes had been tagged for five runs in just two innings, while Ortiz gave up seven in just 1.2. Whatever people expected to happen coming into the game, it didn't happen. With the Giants up 5–0 and the Angels batting in the bottom of the seventh, Dusty Baker thanked Ortiz for his Herculean effort and, as the story goes, gave him a ball to take back to the dugout, saying he earned it. Felix Rodriguez entered the game and immediately gave up a three-run homer to Scott Spezio that barely—I mean, by 18 inches at most—cleared the fence. In the bottom of the eighth, Erstad led off with home run, Salmon singled, Anderson singled, and then Glaus Boss knocked 'em in with a double, putting the Angels up 6–5. After that choke job, the Giants never had a chance in game 7.

When the Angels won the 2002 World Series, they overcame a greater curse than any Cubs or Red Sox fan can claim. Tragedy seemed to follow the franchise from the very beginning. When the team moved to Anaheim in 1966, some said their new stadium was built on an ancient Indian burial ground. Sounds strange, but former general manager Buzzie Bavasi thought enough about the rumor to consult a Roman Catholic priest. Need more convincing? Check out this list of Angels who fell to the curse.

10. Dick Wantz. The curse of the Angels started with the fate of this young pitcher. The 25-year-old made the Halos opening-day lineup in 1965 and made his major league debut on April 13. He pitched one inning, striking out two, but gave up two runs on three hits. After the game he complained about a severe headache and doctors diagnosed him with a brain tumor. He died on May 13, exactly one month to the day after his only major league game.

9. Mo Vaughn. It took Vaughn exactly one game to fall victim to the Angels' curse. Actually, he *fell* victim, tumbling into the dugout going after a fall ball on opening day in 1999. He missed the next 15 games and never came close to fulfilling his potential in his two seasons with the team.

8. Ken McBride. McBride was the first pitching ace for the Angels, earning the starting nod for the American League in the 1963 All-Star Game. That season he ran off a streak of nine wins in 10 decisions, capped by a three-hit shutout of the mighty Yankees. The following spring, McBride injured his back and neck in a spring training auto accident. He won opening day, but lost his next 10 decisions. He went on to win only three more games in his major league career.

7. Tony Conigliaro. One of the most tragic figures in baseball history, "Tony C" overcame a horrific beaning in 1967 to reemerge as one of the American League's most feared sluggers. In 1970, he hit 36 home runs with 116 RBIs for the Red Sox before being traded to the Angels. On the night of July 9, 1971, Conigliaro struck out five times in a 0–8 performance against Oakland. He never played another game as an Angel, retiring immediately because of recurring eye problems stemming from the beaning.

6. Bobby Valentine. When Tommy Lasorda was a minor league manager for the Dodgers, he schooled some amazing talent. Steve Garvey, Bill Buckner, and Ron Cey were just a few of the players he managed that would go on to big league greatness, but the best player he had on those minor league teams was Bobby Valentine. The Angels thought they got a steal when they acquired the 23-year-old from the Dodgers in 1973. By May 2 of that season, Valentine was hitting .397 with visions of Cooperstown in his future. It wasn't meant to be. Two weeks later, Valentine crashed into the outfield wall and shattered his leg. Let's just say he became a better manager than he was a player.

5. Mike Miley. The Angels made Miley their top choice in the 1974 draft after a stellar career at LSU. He was such a great athlete in college that he played both baseball and football. In fact, he was LSU's starting quarterback in the 1974 Orange Bowl. He was projected to be the team's shortstop of the future when he made his big league debut in July 1975, but his promising future came to an end on January 6, 1977, when he was killed in a dune buggy accident in Baton Rouge. Miley died two months short of his 24th birthday.

4. Rick Reichardt. Reichardt was *the* can't-miss player that only comes around once in a lifetime. As both a baseball and football star at the University of Wisconsin, Reichardt was so sought after that the Angels paid an astronomical $200,000 to sign him in the pre-draft days of baseball. In his first full season with the team, he was hitting a solid .288 on July 27 when doctors diagnosed him with a rare kidney ailment. He missed all but one game the rest of the year after having his kidney removed, and never regained his previous form.

3. Minnie Rojas. In 1967, Rojas was the best relief pitcher in the American League, leading the junior circuit with 27 saves while winning 12 others. A year later, Rojas was the victim of a horrific car accident that claimed the lives of his two daughters and left him paralyzed from the neck down. Rojas was confined to a wheelchair for the rest of his life. He passed away in 2002.

2. Lyman Bostock. The Angels signed the promising free agent in 1978 after he hit .323 and .336 in two previous seasons with the Twins. Bostock got off to a slow start in April hitting below .200 and he offered to return his entire salary for the month. He later donated the money to charity. By season's end, however, Bostock had raised his average to .296 when fate dealt him a bad hand. On September 23, 1978, the popular player was killed as an innocent victim in a drive-by shooting. He was 27 years old.

1. Donnie Moore. One pitch changed Donnie Moore's life. It was Game 5 of the 1986 ALCS and the Angels were one strike away from their first World Series appearance. Moore had been suffering shoulder problems, but his sinker seemed to be working fine when he delivered the fateful pitch to Boston's Dave Henderson. When that pitch was deposited into the left field stands, Moore lost it forever. Three years later, still despondent over that October day, Moore shot his wife (she survived) and then killed himself.

The 10 Best Baseball Players to Attend High School in Los Angeles or Orange County

We all know that the Dodgers and Angels have fielded some of the best players in baseball over the past 50 years, but how many great players actually attended high school in the area? As it turns out there's a list of Hall of Famers that attended local schools. By the way, we did not cheat by adding the names of Hall of Famers who played within shouting distance of L.A, such as Ted Williams (San Diego), Tom Seaver (Fresno), and Eddie Mathews (Santa Barbara). Our list includes some surprises.

10. Gary Carter, Fullerton Sunny Hills. "The Kid" was such a good prep athlete that he committed to UCLA to play quarterback. Instead of becoming a Bruin, he opted to sign with the Montreal Expos out of high school. He would go on to be named to 11 All-Star teams, win three Golf Gloves, and help the Mets to the 1986 World Series title. He currently manages a minor league baseball that plays its home games in Fullerton. Talk about coming full circle!

9. Ralph Kiner, Alhambra. The pride of the San Gabriel Valley, Kiner became one of baseball's all-time home run kings. He hit an amazing 369 home runs in just 10 major league seasons, leading the National League in each of his first seven years. What made his home run totals even more imposing was the fact that he played on terrible Pittsburgh teams from 1946 through 1953. He has since become a legendary announcer for the New York Mets. The city of Alhambra immortalized Kiner with a statue that was dedicated in 2008.

8. Don Drysdale, Van Nuys. "Big D" was plenty happy when the Dodgers left Brooklyn for Los Angeles in 1958. It was a perfect homecoming for the Van Nuys High School product, although his prep career was not all that distinguished. It turned out that Drysdale's dad did not permit his son to play high school ball until his senior season. Nonetheless, the Dodgers signed him and he was in the big leagues by age 19. The Cy Young winner went on to set records with six straight shutouts and 58.2 shutout innings in 1968.

7. Duke Snider, Compton. Here is a little known fact: The great Duke Snider was a classmate of former NFL commissioner Pete Rozelle at Compton High School. The Duke may have been a better quarterback in high school, but Branch Rickey saw the gifted athlete as a perfect fit in Brooklyn. Snider is the Dodgers' all-time home run leader and he hit 11 World Series round-trippers. He will forever be linked with the other great New York center fielders of that era—it will always be Willie, Mickey, and the Duke.

6. Robin Yount, Los Angeles Taft. Larry Yount, Robin's brother, first played at Taft and pitched. He would appear in one major league game, but never throw a pitch. That's right—on September 15, 1971, Larry was called on to pitch the ninth inning, but he was replaced before throwing a pitch. Brother Robin would go on to have a much better career. He won two MVP awards and registered more than 3,000 hits. Robin played more games as a teenager than any player in major league history. In fact, less than a year out of high school, he was the opening day shortstop for the Brewers in 1974.

5. George Brett, El Segundo. Like Yount, Brett had an older brother who attended the same high school, but with much more bravado. Ken Brett became an All-Star pitcher during a 14-year big league career. He also was the youngest pitcher ever to appear in the World Series as a 19-year-old in 1967 with the Red Sox. George was considered the lesser of the brothers in baseball, but he would prove the doubters wrong with 21 amazing seasons with the Kansas City Royals. He was the American League MVP in 1980 when he flirted with hitting .400 before finishing the season at .390.

4. Tony Gwynn, Long Beach Poly. Gwynn will always be associated with San Diego as a college star at San Diego State, an eight-time batting champion with the Padres, and now the head coach of his alma mater. But his athletic career really took notice at Long Beach Poly, where he played both baseball and basketball. In fact, Gwynn decided to attend San Diego State because it was the only school to allow him to play both sports. He went on to become one of the best point guards in school history.

3. Eddie Murray and Ozzie Smith, Los Angeles Locke (tie). These two baseball immortals played on the same high school team! Think about the odds! Murray and Smith were not only teammates in baseball, but basketball as well. In fact, Ozzie may have been better known in high school for his skills on the court. It's sad that inner city baseball has declined since this duo graced the field at Locke, but both are committed to bringing the game back to the neighborhood. Murray became just the third player to collect both 500 home runs and 3,000 hits while the Wizard earned an amazing 13 Gold Gloves at shortstop.

2. Walter Johnson, Fullerton. How many people know that the "Big Train" went to high school in Orange County? At the turn of the 20th century, Orange County was just that—nothing but a huge orange grove. It was there, however, that one of baseball's greatest pitchers and perhaps the hardest throwing pitcher of all time grew up. He once struck out 27 batters in a 15-inning game against Santa Ana High School. That was just a precursor of things to come. Johnson would win a mind-boggling 416 games while posting a staggering 110 shutouts. He was one of the first five players elected to the Baseball Hall of Fame.

1. Jackie Robinson, Pasadena Muir. Anyone who saw Jackie Robinson at Muir High School, Pasadena City College, or UCLA will tell you that baseball was his worst sport. Robinson was a four-sport star at every level, starring in football, track, basketball, and baseball. His brother Mack ran in the 1936 Olympics as a sprinting teammate of Jesse Owens. Jackie set records in the long jump while leaving opponents grasping for air on the football field. He was simply one of the greatest athletes who ever lived. Jackie Robinson is also an icon who changed the game forever.

The 10 Best High School Athletes in the Past 30 Years
:: Eric Sondheimer

Note: The *Los Angeles Times'* Eric Sondheimer has covered high school sports in Southern California for the past 30 years. He has become the expert on all things pertaining to prep sports. Here is his list of the 10 best high school athletes since he took over the beat.

10. John Williams, Crenshaw. Some still consider Williams the best high school basketball player to ever play in Southern California. His big body—250 pounds—made him a target of fat jokes, but his skills were second to none. He went on to lead LSU to the Final Four as a sophomore before departing for the NBA. His increasing girth got the best of him at the professional level where he earned the nickname "Hot Plate."

9. Dwayne Polee, Manual Arts. Polee is another high school basketball legend that never really reached his promise. As a senior, he scored 43 points in the 1981 city title game and headed to UNLV with the hopes of collegiate glory. His stay with the Rebels lasted just one season before he transferred to Pepperdine. He had three solid seasons with the Waves, but that would not translate into future professional success. His entire NBA career consisted of one game as a Clipper.

8. Russell White, Crespi. An unbelievable high school football talent, White led Crespi to a Division 1 title as a sophomore—the only Valley school to achieve that distinction. He went on to star at the University of California. The nephew of former Heisman Trophy winner Charles White, White never fulfilled his early promise at the professional level and played just five games in his only NFL season with the Rams.

7. Jack McDowell, Sherman Oaks Notre Dame. One of the dominant high school pitchers of his era, McDowell went on to an All-American career at Stanford. He was the fifth overall pick in the 1987 baseball draft and went on to win 127 games in his major league career. He was a two-time 20-game winner with the White Sox and won the 1983 American League Cy Young award. He was also an accomplished guitar player for several alternate rock bands while still playing baseball.

6. Quincy Watts, Taft. In high school, Watts was a complete athlete competing in both basketball and track. It was the latter, however, where he made the most noise winning the 1987 state title in both the 100- and 200-meter races. His time in the 200 (20.50) is still a state record. Ironically, Watts would achieve Olympic fame in another race, winning the 400-meter gold medal in Barcelona in 1992. He later returned to his former high school as a coach.

5. Marion Jones, Thousand Oaks. She may now be known as one of the biggest cheaters in Olympic history, but she was, by all accounts, clean when she excelled in both track and basketball at Thousand Oaks. In two years at Thousand Oaks, Jones led the basketball team to a 60–4 record averaging 22.8 points and 14.7 rebounds. She also set a national record in the 200 meters and almost qualified for the Olympic team as a 16-year-old.

4. Cheryl Miller, Riverside Poly. Still considered one of the best female basketball players of all time. A member of the Basketball Hall of Fame, Miller's career ended before the start of the WNBA, but her four-year run as an All-American at USC clinched her place in basketball lore. It all started, however, at Riverside Poly, where she became the first player, male or female, to be named a *Parade* All-American four times. She averaged 33 points and 15 rebounds during her prep career and led her team to a combined 132–4 record. She also scored an amazing 105 points in one game!

3. Bret Saberhagen, Cleveland. Talk about meteoric rises. Saberhagen pitched the most memorable game in Los Angeles City Section history when he threw a no-hitter in the championship game at Dodgers Stadium in 1982. Just three years later, Saberhagen shut out the St. Louis Cardinals in Game 7 of the World Series to clinch the title for his Kansas City Royals. He also won the Cy Young award that season at the ripe old age of 21. He would add another Cy Young award in 1989 before injuries cut short what could have been a Hall of Fame career.

2. John Elway, Granada Hills. How good of a high school athlete was Elway? Consider that he was the City Player of the Year—in baseball! He would have won the award in football, but he broke his leg midway through his senior season. Elway, of course, would do a few things after high school like finishing second in the 1982 Heisman Trophy voting while at Stanford and then having enough success in the NFL to earn a spot in the Pro Football Hall of Fame on the first ballot. It's hard to imagine how gifted Elway was as an athlete, but those who saw him at Granada Hills never had a doubt about his future success.

1. Tiger Woods, Anaheim Western. Woods is the greatest golfer of all time, but just consider how dominant he was in high school! He became the youngest ever winner of the National Junior Amateur Championship at age 15 and never looked back. In fact, Woods had just graduated from Western High School when he won his first U.S. Amateur title in 1994. Perhaps there have been better all-around athletes, but no one has ever dominated their high school sport like Eldrick "Tiger" Woods.

Top 10 Los Angeles Area Sporting Venues

Turns out we're pretty lucky when it comes to places to watch a game. When measuring the best Los Angeles venues you have to take into consideration a number of factors. One is the number of history-making moments. For that purpose the Home Depot Center and Galen Center—both of which are relatively new and have no real significant sporting moments—were intentionally excluded. While some soccer fans would like to point out some remarkable matches at the beautiful Carson, CA facility, but when you're talking about Los Angeles, it pales in comparison to the rest of the list.

10. Honda Center. Formerly known as the Arrowhead Pond, this venue is the home of the Anaheim Ducks, although it'd be willing to also host an NBA franchise. There hasn't been a ton of history at the Honda Center, but two Stanley Cup finals— including one championship—are enough to get it onto this list. It's a beautiful arena with great sightlines, plenty of amenities, and it happens to be in the same location as Angels Stadium, which is one of the most accessible in Southern California. If they didn't hand out the Duck calls back in the day, I might have put it a spot higher.

9. L.A. Sports Arena. The one-time home of the Lakers, Clippers, Kings, and Trojans basketball is knocked down the list because of its irrelevancy today. While it hosted boxing matches during the 1984 Summer Games and the 1960 Democratic National Convention, it may be better known as the spot for the annual Warped Tour, massive raves, and Hollywood staging for filmed sporting events.

8. Angels Stadium. Since they carved out a quarter of the bowl in 1997, it is, pardon the pun, a whole new ball game. With the new view of the mountains in the stadium's background, it's almost hard to believe it was once enclosed and a two-sport venue. Angels Stadium is arguably the most accessible of all the venues on this list, which here in Southern California is a giant bonus. It's also probably home to the best-looking crowd, which doesn't hurt either. The 2002 World Series victory and the team's consistent success solidify its place on this list.

7. Riviera Country Club. This one-time site of the U.S. Open and PGA Championship, is also the annual home of the historic Los Angeles Open. Often referred to as "Hogan's Alley" after three-time winner Ben Hogan, it is truly Hollywood's course. Howard Hughes, Elizabeth Taylor, and Humphrey Bogart all sipped bourbon while watching the golfers stroll by, as the stories go. The course's par-3 sixth, with a bunker in the middle of the green, and the two fairways to choose from on the eighth help make it the seemingly only Tiger-proof course in the world. Woods has never won at Riviera, technically his home tournament (I don't count the Tiger World Challenge at Sherwood). But it's the course's great history and beautiful surroundings that make it seventh on this list.

6. Staples Center. In a city that hasn't had a newly constructed arena or stadium for decades, Staples Center made a major impact simply because it was the first to offer some of the modern conveniences common in new venues. When I say downtown Los Angeles was a ghost town before Staples Center was built, I mean it literally. Nothing happened in the city center past 4 p.m. Now, with countless premium restaurants, bars, clubs, hotels, and the just opened Nokia Theatre, we actually have a place to call downtown. The Staples Center itself was a bit sterile thanks to the lighting patterns, but the Lakers' "lights out" adjustment made it much more tolerable. With the last three Lakers titles all won there and, most recently, a NBA Finals match-up against the Boston Celtics, Staples Center represents the best modern arena in town.

5. Pauley Pavilion. Built in 1965 after consecutive UCLA men's basketball championships, Pauley Pavilion might not be all that much of a looker, but the history is inescapable. Consider the first game ever played in the building was an exhibition in which Lew Alcindor led the freshmen against a varsity team that was the consensus pre-season No. 1 in the nation. The freshmen won the contest 75–60. A 149–2 record was amassed in the John Wooden era at Pauley Pavilion, including a 98-game winning streak. The team won eight championships over that span, making it the greatest home court advantage in town.

4. Dodgers Stadium. I'm not sure what the bigger draw to Dodgers Stadium is—the park itself and the beautiful Chavez Ravine surrounding area, or the fact that eight World Series have been played there featuring legendary names like Sandy Koufax, Don Drysdale, Steve Garvey, Maury Wills, and Fernando Valenzuela. It doesn't hurt that the most dramatic play in baseball history occurred October 15, 1988, when Kirk Gibson, barely able to walk, hobbled into the batters box as a pinch hitter facing Dennis Eckersley and, with one runner on-base and two out, he launched an opposite field, game-winning home run. That led Jack Buck to scream his famous line: "I don't believe what I just saw." With the team winning just one playoff game since that 1988 World Series, you have to credit the ballpark for still bringing out nearly four million fans every season.

3. The (Great Western) Forum. When Dr. Jerry Buss purchased the Forum, along with the Kings and Lakers, from Jack Kent Cooke in 1979, it was still known by a number of names—The Fabulous Forum, the L.A. Forum, the Los Angeles Forum. But in 1988 all the variety came to an abrupt halt when the Doc sold the naming rights to Great Western Bank, making the arena the Great Western Forum. It was rare in 1988 to have naming rights on a venue, and many thought it was a moniker referring to the west coast, not a local business. Either way, the Forum was home to 14 NBA Finals—six of them ending with a Lakers championship—and one Stanley Cup series. The Forum became internationally known thanks to the "Showtime Lakers" and the celebrities who filled courtside seats to watch them play. Add in the typical "there wasn't a bad seat in the house" refrain from fans, and it was a one of a kind venue.

2. Rose Bowl. A National Historic Landmark designation and as much of a national presence as a local one, the Rose Bowl has hosted five Super Bowls, a World Cup, the Women's World Cup (which was the highest attended women's sporting event in history), and the greatest annual college football bowl game, often referred to as "the granddaddy of them all." It was mainly a post-season venue until 1982 when the UCLA Bruins made it their home football field. Settled into the Arroyo Seco canyon, the surrounding view when sitting inside the stadium is rivaled by few. And it doesn't hurt that the flea market held there every weekend in the off-season is the largest in the world.

1. The Los Angeles Memorial Coliseum. The only stadium in the entire world that's hosted the Olympics, the Super Bowl, and the World Series is a no-brainer when it comes to topping this list. Opened in 1923 and declared a National Historic Landmark in 1984, we could write an entire chapter on the greatest Coli moments in history. Today it's known as the home of USC football, but for nearly 60 years—from 1928 to 1982—it was also the home of UCLA football. The first of two Olympic Games was hosted there in 1932, and the cauldron from that competition remains. The 1984 Olympics saw the addition of the bronze male and female statues atop the Olympic Gateway. It's also been host to the NFL's Rams, Raiders, and even the Chargers for a season, as well as a World Cup, Super Bowl I, JFK's acceptance speech at the 1960 Democratic National Convention, and countless memorable concerts. It's a runaway to top this list.

A person's bar is like their child, so I anticipate this being one of the most hotly contested lists in the book. The only thing missing from what we've compiled below is an official USC bar, but because of the school's location, there isn't much near campus. Other caveats about this list: The pre-game festivities at Traddy's and the 9-0 don't qualify since neither is a bar/restaurant, and listing the Fox Sports Skybox at Staples Center or Casey's is a bit ridiculous. All that being understood, we present the best places to watch a game in the greater Los Angeles area.

10. Tin Horn Flats, 2623 W. Magnolia Blvd., Burbank. I know, I know, I know—it's the "Official Chicago Bears Bar" in Southern California, and I've grown to love watching my favorite NFL team play there on some Sundays. But there is so much more to this spot that goes beyond their great taste in football teams. It's been around since 1939, which I think is longer than Burbank has been a city. It also features Old West-style swinging doors and one hell of a cowboy motif.

9. JT Schmid's, 2610 E. Katella Ave., Anaheim. Almost makes it by default. There really isn't a "Ducks Bar" in Orange County. That's nothing against their fan base, it just isn't the type of crowd that decides to go to a bar and watch the game together. Schimd's makes this list mostly because it's a great place to pre-game before walking over to Honda Center. There's a bar on the patio outside, which avoids the in-and-out nightmare, and the people inside are all right.

8. Hooters, 321 Santa Monica Blvd., Santa Monica. What's a Hooters doing on the list? As I've already said, Kings fans are the best in town and this happens to be their largest gathering place. It might be the only spot that regularly fills up for a franchise's road games. Needless to say, the surroundings are friendly and you know what you're getting when it comes to food. Consider this your best bet if you have the urge to put on a "sweater" and cheer on your favorite NHL team.

7. Leo's All-Star Sports Bar & Grill, 2941 Honolulu Ave., La Crescenta. I hear from more people that Leo's is the place to be when it comes to watching the Lakers. It's routinely voted the best sports bar in the 818, and it's a notch above some of the other places on this list—definitely not a dive. You'll actually get some attractive ladies in the mix, and the weird karaoke/"Rock Band" crowd balances it out. Eat the Chicken Philly.

6. O'Hara's, 1000 Gayley Ave., Westwood. This used to be Maloney's back in the day and is now the king of the Westwood sports bar scene. I would have listed Stratton's Pub of it was still open, but today O'Hara's gets the title. I prefer the basement with the long narrow tables and multiple TVs to the main level. You want to watch a game with UCLA students, this is the spot.

5. Phil Trani's, 3490 Long Beach Blvd., Long Beach. This place is all about Phil. Without him it doesn't make this list. Phil is the owner/operator, Phil is in the kitchen, Phil is on the floor talking with everyone, and that's what makes Trani's. Hang out in the bar and you'll find yourself watching the game with former UCLA O-linemen, defensive ends that played with the Rams, and 20-game winners from various MLB teams. Trani's has long been a spot for Southern California athletes to catch up, and after they leave town it seems like every time they return, a trip to Trani's is on the schedule.

4. National Sports Grill and Bar, 450 N. State College Blvd., Orange. Possibly the only spot on this list that actually includes players stopping by after the game on a regular basis. Right across from the main entrance to Angels Stadium, the National is in a good location and it's huge. The perfect pre-game spot to watch some of the east coast games and have one of their many draft beers. The only bummer is the shuttle to Honda Center is apparently no longer in service.

3. Ye Olde Kings Head, 116 Santa Monica Blvd., Santa Monica. When it comes to soccer/futbol, this is far and away the best place. Not only is it the best British pub in town, but it's also a block from the ocean. You want bangers and mash? Done. Traditional English breakfast is ready and waiting for those early-morning EPL kickoffs, and there's always a good crowd of like-minded soccer enthusiasts to cheer with you— or, if your rooting interests aren't the same, threatening to gouge out your eyes.

2. Sports Harbour, 13484 Washington Blvd., Marina Del Rey. It takes me all of a fraction of a second to nominate this as the best sports bar on the west side. Football Sunday brings in more Raiders and Eagles fans than anything else, but outside of that it's fair game—anything and everything will pull a crowd to this retro dive. They boast U.S.A. vs. U.S.S.R. hockey, shuffleboard, darts, pool, cheap beer, and the world's greatest pop-a-shot player. That's not hyperbole—Rahim, the bar's owner and a former UCLA wrestler, is the world champion pop-a-shot player with 180 points in one game.

1. Short Stop, 1455 W. Sunset Blvd, Los Angeles. In the interest of full disclosure, one of the owners (Chuck) used to work with me and left a sweet music business accounting gig to get this place going. Sure, it's sort of an LAPD bar and used to exclusively cater to that crowd, but I'm all right with cops and the guys who hang out at this place are good by me. Add to that, on game nights PBR is your drink special, you get free jukebox plays and free pool, and it's the runaway winner.

There have been dozens of players, coaches, and executives who have swung both ways—contributing to both the Dodgers and Angels. Here's a list of those who made a definite impact on both local baseball teams.

10. Jeff Torborg. He's probably best known as a manager, but Torborg was an excellent defensive catcher in his playing days. He also had the unique distinction of catching three no-hitters in his career. He was behind the plate for Sandy Koufax's perfect game in 1965, Bill Singer's no-no for the Dodgers in 1970, and Nolan Ryan's first no-hitter as an Angel in 1973. Considering he only caught 559 games in his entire career, Torborg's no-hitter percentage is amazing.

9. Fernando Valenzuela. This may surprise some people since few remember Fernando pitching with the Angels. After a decade of great pitching with the Dodgers, Valenzuela was released in spring training of 1991 and no other teams showed any interest in the former Cy Young award winner. That changed on May 20 when the Angels signed the local favorite. Almost 50,000 showed up for his first start on June 7, the largest crowd of the season to date. He lasted just five innings and took the loss. Five days later, Fernando didn't last through the second inning and the Angels released him. His record as an Angel was 0–2 with a 12.15 ERA, but the number that counted most was 82,492 fans showing up to see him pitch. That was the impact the Angels needed most.

8. Jay Johnstone. Johnstone played 20 years in the major leagues without a single All-Star Game appearance. In fact, he spent most of his career as strictly a platoon player. How does a guy like that last so long? By being a fun guy to have in the clubhouse and someone who could deliver a hit off the bench. Johnstone started his career as an Angel in 1966 and played five years with the Halos. The Dodgers picked him up in 1980 and a year later he played a key role off the bench to help the team win a World Series. His career post-season average was an amazing .435!

7. Don Drysdale. One of the greatest pitchers in Dodgers history, Drysdale earned a spot in the Hall of Fame in 1984. His record included 209 wins, three strikeout titles, one Cy Young award, and two amazing streaks during the 1968 season—six straight shutouts and 58 scoreless innings. Although he never pitched for the Angels, he did "pitch" the team as the club's announcer from 1973 through 1979. He also served as a Dodgers' play-by-play guy until his sudden death of a heart attack in 1993. He was just 56 at the time.

6. Tommy John. When you mention the name of Tommy John you think of one thing—Tommy John surgery. Hundreds of players have had the career-prolonging procedure, but none had more post-surgery success than John himself. He had seven great seasons with the Dodgers, including his 20-win season in 1977 after the surgery. He later joined the Angels during their run to the 1982 ALCS, winning four of his seven starts. He won Game 1 of the ALCS against Milwaukee and threw a complete game, but he lost Game 4 when Gene Mauch forced him to pitch on three days rest. His 288 career wins is the most by a pitcher not in the Hall of Fame.

5. Don Sutton. Sutton was a 324-game winner over a 23-year Hall of Fame career. He was also the winningest pitcher in the history of the Dodgers. His greatest achievement, however, occurred with the Angels. On June 18, 1986, Sutton threw a complete game three-hitter against Texas to notch his 300th career victory. He went on to win 15 games that season for the Halos at the age of 41. Although he never dominated like his contemporaries Steve Carlton and Tom Seaver, Sutton's consistency was amazing. He never missed a start due to an injury in his entire career.

4. Bill Singer. Bill Singer was a very good pitcher who could have been a great pitcher had he not been beset with so many injuries. He won 20 games for the Dodgers in 1969, striking out 247 batters and posting a 2.34 ERA. The next season he threw a no-hitter against the Phillies. However, 33 losses over the following two years convinced the Dodgers to trade him to the Angels. Singer responded with his second 20-win season, giving the Angels two 20-game winners in one season for the first time (Nolan Ryan was the other). He won only 29 games over the next four seasons before retiring at age 33.

3. Andy Messersmith. Like Singer, Messersmith's promising career was cut short due to injuries and he was a 20-game winner for both the Angels and the Dodgers. Actually, Messersmith duplicated many of Singer's accomplishments, but in reverse order. He started his career with the Angels and won 20 games in 1971. Two years later, he was traded to the Dodgers and his 20-win season in 1974 helped the team win its first National League title in eight years. He later became one of the game's first free agents, signing with the Atlanta Braves in 1976.

2. Mike Scioscia. Scioscia was the best plate-blocking catcher in baseball during his 13-year career in baseball—all with the Dodgers. He seemed destined to be a Dodger for life when he started his managerial career in the Dodgers' farm system. However, a fall-out with a since departed Dodger executive led him to leave the only organization he had ever known since being the team's top pick in the 1976 draft. The Angels jumped on the opportunity to snag Scioscia and named him manager in 2000. Three years later, he led the Halos to the team's only World Series title. Dodgers fans have never let the organization forget about the man that got away.

1. Buzzie Bavasi. The Baseball Hall of Fame has been reviewing the executive career of Bavasi for years, but they can't seem to get it right. This is a man who belongs in the game's greatest shrine. He started with the Dodgers in 1939 and was named the team's general manager in 1951. Under his tutelage, the team won eight pennants and their first four World Series. He left the team in 1968 to become the team president of the expansion San Diego Padres and then moved back up the freeway to become general manager of the Angels in 1978. The following year, he put together the first Angels team to win a division title. They won another in 1982 and Bavasi retired in 1984.

The 10 Best Rookie Seasons in Los Angeles Dodgers History

No team has had more players win the Rookie of the Year award than the Dodgers. In fact, the award is named after former Brooklyn Dodger Jackie Robinson. With that in mind, here are the best rookies seasons since the Dodgers moved to Los Angeles in 1958. Apologies to the those Dodgers who won rookie honors and didn't make this list: Frank Howard (1960), Ted Sizemore (1969), Rick Sutcliffe (1979), Steve Sax (1982), Eric Karros (1992), and Raul Mondesi (1994).

10. Todd Hollandsworth, 1996. Perhaps the most obscure Dodger to win this award, Hollandsworth was a clutch hitter during the team's run to the wild card. He hit .304 after July 1, including a four-game stretch in mid-September when he had 11 hits in 18 at bats. Hollandsworth spent the next decade bouncing from team to team as a quality utility player.

9. Steve Howe, 1980. The team's only relief pitcher to win rookie honors, Howe will always be remembered as a tortured person with a never-ending drug problem. His death in a car crash in 2006 was tragic, but not unexpected. In 1980, he emerged from obscurity to save 17 games for the Dodgers. In July of that season, he had yet to allow an earned run. Howe helped the Dodgers win the World Series the following year before his drug abuse took control of his life and career.

8. Mariano Duncan, 1985. Duncan lost out on rookie honors in 1985, finishing behind Vince Coleman (110 stolen bases) and Tom Browning (20 wins). However, he was perhaps the most valuable rookie that season, helping the Dodgers improve from 79 wins the previous season to 95 wins and a division title. Playing shortstop, Duncan hit just .244, but he stole 38 bases, including 16 the final month of the season. He even got some MVP votes. He would later hit .340 and win a title in 1996 with the New York Yankees.

7. Tim Belcher, 1988. Everyone remembers the heroics of Kirk Gibson and Orel Hershiser during the Dodgers' magical 1988 championship season, but they wouldn't have survived without the pitching of Belcher. The rookie won 12 games while saving four others. He was also 3–0 in the post-season in four starts with 26 strikeouts in 24 innings. He would go on to win 146 games in his major league career.

6. Jim Lefebvre, 1965. The Dodger's 1965 championship team was more than just Sandy Koufax, Don Drysdale, and Maury Wills. They also had a rookie second baseman that ended up beating out a Hall of Famer for top rookie honors. Lefebvre clinched the award by hitting .320 in September as the Dodgers won 15 of their last 16 games to earn the National League pennant. The following season he was an All-Star, but for the balance of his career he was just a decent utility player.

5. Bob Welch, 1978. Welch did not join the team until June and he didn't become a regular in the starting rotation until August, but his impact on the team's run to the pennant was immeasurable. He won seven games, saved three others, and sported a 2.02 ERA. Three of his victories were shutouts. He went on to World Series glory, striking out Reggie Jackson to save Game 2 of the series. Welch would overcome alcohol problems to win 211 major league games and earn the 1990 American League Cy Young award.

4. Hideo Nomo, 1995. As the first full-time major league starting pitcher from Japan, Nomo was simply sensational in 1995. He posted a 13–6 record and was named the starting pitcher for the National League All-Star team. He led the league in strikeouts, was second in ERA, and finished fourth in the Cy Young voting. Nomomania swept the Asian community in Los Angeles. Others have followed, but Nomo was the most consistent Japanese import pitcher. He went on to win 123 games, including two no-hitters.

3. Larry Sherry, 1959. Sherry was an unheralded rookie entering the 1959 World Series, but over the course of six games he became a national phenomenon. The Dodgers beat the Chicago White Sox and Sherry had a hand in all four wins, earning two victories and two saves for MVP honors. Sherry would go on to have a solid career with both the Dodgers and the Tigers. He passed away in 2006.

2. Mike Piazza, 1993. His story is now part of the Dodgers' lore. Piazza was an obscure 62nd round pick who was only chosen because his father was a friend of Tommy Lasorda. As a rookie in 1993, he hit .318 with 35 home runs and 112 RBIs. Over the next four years he established himself as perhaps the greatest hitting catcher in the game. He may have gone down as the greatest Dodger catcher of all time, but the new Fox ownership decided to trade him instead of pay him. Dodger fans have never forgotten. Piazza's next stop will be the Hall of Fame.

1. Fernando Valenzuela, 1981. Forget that he is still the only rookie to win the Cy Young. Forget that he started his rookie season with eight straight wins, including five shutouts. Forget that he saved the World Series by winning game three when the Dodgers were down 2–0 to the Yankees. No, the big story of Fernando's rookie year was Fernandomania. Never before and never since has any athlete captivated the city of Los Angeles like Fernando did in 1981. You had to be here to believe it.

The 10 Best Nicknames in Los Angeles Dodgers History

Whatever happened to baseball nicknames? Back in the day it seemed like every player was better known for his nickname rather than his birth name, and the Dodgers were no exception. Here are the best of what was a glorious era in nicknames.

10. Walter "Smokey" Alston. The Hall of Fame skipper is often overlooked when great managers are discussed. He won seven pennants and four championships during his 23-year reign with the Dodgers. He also had a mystique befitting his nickname "Smokey." There were two main reasons for the moniker. First, Alston was rarely seen without a cigarette in hand. Second, Alston was as tough as a bear—a Smokey Bear, perhaps—and willing to challenge any player who questioned his authority.

9. Don "Big D" Drysdale. It's not that uncommon to call a tall or large player "Big" and the nickname fit Drysdale perfectly. "Big D" pitched big. He was 6-foot-6, threw sidearm, and had a mean streak second to none. He still holds the National League record for hit batsmen even though he pitched only 12 full seasons. Off the field, "Big D" had a big heart that gave out all too soon at the age of 56.

8. Tom "Wimpy" Paciorek. Paciorek is best known for his many years as a White Sox announcer, but his major league playing career started with the Dodgers. He was one of the star minor league players of the late 1960s managed by Tommy Lasorda and it was Lasorda who gave Paciorek the nickname that stayed with him for 40 years. It all stemmed from a night out with his minor league teammates, when everyone ordered a steak for dinner and Paciorek chose a hamburger. Lasorda called him "Wimpy" after the Popeye character and the nickname stuck.

7. Phil "The Vulture" Regan. It was Sandy Koufax who proclaimed the previously anonymous pitcher "The Vulture" during a memorable 1966 season. Regan had been a journeyman starter in Detroit, but he became an All-Star when the Dodgers moved him to the bullpen. He finished the season with 21 saves and a 14–1 record with most of the victories coming courtesy of late rallies. When's the last time you heard of a relief pitcher winning 14 games in a season? We'll never see the likes of "The Vulture" again.

6. Don "Black & Decker" Sutton. The Hall of Famer and winningest pitcher in the team's history was also an alleged cheater. The legend goes that Gaylord Perry, another alleged Hall of Fame cheater, offered some Vaseline to Sutton to improve his pitching. Sutton countered with a sample of sand paper, thus the "Black & Decker" nickname for the alleged "sander." Whatever the truth is, Sutton won 324 games and earned a spot in Cooperstown.

5. Orel "Bulldog" Hershiser. Normally a nickname like "Bulldog" goes to a player who resembles a bulldog. That could not have been further from the truth when it came to Hershiser. His "Howdy Doody" looks and disarming name hardly fit the mold of previous "Bulldogs," but manager Tommy Lasorda saw it differently. What he saw was a pitcher with a relentless desire to win. Hershiser led the National League in innings pitched for three consecutive seasons and posted more than 200 victories in his outstanding career. Hershiser proved to be the ultimate "Bulldog" during his 18-year career.

4. Steve "Popeye" Garvey. Oh, those forearms! Garvey was a perennial All-Star with the Dodgers and had an unusual physique for a first baseman. When you think of All-Star first-baggers you think of tall, left-handed hitting behemoths with slick gloves and relentless power. Garvey was a relatively short player with no arm and marginal power. But, he had those forearms! Garvey got enough power out of those forearms to post six 200-hit seasons and win the 1974 MVP trophy.

3. Willie "3-Dog" Davis. There has never been a major league player with more speed than Willie Davis. He was also a vastly underrated player with more than 2,500 career hits and three Gold Gloves in center field. His "3-Dog" moniker traces back to his ability to race out triples—138 in his career—and the fact that many would have been doubles for a player of normal speed. Davis reached his zenith in 1970 with a league-leading 16 triples, still the most of any Dodger in history.

2. "Sweet" Lou Johnson. He may have played just three seasons with the Dodgers, but "Sweet Lou" remains one of the most popular figures in team history. Even today, at age 75, he is still recognized by fans. Johnson started his playing career in the Negro Leagues and appeared unlikely to ever get a fair shot at major league baseball until an injury to Tommy Davis created an opening. The Dodgers put "Sweet Lou" in left field to replace Davis in 1965 and he helped the team win the World Series. "Sweet Lou" even hit the winning home run in Game 7 that season.

1. Ron "The Penguin" Cey. Cey remains the greatest third baseman in the history of the Dodgers and no one else is even close. He also possesses of the greatest nickname in team history and no one else is even close. "The Penguin" got his nickname for one obvious reason—his running style. With relatively short legs and a waddling style, "The Penguin" emerged from the pages of *Batman* to become a six-time All-Star with the Dodgers. He may not have been crazy about the nickname, but he had no choice.

The 10 Best Los Angeles-Area Athlete Nicknames
:: Jimmy Kimmel

After eight months of research and six minutes of intense thought, here are my choices for the 10 greatest LA-area nicknames.

10. Jerome "Pooh" Richardson. It takes a secure individual to accept a nickname that brings to mind feces.

9. Ted "The Stork" Hendricks. Storks don't look tough, but they will mess you up if you cross them.

8. "Big Game James" Worthy. I think Chick gave him this moniker—fitting, great, and, best of all, it rhymes.

7. "Love Shaq" O'Neal. Kobe may not agree.

6. "Pee Wee" Reese. A pre-steroid-era nickname if ever there was one.

5. Ron "The Penguin" Cey. He didn't look like a penguin, but somehow he also looked exactly like a penguin.

4. "Dusty" Baker. I'm not sure why I love this one, but I do.

3. Mike "Squatting Jesus" Piazza. I made this one up—and I dare say, it is incredible.

2. Wayne "The Great One" Gretzky. The sort of title you'd give an emperor.

1. Earvin "Magic" Johnson. This might be the best nickname ever.

The Dodgers have had many legendary players in their history, many of whom displayed their skills over an extended period of time. There were other players, however, who had just one magical season in the team's uniform. Here are the best of the one-and-done guys.

10. Billy Grabarkewitz, 1970. His name was tough enough to pronounce, but for one year he was an All-Star. As late as May 27, Grabby was hitting .402 and was the talk of the National League. He was named to the All-Star team and his single set up Pete Rose's famous home plate collision with Ray Fosse. By season's end, however, Grabby's average was down to .289. Two years later he hit just .167 and the Dodgers dumped him to the Angels.

9. Norm Larker, 1960. A platoon player for most of his career, Larker caught fire in 1960 and was leading the National League in hitting for much of the season. He finished the year a close second to Dick Groat with a .323 batting average. He also was named to his only All-Star team. His average dove more than 50 points the following year and the Dodgers dumped him in the Houston expansion draft.

8. Terry Forster, 1978. Forster came to the Dodgers in 1978 with some impressive credentials. As a member of the White Sox, he led the American League in saves in 1974. His first year with the Dodgers was equally impressive with 22 saves and a 1.93 ERA. He had one stretch in late August and early September where he won one game and saved eight others in nine consecutive appearances. However, his next four years with the Dodgers produced just five saves and a bomb to Joe Morgan to lose the 1982 NL West crown.

7. Rick Sutcliffe, 1979. Sutcliffe's career was a roller coaster ride. He won 17 games for the Dodgers in 1979 to earn the Rookie of the Year award. The following season his record fell to 3–9 and one year later the Dodgers traded him to Cleveland. By 1984, Sutcliffe was back on top, winning the Cy Young with the Cubs. If the Dodgers had shown a little more patience, Sutcliffe would not have made this list.

6. Tommy Davis, 1962. How can a two-time batting champion make this list? Check out Davis' 1962 season for the answer. That year he hit a stunning .346 with 27 home runs and 153 RBIs. The following year he repeated as batting champion, hitting .326 with 16 home runs and 88 RBIs. That's a drop of 65 RBIs in one year. In fact, Davis never had 100 RBIs in the remaining 15 years of his solid career. His career with the Dodgers ended when he never fully recovered from a broken ankle and he played for nine other teams before retiring.

5. Jimmy Wynn, 1974. The "Toy Cannon" could easily have won the 1974 National League MVP award after the Dodgers picked him up in a trade with the Houston Astros. Only a late season slump cost him the honor, but he still finished with 32 home runs, 108 RBIs, 108 walks, and 18 stolen bases. However, the next season Wynn seemed to age overnight, hitting just 18 homers with 58 RBIs. The Dodgers traded him to Atlanta for Dusty Baker—one of the great trades in team history.

4. Al Downing, 1971. "Gentleman Al" was considered washed-up when the Dodgers traded for the lefty from Milwaukee in 1971. All he did that first year was win 20 games and finish third in the Cy Young voting as the Dodgers finished just one game short of a division title. His back-to-back shutouts in late September were pure brilliance. Downing spent six more years with the Dodgers, but would never win more than nine games in any season. He also gave up Hank Aaron's 715th home run to secure his baseball immortality.

3. Phil Regan, 1966. "The Vulture" was little more than a journeyman starting pitcher for the Detroit Tigers when the Dodgers traded for him before the 1966 season. By year's end, he was the talk of baseball. The Dodgers made him their closer and he saved a league-high 21 games while fashioning an amazing 14–1 record. He even finished seventh in the MVP voting. The high would not last, however. Regan's record fell to 6–9 the next year with just six saves. The Dodgers traded him to the Cubs.

2. Mike Marshall, 1974. There may never be another relief pitcher like Mike Marshall. The Dodgers traded fan favorite Willie Davis for the enigmatic pitcher, who proceeded to have a huge season. Pitching in a record 106 games, including a record 13 consecutive games, Marshall won the Cy Young with 15 wins and 21 saves. His save total would have been much higher under current rules when you consider he finished 83 games. His abrasive personality proved to be his undoing. His record fell to 9–14 the following year and the Dodgers dumped him to Atlanta.

1. Kirk Gibson, 1988. Gibson's heroics during the 1988 World Series will forever cement his place in Dodgers' lore, but he should have walked away after that legendary feat. The injuries he suffered during that 1988 MVP season never fully healed. After hitting .290 with 25 home runs and 31 stolen bases in 1988, Gibson's numbers fell to .213, 9, and 12 in 1989. His explosive temper also got the best of him with the media and teammates. But for one year he may have been the most valuable Dodger of all time.

The legend of the revolving door at third base for the Dodgers is alive and well. When catcher Russell Martin was forced to fill in at third for an inning in 2008 it just illustrated how futile the search for stability has been. In fact, the only third basemen ever to hold down the job for any significant time were Ron Cey (1973–1982) and Adrian Beltre (1998–2004). Dozens of others have tried and failed to secure a spot at the hot corner. Here are the worst of those who were considered, at least for one year, to be the Dodgers "starting" third baseman.

10. Wilson Betemit, 2006–2007. The Dodgers traded two players and cash mid-season to Atlanta for Betemit in hopes of finding a permanent replacement at third following the free agency departure of Adrian Beltre. Betemit quickly established himself as nothing more than a journeyman, hitting .241 and .231 in two partial seasons with the Dodgers. Almost one year to the day after the Dodgers acquired Betemit, they traded him to the New York Yankees.

9. Jeff Hamilton, 1986–1991. Quick now, who was the Dodgers starting third baseman when they won their last championship in 1988? If you guessed Jeff Hamilton consider yourself a true Dodgers trivia buff. Hamilton inherited the starting job that year when Pedro Guerrero was dealt to St. Louis in mid-season. He hardly set the world on fire, hitting just .236 with six home runs. Hamilton was even worse during the World Series, batting just .105. The following season proved that Hamilton would never be the answer at third—a .245 batting average and 12 home runs in 151 games wasn't exactly what the Dodgers were hoping for. He was banished to the bench for the next two years and faded into obscurity.

8. Pedro Guerrero, 1978–1988. When Ron Cey was let go by the Dodgers after the 1982 season, management decided to put rising star Pedro Guerrero at third base. The idea was to hide his sub-par glove while giving him an opportunity to flash his potent bat. Offensively, the experiment worked. Guerrero had a huge year at the plate, but his defensive work at third was worse than anticipated. He led the league with a staggering 30 errors, many of which proved costly. After posting 16 more errors in just 76 games the next year, Guerrero was shipped to the outfield for good.

7. Dick Gray, 1958–1959. The man who started the revolving door at third base for the Los Angeles Dodgers was this obscure rookie. Gray was the Dodgers' first opening day starter after the move from Brooklyn—and he was also the first starting third baseman to lose his job. Playing in 58 games that season, Gray batted just .249 while being charged with 15 errors in the field. He was traded to St. Louis the next season after hitting just .154 in 21 games. His career ended for good in 1960.

6. Bob Bailey, 1967–1968. The Dodgers did the unthinkable after the 1966 season when they traded shortstop Maury Wills to the Pittsburgh Pirates for a promising third baseman named Bob Bailey. Bailey was considered a player on the rise after being a huge "bonus baby" in 1961. He showed some progress in four years in Pittsburgh, but that came to a screeching halt when he put on a Dodgers' uniform. Amazingly, his two years with the Dodgers were exactly the same in one respect. In both 1967 and 1968, Bailey had 322 at-bats with 73 hits and a .227 batting average. The Dodgers ended up selling Bailey to the Montreal Expos, where he would play a solid third base for the next seven years.

5. Steve Garvey, 1969–1982. Before he became the best first baseman in the National League, Garvey was perhaps the league's worst third baseman. Everyone knew Garvey could hit, but no positions were open until Billy Grabarkewitz hit the skids at third in 1971. Garvey started 60 games at third base that season and hit just .227. The following season was one that Garvey would like to forget. Although he hit a respectable .269, Garvey posted a league-worst 28 errors in just 73 starts at third. Most of his errors came from throwing the ball past helpless first basemen. Fortunately, the Dodgers realized their mistake and they moved Garvey to first base. The rest was history.

4. Daryl Spencer, 1961–1963. Spencer was one of many third basemen the Dodgers acquired late in their careers, when there was no gas left in the tank. Another classic example was former MVP Ken Boyer, who the Dodgers employed in 1968 and 1969. At least Boyer could still hit. Spencer was the Dodgers' regular third baseman during the 101-win 1962 season, but the team lost a three-game playoff to the Giants for the National League title. Spencer hit just .236 that season with only two home runs. After August 1, his batting average was a pathetic .129. Spencer was dumped the following year after hitting .111 in seven games.

3. John Kennedy, 1965–1966. How many people know that John Kennedy played third base for the Dodgers? Not that John Kennedy, of course, but a career journeyman who the Dodgers acquired before the 1965 season. Kennedy had a decent glove, but his bat was beyond quiet even by Dodgers' terms. He batted just .171 in 1965 and .201 in 1966 before being shipped to the New York Yankees. Kennedy even started a couple of games for the Dodgers in the 1966 World Series. Amazingly, Kennedy lasted 12 seasons in the major leagues with a career .225 batting average.

2. Derrell Griffith, 1963–1966. In 1964, the Dodgers called up a 20-year-old rookie named Derrell Griffith to start at third base and for a the better part of three months it appeared to be a solid decision. Griffith came out on fire, batting .337 through his first month before slowing down the stretch. Still, he finished with a respectable .290 batting average. So why did his career with the Dodgers stall after that one season? Perhaps it was his glove that did him in. In 35 games at third base, Griffith had a staggering 21 errors. That adds up to a .769 fielding percentage that has to rank with the worst of all time. Griffith played a few games in 1965 and 1966, but his bat went silent and there was no excuse to hide that glove.

1. Jose Valentin, 2005. Without question, the worst season ever posted by a Dodgers third baseman belongs to Jose Valentin, who signed as a free agent before the 2005 season. The year before he joined L.A., Valentin hit 30 home runs for the Chicago White Sox, his fifth straight season of hitting at least 20 home runs. But Valentin struggled from day one, hitting just .170 for the season with two home runs. His "slugging" percentage was a pathetic .265. To make matters worse, the Dodgers had let Adrian Beltre get away in free agency after his staggering 2004 season, which featured a league-leading 48 home runs. Valentin's one-year stint assured that the Dodgers were right back where they started in 1958—searching for a permanent answer to their third base problems.

The 10 Former All-Stars Who Wished They Never Played for the Dodgers

For more than a decade, Andruw Jones was one of the most honored center fielders in baseball with five All-Star selections and 10 Gold Gloves. That run of success came to a screeching halt when he donned a Dodgers uniform in 2008. Suddenly, a consistent All-Star became a broken down player. It's not the first time that has happened in the team's history. Here's a list of players who hit the wall wearing Dodger blue.

10. Bill Skowron. "Moose" was one of the best first basemen in the American League for nearly a decade when he came to the Dodgers in 1963. A seven-time All-Star with the Yankees, Skowron was a model of consistency until his arrival in Los Angeles. By season's end he was batting just .203, 91 points below his career average. Amazingly, Dodgers manager Walter Alston still had the instinct to put Skowron in the lineup for that year's World Series and "Moose" responded by hitting .385 in the Dodgers four-game sweep of the Yankees. Unimpressed, the Dodgers traded Skowron before the 1964 season.

9. Ken Boyer. The National League MVP in 1964, Boyer is a prime example of a player losing "it" overnight. The season after his MVP campaign, Boyer's numbers dropped across the board and the St. Louis Cardinals dumped him to the lowly New York Mets. Boyer recovered somewhat in New York and the Dodgers took notice, picking him up during the 1968 season. His hitting was adequate, but the former five-time Gold Glover was a butcher at third base with seven errors in just 34 games. He came back the following season, but hit just .206 before calling it a career.

8. Mudcat Grant. One of baseball's great characters, Mudcat beat the Dodgers twice during the 1965 World Series as the Minnesota Twins' staff ace. That seemed like ancient history when the Dodgers acquired him for the 1968 season. He started just four games all season long before finding a role as a set-up man. It wasn't what the Dodgers expected so they dumped Grant in the expansion draft at season's end.

7. Al Oliver. Oliver is one of the best players not in the Hall of Fame. He was a seven-time All-Star with 2,743 hits and a .303 career batting average. In fact, Oliver hit at least .300 for nine straight years when the Dodgers acquired him before the 1985 season. That streak ended abruptly as Oliver hit just .253 in 35 games with the Dodgers before they traded him in mid-season to Toronto. He never played again after 1985.

6. Jim Bunning. Few players have had a post-career resume like Jim Bunning. The Hall of Fame pitcher became a senator from Kentucky after serving as a congressman for several years. He once pitched a perfect game for the Phillies in 1964, but by the time he put on the Dodgers' uniform in 1969 his best days were long gone. He started just nine games for the Dodgers, winning three, before getting his pink slip as season's end.

5. Rocky Colavito. One of the great power hitters in the American League during the late 1950s and early 1960s, Colavito was on the down side of his career when the Dodgers acquired him for the 1968 season. Still, he had led the AL in RBIs just three years earlier so the thinking was he still had some gas left in the tank at age 34. But that was not the case. He hit just .204 with three home runs before the Dodgers released him in July. A nine-time All-Star was finished by season's end after a brief stint with the Yankees.

4. Boog Powell. In 1975, Powell hit 27 home runs with the Cleveland Indians to earn Comeback Player of the Year honors. Of course, he was best known for his years with the Baltimore Orioles, earning MVP honors in 1970. When the Dodgers picked up "Big" Boog before the 1977 season they were hoping for yet another comeback by the loveable giant. Instead they got a washed up player with less pop in his bat than a 90-year-old grandma. His final numbers included just 10 hits in 50 games—all singles.

3. Zoilo Versalles. The Dodgers seemed to have a short memory when they acquired the 1965 American League MVP before the 1968 season. They traded legends Ron Perranoski and Johnny Roseboro for two players that had led the Minnesota Twins to the 1965 American League pennant. Versalles, just three years removed from being the best player in the AL, was an absolute disaster. He butchered the shortstop position all year with 28 errors and a .196 batting average. At age 28, he seemed to lose whatever spark he had during that magical 1965 season. The Dodgers dumped him in the expansion draft after the season.

2. Frank Robinson. It was a huge story when the Dodgers traded four players to the Baltimore Orioles to acquire the future Hall of Famer in 1972. Robinson had been MVP of the 1966 World Series when the Orioles swept the Dodgers. He was supposed to supply some much needed power for a team known more for its speed, but it never came to be. Robinson hit just 19 home runs, the second lowest total of his career to date, with a career-low .251 batting average. The Dodgers traded him to the Angels after the season. Ironically, Robinson found his power in Anaheim, hitting 30 home runs for the Halos in 1973.

1. Juan Marichal. It should never have happened. How did the Dodgers expect to sell Juan Marichal to their fans? This was the guy who bashed Johnny Roseboro in the head with his bat. This was the guy who beat the Dodgers more times than any other active pitcher. This was the guy who wore the Giants uniform for 14 years. Still, the Dodgers thought Marichal could help the team when they signed him as a free agent in 1975. Two starts proved otherwise. His final line for the Dodgers read like this: six innings, one strikeout, five walks, zero wins, and a 13.50 ERA. How's that to cap a Hall of Fame career?

Note: Eric Karros is the Los Angeles Dodgers' all-time leading home run hitter with 270 during his 12-year run with the Big Blue. He also played one season with the Cubs and one season in Oakland before calling it a career. All told, Karros hit 284 home runs with 1,027 RBIs. The 1992 National League Rookie of the Year has gone on to become one of baseball's most respected analysts for the Fox network, demonstrating a style that is straight to the point. Along those lines, Karros offered this list of his favorite teammates. He wanted to make clear that this list is about teammates and not necessarily "friends."

10. Tom Prince, Dodgers, 1994–1998. Prince played 17 major league seasons as a back-up catcher, totaling just 519 games and a .208 career average. But he was a true manager on the field. It was amazing how he knew everything happening even though he rarely played. I'd hire him to manage my team anytime.

9. Paul Bako, Cubs, 2003. Paul was another career back-up catcher. I think guys like this are the backbone of any team. No one was more prepared to play probably because he never knew when he was going to play. You always appreciate guys who know how lucky they are to be in the big leagues.

8. Tom Goodwin, Dodgers, 1991–1993 and 2000–2001. Tom and I were teammates before and after he was a regular player. We were kids coming up, but he never really got a chance to play until he left the Dodgers. He had some solid seasons in Kansas City and Texas and then returned to the Dodgers as a utility player. It can be tough when you've been a starter to sit on the bench, but Tom always accepted his role without complaining. That's a good teammate.

7. Lenny Harris, Dodgers, 1991–1993. He became baseball's all-time leading pinch hitter, breaking the record of legendary Dodger Manny Mota. He played for eight teams in his career and I can guarantee you anyone who crossed his path will tell you how funny Lenny could be in and out of the clubhouse. I think that's what made him so good as a pinch-hitter. He was always loose.

6. Mark Kotsay, Athletics, 2004. When I went to Oakland it was a whole new environment coming from the National League. The guy who impressed me the most on that team was Kotsay. He had also come over from the National League that year and he put up some impressive numbers. He may not have fulfilled all his potential in the major leagues, but when it came to being a solid guy and teammate, Kotsay was among the best.

5. Kerry Wood, Cubs, 2003. Kerry was this guy who could blow anyone away with some of the nastiest stuff you will ever see—or not see. He struck out 20 batters in one game as a rookie and was considered one of the best pitchers in baseball by the time I joined the team. It was an amazing season, as we came so close to getting to the World Series. Kerry started games and came in to relieve games throughout that post-season. He would do anything for the team. I'm so happy he has fought back from injuries. To see him as an All-Star again in 2008 made me feel good because he deserved it.

4. Roger McDowell, Dodgers, 1991–1994. Roger had played several seasons with the Mets and Phillies before he joined the Dodgers. I was a rookie with a lot of expectations and it would have been real tough to live through the pressure had I not had teammates like Roger. He kept everyone in the clubhouse loose. It was amazing how he could have a good game or bad game and stay the same fun-loving guy. I learned from him that a bad day is not a total disaster.

3. Tim Wallach, Dodgers, 1993–1996. Wallach had been one of the best third basemen in baseball for more than a decade when we acquired him in 1993. He had a couple of good years with the Dodgers, but what impressed me most was his "quiet" leadership. There's a lot to be said about someone who comes to the park everyday doing their job and doing it right. There was never a time when Wallach disrupted the team. He understood what it means to be a great teammate without trying to be everyone's friend.

2. Marquis Grissom, Dodgers, 2001–2002. I think if you polled players from my era about who were the best "teammates," Marquis Grissom would be on almost everyone's list. I had heard good things about him in Montreal and Atlanta, and when he joined us in 2001 I immediately understood what the fuss was all about. Marquis is the guy who takes care of everybody. If you need something, Marquis will deliver. I'm not just talking about some of the time. You could count on Marquis *every* time.

1. Moises Alou, Cubs, 2003. Everyone remembers Moises from the Steve Bartman play that did *not* cost us the National League pennant. He was frustrated to not catch that foul ball, but that's not the reason the Marlins came back to win that series. We just got beat. Moises was the first to understand the situation. He reminded me of what I call "old school" players. I hate excuse makers and Moises was the kind of guy who was always accountable. If more players were like Moises Alou, baseball would be a better game.

The 10 Greatest Pitching Achievements in Los Angeles Dodgers History

Great pitching has been synonymous with the Dodgers ever since their move to Los Angeles in 1958. Dodgers Stadium was specifically built to help pitchers achieve great success. Here's just as sampling of great pitching performances that have set the Dodgers apart from the rest.

10. Phil Regan. In 1966, the Dodgers unleashed "The Vulture" on the National League. He finished the year with a 14-1 record, a league-high 21 saves and a 1.62 ERA. But his most impressive stat was his 13 consecutive victories in relief. He lost a game to Pittsburgh on May 13 and did not lose again. Amazingly, he did not allow an earned run in 50 of his 65 appearances that season.

9. Ramon Martinez. There have been many young pitching phenoms that wore a Dodgers' uniform, but few have made the immediate impact that Martinez exhibited back in 1990. He didn't turn 22 until August of that season, but he finished with a 20-6 record and placed second in the Cy Young voting. The highlight that season was his 18-strikeout game June 4 against Atlanta. He pitched a three-hit shutout that day, walking just one, and became the youngest pitcher since Bob Feller to strike out that many batters in a game.

8. Hideo Nomo. After a spectacular rookie campaign in 1995, Nomo settled in as one of the best pitchers in the National League during his sophomore campaign. He took that status to new heights when he threw a no-hitter on September 17, 1996 on the road against the Colorado Rockies. This may have been the most impressive no-hitter in history. The Rockies had a team batting average of .343 in 81 home games that season. They averaged eight runs per game at home that season. Nomo's no-no that day still defies all logic.

7. Larry Sherry. The World Series MVP award was first presented in 1955 when the Dodgers' Johnny Podres earned the honor for his pitching heroics. Since then only one rookie has ever been singled out as the star of the World Series. That would be Sherry, who stunned the baseball world with his performance against the White Sox in the 1959 World Series. He appeared in all four games the Dodgers won, winning two and saving the other two. He pitched 12.1 innings, giving up just eight hits and one run. It remains the single most dominant relief performance in World Series history.

6. Fernando Valenzuela. Will there ever be another pitcher who can match Fernando's first eight career starts? As a late substitute to start opening day for the Dodgers in 1981, Valenzuela pitched a shutout against the Astros. He followed that game with seven more victories, including six complete games and four additional shutouts. His stats through his first eight major league starts read like this: An 8–0 record, 72 innings pitched, 43 hits allowed, 68 strikeouts, 17 walks, seven complete games, five shutouts, and a 0.50 ERA. No one will ever top that start to a career.

5. Mike Marshall. These days Dr. Marshall tries to teach young pitchers how to throw a baseball properly, without hurting their arms. They should listen to this guy. In 1974, Marshall won the Cy Young for the Dodgers by pitching in a record 106 games and throwing more than 208 innings in relief. In one 30-day stretch he pitched 20 games with a 9–0 record and three saves. His most amazing stretch occurred between June 18 and July 3, when he appeared in a record 13 consecutive games. In the 12th game of that streak, Marshall pitched four innings of shutout relief to earn the victory. When was the last time you saw a closer do that?

4. Eric Gagne. For three years, Gagne was the most dominant relief pitcher in major league history. From 2002 to 2004, he appeared in 224 games, saving 152, including a record 84 consecutively. The numbers are even more mind-numbing when you take a closer look. In those three years, Gagne pitched 247 innings and gave up just 145 hits. He struck out 365 batters and walked just 58. His ERA for those three years was 1.79. Accusations of steroid use have somewhat diminished his legacy, but anyone who was there to sing "Wild Thing" when he emerged from the bullpen will never forget his dominance.

3. Don Drysdale. "Big D" was one of the most feared pitchers in baseball history with his 6-foot-6 frame and sidearm delivery. He also set a record that is likely to stand the test of time. In 1968, Drysdale pitched six consecutive shutouts. The streak started on May 14, 1968, when he two-hit the Pittsburgh Pirates. Five more shutouts followed with the last one coming against those same Pirates on June 4. All told, Drysdale pitched 54 innings during the streak, allowing just 27 hits and no runs. His ERA fell from 2.52 at the start of the streak to 1.21. Consider that no pitcher has had six shutouts in a *season* since 1989 and that Brandon Webb led the National League in complete games with four in 2007 and you'll understand why Drysdale's mark is safe.

2. Orel Hershiser. The man with the funny name had one of the greatest seasons ever by a pitcher in 1988. He was a unanimous choice for the Cy Young after winning 23 games with a 2.26 ERA. In the post-season, he was both the NLCS and the World Series MVP, winning three games and saving another. That said, he will always be remembered for one great event that season—his streak of 59 consecutive scoreless innings. Twenty years earlier, Drysdale had run his streak to 58 innings and no one thought that record would fall. Hershiser did it in style with five shutouts and a 10-inning scoreless appearance, all during a pennant race.

1. Sandy Koufax. I could make a top 10 list just with Koufax's mind-boggling numbers. But which one stands out from the rest? Throwing four no-hitters in four years? The three unanimous Cy Young awards? The 0.95 career World Series ERA? Pitching two shutouts in three days during the 1965 World Series? Striking out a record 382 batters in 1965? All of these accomplishments were great, but none compare with Koufax leading the National League in ERA for five consecutive years. Even more remarkable was his collective ERA over those five seasons—2.02. Koufax was the greatest left-hander of all-time, period.

The Best and Worst Post-Season Starts in Los Angeles Dodgers History

The Los Angeles Dodgers have always been known for their great pitching, but it hasn't always shown up when it counts the most. For every great game pitched by the likes of Sandy Koufax, there's a meltdown by some mere mortal. Here is a list of the five best and the five worst post-season starts by a Dodgers' pitcher.

Five Best

5. Fernando Valenzuela, 1981 World Series, Game 3. It was the year of Fernando-mania and the rookie left-hander was the toast of baseball. His biggest start of the season occurred in Game 3 of the World Series, the Yankees up by one game and the Dodgers needing a win. Valenzuela struggled at first, giving up four runs in the first three innings. The Dodgers rallied, however, and Valenzuela hung on for a gutsy 5–4 win. The 20-year-old threw a staggering 141 pitches, walked seven batters, and gave up nine hits, but his grit inspired the Dodgers to win three straight and earn their first World Series title since 1965.

4. Jose Lima, 2004 Division Series, Game 3. The Dodgers have had little to brag about since their last World Series win in 1988. Over the past two decades, the once dominant franchise has appeared in just four playoff series and posted a cumulative record of 1–12. That one win occurred in the 2004 Division Series against the eventual National League champion St. Louis Cardinals. On that October day, veteran right-hander Jose Lima pitched the game of his life. The journeyman shut out the Birds on just five hits while walking just one. The Dodgers rewarded him by letting him go as a free agent. It turned out to be a good move because Lima went 5–20 the rest of his career.

3. Don Drysdale, 1963 World Series, Game 3. Most people remember Sandy Koufax as the hero of the Dodgers' 1963 World Series sweep of the Yankees as he struck out 23 batters in two complete game victories. But, according to Yankee legend Mickey Mantle, the best game pitched during that World Series belonged to the "other" Hall of Famer, Don Drysdale. "Big D" shut out the Yankees in Game 3, giving up just three hits and one intentional walk while striking out nine. The only scare came with two outs in the ninth, when Joe Pepitone hit one deep to right and Ron Fairly made the catch to preserve a 1–0 win.

2. Orel Hershiser, 1988 League Championship Series, Game 7. Few pitchers have had a season that matches Orel Hershiser's 1988 dominance. The Cy Young winner won 23 games, including five straight shutouts in September. His 59 consecutive scoreless innings to conclude the regular season set an all-time MLB record. That phenomenal finish set the stage for an even more impressive post-season in which Hershiser won both NLCS and World Series MVP honors. His most impressive start was a five-hit shutout against the Mets in the decisive Game 7 of the 1988 NLCS. He also won two games against Oakland in the World Series, including another shutout in Game 2.

1. Sandy Koufax, 1965 World Series, Game 7. Picking just one Koufax performance as his post-season best is a daunting task, but this Game 7 against the Minnesota Twins is a safe choice. Pitching on just two days rest, the legendary left-hander pitched a three-hit shutout to secure the Dodgers second championship in three years. What made Koufax's performance even more remarkable was his inability to throw a curveball for a strike. Catcher John Roseboro told him to throw nothing but fastballs and the rest was history. Koufax struck out 10 Twins, including the last two batters of the game. He finished the Series with a 0.38 ERA in three starts.

Five Worst

5. Don Drysdale, 1965 World Series, Game 1. The aforementioned dominance of Koufax in the 1965 World Series was even more noteworthy when you consider a scheduling conflict due to his religious convictions. The opening game of the series fell on Yom Kippur, the holiest of Jewish holidays. Koufax requested the day off and Dodgers skipper Walter Alston chose Drysdale, a 23-game winner, to start against the Twins. "Big D" didn't get through the third inning and gave up seven runs, including six in the third inning alone. After the game, a reporter said to Alston, "I bet you wish Drysdale was Jewish too."

4. Roger Craig, 1959 World Series, Game 1. The Dodgers shocked the baseball world when they won the National League pennant in 1959, just one year after they finished seventh in an eight-team league. One of the key pitchers that season was Roger Craig, who posted an 11–5 record after being recalled from the minors in June. He finished the season with three straight complete game victories, earning him the opening game assignment in the World Series against the Chicago White Sox. The magic ran out that day when he was bombed for 5 runs in 2.1 innings. Ted Kluszewski knocked Craig out for good with a monster home run in the third inning. The White Sox won 11–0, but the Dodgers came back to win the title.

3. Jerry Reuss, 1985 League Championship Series, Game 4. Reuss won 220 games during a 22-year career that included eight full seasons with the Dodgers. He was a solid starter who could be counted on in big games—unless they occurred in the NLCS. It is one of baseball's all-time anomalies. Reuss started seven games in the NLCS over his career and posted a stunning record of 0–7. His final NLCS start was his worst. The St. Louis Cardinals bombed him for seven runs in less than two innings. To make matters worse, the Dodgers blew a 2–0 series lead to lose the National League title.

2. Doug Rau, 1974 League Championship Series, Game 3. From 1974 through 1978, Doug Rau posted a 73–49 record with the Dodgers as a solid third starting pitcher. The left-hander earned three post-season starts during that run and none of them came close to matching his regular season success. His biggest disaster occurred in Game 3 of the 1974 NLCS against the Pittsburgh Pirates. The Dodgers were one win away from wrapping up their first National League crown since 1966 and Rau was pitching before a full house at Dodgers Stadium. He didn't survive the first inning, giving up five runs on three hits, including two home runs. Rau's overall post-season record was 0–2 with a 6.55 ERA.

1. Bob Welch, 1981 World Series, Game 4. Bob Welch is best remembered in post-season play for striking out Reggie Jackson to end Game 2 of the 1978 World Series. That strikeout came in a relief appearance that would provide a sharp contrast to the three post-season games Welch started for the Dodgers. His ERA in those starts was a whopping 11.25! His first post-season start came in Game 4 of the 1981 World Series against the Yankees. He faced just four batters and gave up a triple, double, walk, and single. Amazingly, the Dodgers came back to win that day thanks to some outstanding relief pitching. Welch's career numbers for his post-season starts with the Dodgers read like this: four innings, eight hits, eight runs (five earned), nine walks, and just two strikeouts.

When Steve Garvey retired from baseball in 1987, most people assumed he was a lock for the Hall of Fame. Now after 15 years on the writer's ballot, Garvey's only hope for immortality falls into the hands of the Veteran's Committee, which is comprised of current members of the Hall of Fame. With the next election coming in 2009, let's remind those who vote why Garvey should have been a Hall of Famer long ago.

10. 200 Hits. Only 13 retired players have had six or more 200-hit seasons during their career. All are in the Hall of Fame except Garvey. He had six 200-hit seasons in a seven-season stretch between 1974 and 1980. Imagine a pitcher with six 20-win seasons not in the Hall of Fame. There have been far fewer 200-hit seasons than 20-win seasons.

9. MVP Voting. Garvey was the National League MVP in 1974 and finished second in 1978. He also placed sixth in the balloting on three separate occasions. His career MVP award shares are calculated at 2.46. All but two retired players—Jim Rice and Dave Parker—with a better MVP share are in the Hall of Fame. Hall of Fame first baseman Willie McCovey had a MVP share of 1.63 and he was elected on the first ballot.

8. Gold Glove. Garvey started his career as a butcher at third base, but he became a fielding wizard once he moved to first base. His ability to dig out bad throws was legendary. He won four Gold Gloves and set an all-time record with 193 consecutive errorless games (since broken). In fact, Garvey is the only infielder in history to play an entire season without committing an error, something he accomplished with the Padres in 1984.

7. All-Star Games. If the Hall of Fame were a vote of baseball fans, Garvey would have been a lock. He was voted the National League starting first baseman in nine All-Star Games by the fans and played in a 10th when added as a reserve. Garvey delivered against the biggest stars in the game with two All-Star Game MVP awards in 1974 and 1978. He is also the last player to be selected as a starter as a write-in candidate.

6. Post-Season Games. If the value of a player is measured by what he does on the grandest stage, then Garvey stands among the greatest to ever play the game. In 55 post-season games, he hit .338 with a .550 slugging percentage. His NLCS numbers were even more impressive. Garvey was a two-time NLCS MVP in 1978 and 1984 with eight home runs and 21 RBI in just 22 games. His game-winning home run for the Padres in Game 4 of the 1984 NLCS is still part of San Diego folklore.

5. Team Success. When Garvey made his move to first base in 1973 the Dodgers had gone seven years without a post-season appearance. The Dodgers went on to finish first or second nine of the next 10 seasons, including four division titles, four National League pennants and one World Series title. He then signed on with the Padres and led them to their first World Series appearance. The man was a flat-out winner.

4. Iron Man Record. Cal Ripken Jr. may be baseball's all-time Iron Man, but Garvey still holds the National League record with 1,207 consecutive games from 1975 through 1983. He broke Billy Williams' league record of 1,117 and it was a big story at the time. It's interesting that Williams' place in the Hall of Fame was bolstered by his then-record. Apparently Garvey did not receive that same consideration from baseball writers.

3. Community Service. Two of baseball's most prestigious honors are the Lou Gehrig Award and the Roberto Clemente Award. Both of these trophies are given to players whose contributions off the field matched their success on the field. Only a select few have won both and Garvey is in that select class. The Hall of Fame professes to judge players on character as well as statistics and Garvey excelled in both departments.

2. Star Appeal. Garvey was the complete package. He had the skills and he had the looks that make a star. It's interesting that baseball writers would sometimes look down on Garvey because he was too good to be true. The fact that his post-baseball life included some controversy, including the fathering of at least two children out of wedlock, should not have a bearing on his Hall of Fame candidacy. As far as we know, Garvey never did drugs or used steroids. His baseball numbers are clean.

1. Nobody Cares About On-Base Percentage. When you ask writers why Garvey was passed over for the Hall of Fame they love to talk about his .329 career on-base percentage. This is an absolute joke because no one cared about on-base percentage when he played. It was all about batting average, home runs, and RBIs. Garvey hit better than .300 seven times and drove in 100-plus runs in five seasons. His home run numbers were average, but the total package is beyond dispute. Garvey should be—and I predict will be— a member of the Baseball Hall of Fame.

The Los Angeles Frankenstein

We like science, we like medicine, we love monster flicks. So how could we not put together the greatest athlete in the history of the world, one comprised of the best body attributes from every player that ever spent a second in the city?

Left Arm: Sandy Koufax.

Left Hand: Gail Goodrich.

Right Arm: Nolan Ryan.

Right Hand: Jerry West.

Forearms: Steve Garvey.

Elbows: Tommy John.

Fists: Stu Grimson.

Wrists: Howie Long.

Biceps: Corey Maggette.

Shoulders: Michael Cage.

Back: Jackie Slater.

Abs: Reggie Bush.

Chest: Lyle Alzado.

Ass: Elton Brand.

Asshole: Jeff Kent.

Heart: Kobe Bryant.

Belly: Tommy Lasorda.

Guts: Marcus Allen.

Balls: Christian Hosoi.

Feet: Landon Donovan.

Right Leg: Ray Guy.

Left Leg: David Beckham.

Thighs: Bo Jackson.

Calves: Kwame Brown.

Brains: Kareem Abdul-Jabbar.

Eyes: Earvin "Magic" Johnson.

Sideburns: Mike Marshall.

Moustache: Ron Cey.

Nose: Ian Laperriere.

Mouth: Milton Bradley.

Beard: Scott Niedermayer.

Neck: Kurt Rambis.

Ears: John Wooden.

Fluid in the Veins: Tiger Woods.

Hair: Pat Riley.

Most cities have franchises that have gone belly-up or left for greener pastures, but this is Los Angeles. Where could teams possibly want to go from here? St. Louis? Oakland? We'll leave those discussions for another list. In the meantime, here's a group of teams that you might remember—or might not if you weren't up to speed on professional tennis or various challengers to the NFL. There's a handful we could have added to this list, but that would have led to some serious questioning of whether the team actually existed.

7. L.A. Aces/Sharks, World Hockey Association. This team debuted as the Aces in 1972, but once the San Francisco Sharks left No Cal, they stole the Sharks moniker and created quite possibly the coolest jersey in city history. Too bad every big name player they went after refused to spurn the NHL and the L.A. installment of the World Hockey Association went down as one of the league's worst franchises. Marc Tardif, who was twice named the WHA MVP, was perhaps the team's best player.

6. L.A. Aztecs, North American Soccer League. The Toros and Wolves were also part of Los Angeles and NASL history, but the Aztecs were the city's most memorable NASL team. A couple of big names graced the pitch: Javier Aguirre, 1979 league MVP Johan Cruyff, and, in the decline of his career, George Best. But the most popular Aztec was no doubt part-owner and Hall of Famer—well, Rock and Roll Hall of Famer—Elton John.

5. Southern California Sun, World Football League. The WFL only lasted two seasons at Anaheim Stadium, but with local legend and former USC workhorse Anthony Davis running the rock and former Raiders quarterback Daryle Lamonica slinging it, the team made a lasting impression during its 13–7 1974 season. I'll always have a soft spot in my heart for that sun in the center of the universe on their white helmet.

4. L.A. Blades, various teams/leagues. I'm not referring to the current gay and lesbian ice hockey team, but rather the other three L.A. Blades franchises that have existed. The best known was part of the Western Hockey League from 1961–1967. With the 1967 NHL expansion and the arrival of the Kings, they simply packed their bags and called it a run. In 1979, the Pacific Hockey League briefly included another L.A. Blades. The most recent Blades franchise in L.A. existed from 1993 to 1999 and was affiliated with Jeanie Buss—and participated in the Roller Hockey International league.

3. L.A. Express, United States Football League. Who knows what could
have been? In 1983 the USFL franchise made big money offers to both Eric Dickerson and Dan Marino, both of whom considered taking the money and jilting the NFL
before eventually going with the safer pick. The team came back strong in 1984 and
landed BYU superstar quarterback Steve Young with what was reported to be the
richest sports contract ever—10 years, $40 million. It turned out to be an annuity the
owners bought, which apparently still pays Young $1 million annually. The Express
played at the Coliseum to an average of 8,500 fans and even had games moved to
Pierce College. Yes, Steve Young once graced the Pierce College football field as a
professional.

2. Los Angeles Strings, World Team Tennis. The team struggled from 1974
to 1977, but put together one hell of a swan song. The Strings won the league title in
1978 thanks to Ilie Nastase defeating Tony Roche in the men's singles final, and Chris
Evert defeating Marina Navratilova in the women's singles final. Evert was named
playoff MVP.

1. L.A. Xtreme, XFL. A single season is all it took for this team to go down as the
most ridiculous of all the defunct sports franchises in Southern California history. A
large crowd filled the Memorial Coliseum for the team's 2001 debut and to cheer on
former UCLA quarterback Tommy Maddux. The Xtreme lost 15–13 to San Francisco,
but got their revenge in the Million Dollar Game. Vince McMahon and NBC thought
they had something on the NFL. It turns out it only took one season and some dismal
ratings for them to call an audible and punt the league into history.

While Southern California may not be the fashion capital of the world, our Hollywood connection means we have some interest in what we wear. So do our sports teams. From spandex-like leggings on the Lakers to extra long pants on the Dodgers, our athletes want to look good while they're doing what they do so well. Here's the list of the 10 teams that looked the best doing it.

10. 2004 Titans. I'm breaking from convention and saying Cal State Fullerton's home pinstripe uniforms are bona fide top 10 worthy. They also started a trend—although it's not necessarily a great one—when they busted out the flat bill in multiple College World Series games. That seemed to get things started and unfortunately caught on with the koi fish tattoo sporting, monster truck driving types in Huntington Beach and other O.C. cities.

9. 1982 Angels. The giant head of Don Baylor, the Jheri curl and headband of Rod Carew, the feathered part of Freddy Lynn, and the Stetson glasses of Reggie Jackson were all perfectly complemented by this uniform's cavalcade of colors. The look was gray or white with navy, straight red, and gold accents. I think my favorite part is how elementary the "A" was. It's almost as if a third grader drew it with a ruler before they embroidered each hat. Plus, the ultra-fine gold halo on the hat rules.

8. 1989 Kings. When Wayne Gretzky arrived and Bruce McNall purchased the franchise from Dr. Buss, the team got a uniform makeover. Much to the delight of N.W.A. fans, the Kings went with the popular silver and black combination, a look reminiscent of the Raiders. Not happy to leave their copying ways at that, the "Kings" script that adorned the front of their sweaters looked similar to the "Lakers" written on the local basketball uniforms.

7. 1981 Kings. We'll go with the Triple Crown Line season for our best Kings uniform, and I'm going with the purple sweater as opposed to the gold. Or maybe I should say the "Forum Blue" sweater. While I like the current purple, silver, and black combination, I would be willing to amend my "Why the Kings Will Never Win a Stanley Cup" list should they return to their original regal uniform. Something about that jeweled crown in the middle of a sea of "Forum Blue" was really special.

6. 1966 Rams. I'll go with the best record posted while the team had the fearsome foursome together. Plus, that's the season they went to the navy and white instead of the blue and yellow that preceded it. No question this was the team's best uniform, and much better looking than the Eric Dickerson-era blue and yellowy-gold uniforms.

5. 1973 UCLA Bruins. I'm not sure there's a more beautiful basketball uniform than the light blue and gold UCLA tank top and short-short combo Bill Walton rocked while contributing to John Wooden's 88-game win streak. Don't forget this is the year Walton went 21–22 and hung 44 points on Memphis State in the championship game of the NCAA Tournament.

4. 1967 USC Trojans. Maybe I like things a bit simpler, but I'll take the plain helmet and straight-up cardinal and gold over the dude on the side of the helmet any day. Since USC has/had one of the best looking color combinations of any university ever, the gold pants and deep burgundy top are beautiful without a logo taking away from their charm. And we'll go with 1967 since it's one of John McKay's four national championships and right between the Heisman-winning seasons of Mike Garrett and OJ Simpson. It was also the era that saw USC return to an elite status it had not enjoyed since the 1930s.

3. 1985 Lakers. The team that finally shook the curse of the Celtics also donned the Lakers' best uniforms. The gold uniforms featured a purple sideband and the famous "Lakers" script across the front. Much like the "VH" in Van Halen is unique to the band, so is the "L" and the "R" on the front of the Lakers' jersey. As great as the script was, nothing touches the wannabe 3-D numerals. The shading of each number made games shown on black and white TV look like there was about two feet between Magic's 3 and 2.

2. 1983 Raiders. It's pretty hard to trump the silver and black, especially since everyone seemed to want in on the color scheme after the team's success in the early 1980s. But there will always be just one. There were few better sights than Marcus Allen and his power running game breaking into the open field with those bright silver pants and the most feared helmet in all of football bobbing up and down with every stride.

1. 1988 Dodgers. Nothing is remotely close to the Dodgers' home uni. White jersey and pant, "Dodgers" written in blue cursive at the perfect angle across the chest, and the seemingly out of place shiny red number marks the classic look. Dodger blue is a reference recognized across the country, and likely around the world. And then there's the cap, the Dodger blue "L.A." a perfect answer to the Yankees' "N.Y."

Top 10 Reasons the Raiders Failed in Los Angeles

This one comes from first-hand experience. I worked as the public relations director for the Los Angeles Raiders from 1984 through 1988. Here are the real reasons the Raiders never had a chance to survive in Los Angeles.

10. The Raiderettes. Known as "Football's Fabulous Females," the Los Angeles Raiderettes more than lived up the hype of putting the Dallas Cowboys cheerleaders to shame in the looks department. The problem was not their pom-poms, but how they used them. The Raiders were the only team to permit the cheerleaders to date the players. Unfortunately, the girls often dated the *married* players causing untold scandal. This would make a great book in itself.

9. Marcus Allen. From day one, Marcus Allen and Al Davis were not meant for each other. Allen went directly from winning the Heisman at USC to playing for the Raiders in the same football stadium. His popularity with the fans and teammates was matched only by the distain he received from the Raiders' owner. When Allen was benched in favor of part-time running back Bo Jackson, the team split apart and never recovered. Had Davis embraced Allen from day one, the Raiders' fortunes in L.A. could have been much different.

8. Media Alienation. From the first day I arrived with the Raiders, I was told to *not* help the media in any way. Great idea, huh? The local newspapers turned on Al Davis and his paranoia fueled the inferno to the point that he would often ask me to remove writers from the Raiders' facilities. When you're the new kids on the block, it makes no sense to piss off your neighbors.

7. Firing Mike Shanahan. Davis never intended to hire Shanahan. He interviewed the then-quarterbacks coach of the Denver Broncos to get some insight on how the Broncos were suddenly beating the Raiders. However, when Joe Bugel backed out of the job, Davis took a flyer on Shanahan. Twenty games later, he was fired. Shanahan's subsequent success with the Broncos only proved that Davis should have let a young coach with fresh ideas run the team. Of course, that's not Al's way.

6. The Hollywood Scene. I remember running back Kenny King telling me that the worst thing to happen to the Raiders was moving from Oakland to Hollywood. Technically, he meant Los Angeles, but his message was clear. The Raiders had some larger than life characters that ate up the Hollywood scene. If you go looking for trouble you'll find it in Tinseltown. The only thing that saved certain players from extended jail time was a few payoffs from alert Raider officials.

5. Bad Drafts. The Raiders were one of the NFL's most successful franchises because of their ability to steal players in the draft. Ron Wolf was the genius behind the operation, but when he left all hell broke loose. Remember Jessie Hester, Bob Buczkowski, and John Clay? If not, here's a reminder: They were the Raiders first-round picks for three straight years starting in 1985. Those three drafts set the Raiders back at least a decade.

4. Raiders Fans. The Oakland Raiders were known for their ferocious fans that inhabited the "Black Hole." That may have been fine in the Bay Area, but that influence was not so welcome in Los Angeles. Going to the Raiders games become as competitive as anything happening on the field. Many local football fans feared for their lives, which is why they decided to stay home. The Raiders spent their last five years in Los Angeles playing in a half-empty stadium.

3. Al Davis' legal obsessions. When the Raiders moved to Los Angeles, the NFL fought with a vengeance to send them back to Oakland. Davis became obsessed with beating Pete Rozelle in the courtroom. You could even say winning the legal battles was more important than winning on the field. With Davis distracted by non-football matters, the team's slide was inevitable.

2. John Elway. We all know that Elway and the Broncos regularly beat the Los Angeles Raiders to assume top dog status in the AFC West. What you may not know is that Elway should have been a Raider. When Elway forced the Baltimore Colts to trade the top pick in the 1983 draft, Davis engineered a deal with Chicago for their No. 1 pick, which was then going to be used in a package to acquire Elway. However, the NFL nixed the Raiders-Bears trade and Elway ended up in Denver. Davis is still convinced of a conspiracy.

1. The Coliseum Commission. With all the criticism leveled at Al Davis, the main reason the Raiders left Los Angeles was the ineptitude of the Coliseum Commission. This is the same group that forced the Rams to move to Anaheim and, more recently, they almost lost USC as tenants. There is a reason that Los Angeles, the second biggest television market in the country, has no NFL football. The Coliseum Commission should be abolished forever.

The 10 Worst Draft Picks in Los Angeles Raiders History

The Raiders' fall from football's pinnacle can be traced to some misguided draft choices after the team moved from Oakland to Los Angeles in 1982. Before the move the Raiders were known as a team with a key eye for hidden talent. That all seemed to change when they moved south. The Raiders played just 13 seasons in Los Angeles before moving back to Oakland in 1995, but the damage had been done. Check out this list of bad picks that still haunt the franchise.

10. Tony Caldwell, third round, 1983. Caldwell came out of the University of Washington with the promise of following in the footsteps of Ted Hendricks and Rod Martin. Instead he played special teams for two seasons before the Raiders tossed him to the curb. He played just three games for the silver and black in 1985 and one strike game for Seattle in 1987 before calling it a "career." Caldwell's selection was particularly bad when you consider the Redskins selected Charles Mann, a four-time Pro Bowl defensive end, after Caldwell.

9. Billy Joe Hobert, third round, 1993. Another disaster from Washington, Hobert was one of many bad picks the Raiders made at the quarterback position. Hobert split time with Mark Brunell in college, but unlike his teammate, Hobert never fulfilled his promise in the pro game. He started just five games for the Raiders in two seasons before taking his "game" to New Orleans. His main contribution with the Raiders was filling in as an emergency punter in 1996. Among those drafted after Hobert in 1993 were future Hall of Famers Will Shields (a 12-time Pro Bowl guard) and John Lynch (a nine-time Pro Bowl safety).

8. Jim Romano, second round, 1982. The Raiders had a great tradition at the center position with Hall of Famer Jim Otto and Pro-Bowler Dave Dalby, but that streak ended with the poor choice of Romano in 1982. A Penn State product, Romano played a total of 12 games in three seasons for the Raiders before being shipped to Houston. The Raiders took Romano while passing on Andre Tippett, the Hall of Fame linebacker who could have filled the shoes of Hendricks and Martin.

7. Todd Marinovich, first round, 1991. This pick was a disaster for many reasons. Marinovich played just two seasons at USC and wasn't mentally ready to tackle the rigors of playing pro football. His entire NFL career consisted of just eight games while his post-career has been filled with drug abuse and numerous brushes with the law. Marinovich's story is tragic, but the greater tragedy for the Raiders is what could have been had they selected the quarterback chosen nine picks after Marinovich. Perhaps you've heard of a guy named Brett Favre? Ouch!

6. Tim Moffett, third round, 1985. Most people think Jessie Hester was the biggest bust of the Raiders' 1985 draft, but his 373 career receptions say otherwise. A much worse pick that year was Moffett, a lanky wide receiver out of Mississippi. Moffett played just two years with the Raiders and caught a total of 11 passes. That's

930 receptions less than Andre Reed had in his career with the Buffalo Bills. Why is that significant? Reed was drafted seven picks after Moffett.

5. Calvin Jones, third round, 1994. In their final draft as the Los Angeles Raiders, the silver and black drafted a running back out of Nebraska they hoped would replace the departed Marcus Allen. Jones was not that running back. In two seasons with the Raiders he gained just 112 yards on 27 carries. Including the one game he subsequently played with Green Bay, Jones scored a total of zero touchdowns in his NFL career. Just for the record, Allen scored 145 times in his Hall of Fame career.

4. Joe McCall, third round, 1984. After passing on quarterback Dan Marino in the 1983 draft, the Raiders decided to not miss out another University of Pittsburgh star when they chose running back Joe McCall in 1984. If you've never heard of Mc-Call don't feel alone. Only a diehard Raiders fan would remember his one carry for three yards during that 1984 season. That one carry was also the total sum of his NFL career. If only the Raiders could have had that Marino pick back.

3. John Clay, first round, 1987. Clay was an All-American offensive tackle at Missouri and a well-known fatso. His listed weight of 300 pounds did not do him justice. The Raiders inserted him in the starting lineup as a rookie and after one season he was gone. Amazingly, the Raiders acquired future All-Pro tackle Jim Lachey from the Chargers for Clay, only to trade Lachey to Washington for quarterback Jay Schroeder. Clay played just two games with the Chargers before ending his forgettable two-year career. By the way, 27 players chosen after Clay in 1987 went on to reach the Pro Bowl.

2. Brad Cochran, third round, 1986. Don't bother looking up Cochran, a defensive back, on any NFL website. He doesn't exist. That's because the Raiders drafted a player in the third round who never played a single game in the league. Cochran came from a big program at Michigan, but it turned out he had small-time skills. Imagine using a third round pick on a player so bad that he is cut before his rookie season. It just doesn't get any worse than that.

1. Bob Buczkowski, first round, 1986. Did I say it doesn't get any worse than Brad Cochran? Correction. In the very same draft, the Raiders wasted their first-round pick on a stiff named Bob Buczkowski. The defensive lineman came out of Pittsburgh with very little hype, but a Raiders scout convinced Al Davis that this kid was the second coming of Howie Long. The first day he showed up at Raiders camp it was clear this was no Howie Long. Buczkowski's soft body and limited skills were on display for just two games in 1987. Those were the only games he ever played as a Raider. To add insult to injury, the Raiders were still paying Buczkowski 10 years after he last played because of his deferred contract.

Yes, the city of Los Angeles has celebrated a Super Bowl championship. That title belonged to the 1983 Los Angeles Raiders as they dismantled the Washington Redskins in Super Bowl XVIII. The team was loaded with talent: Hall of Fame players like Marcus Allen, Howie Long, and Mike Haynes were icons that exhibited a certain amount of class both on and off the field. There were also some players who showed less restraint. Here's a list of the greatest "characters" from the championship team.

10. Cliff Branch. Branch is one of the greatest wide receivers not in the Hall of Fame. He was truly dominant from 1974 through 1977, making the Pro Bowl each season and twice leading the league in touchdown receptions. By 1983, Branch had become the consummate veteran who always raised his game when the stakes were high. He even caught a touchdown pass in the Super Bowl win over the Redskins. Off the field, Branch had his fun. He fathered several children and there was also the mystery of why he no-showed for a certain regular season game. His story was he just didn't make it. When you're a great player for the Raiders no other explanation is needed.

9. Greg Townsend. Townsend was a rookie in 1983 and he made an immediate impact with 10.5 sacks as a reserve defensive end. He went on to have an outstanding career with more than 100 sacks and two Pro Bowl selections. The L.A. product also readily admitted that smoking pot was one of the reasons for his success. Townsend talked openly about the benefits of marijuana while working out. The Raiders certainly didn't care as long as he produced. Townsend has gone on to be an actor and already has four grandchildren before the age of 50. You go Greg!

8. Ray Guy. The greatest punter in the history of the game, Guy is one player who should have been in the Hall of Fame years ago. He's been a finalist six times, but the committee somehow misses the impact Guy had for the Raiders. Consider the facts: 14 seasons, first punter selected in the first round of the NFL draft, seven Pro Bowls, six All-Pro selections, and three Super Bowl wins. He was also the team's emergency quarterback. Guy had tremendous athletic skills, which were all the more remarkable when you consider that he was a smoker. There's something strange about an athlete lighting up, but Guy loved to smoke. It must have been a habit he picked up from his Southern roots.

7. Henry Lawrence. "Killer" was a fixture on the Raiders offensive line from 1974 through 1986. He was selected for two Pro Bowls and played on three Super Bowl championship teams. He was also a man with a sweet voice—as in, a singing voice. He was performing at clubs while still an active player and you can still see his act down in Florida these days. Lawrence also had an eating ritual before games that set him apart—he ate a plate of french fries to get his motor running. Maybe not the healthiest diet, but it worked!

6. Rod Martin. One of the most underrated defensive players of the 1980s, Martin burst on the scene when he intercepted a record three passes to lead the Raiders to a Super Bowl XV win over the Eagles. Martin was also crazy. He lived by the Raiders motto, "Don't get mad, get even." He proved he was a man of his word in a 1987 game at Kansas City when one of the Chiefs took a cheap shot at Marcus Allen. Martin responded by almost decapitating Kansas City running back Paul Palmer five yards past the sideline. Flags flew everywhere, but Martin got his point across to the Chiefs—don't mess with a true Raider.

5. Matt Millen. Everyone knows that Millen has become one of the worst executives in NFL history with his embarrassing run as the Detroit Lions general manager, but did you know how he got the job in the first place? Simply put he talked his way into the job just like he talked his way into becoming a top NFL television analyst. Millen is one of the great talkers in history. He was the same way as a player. Writers would regularly confide with Millen for inside dirt on the team. Of course, his talking wasn't always a positive. He probably lost some Pro Bowl votes with opposing players because he would never shut up on the field.

4. Todd Christensen. There has never been a NFL player quite like Christensen. A former running back at BYU, the Raiders picked him off the scrap heap and made him one of the premier tight ends in league history. Twice he led the entire NFL in receptions and he was named to five consecutive Pro Bowls. So why isn't he in the Hall of Fame? Perhaps it was Christensen's habit of putting down the intellect of every sports writer, teammate, or just about anyone that crossed his path. It was as if the Raiders should have been honored by his sheer presence. Christensen was a great player. We just didn't have to know about it all the time.

3. Lester Hayes. "The Judge" was one of football's greatest personalities. He was also one of the premier cornerbacks in league history, as he proved in 1980 when he was named the NFL Defensive Player of the Year after intercepting a near-record 13 passes. Off the field, Hayes had a girlfriend that was a former Raiderette. The only problem was his wife at the time. She too was a former Raiderette. Legend has it she stood over him with a knife while he was sleeping. Her intentions were clear and it had nothing to do with carving the Thanksgiving turkey. Hayes was one of those players who marched to his own tune and you loved every minute of it.

2. Lyle Alzado. Alzado was larger than life even on a team loaded with star players. His steroid use was no secret. He had a raised mound on his right buttocks where he made repeated injections. His mood swings were legendary both on and off the field. Alzado could be a gentle soul with a broad knowledge of many things beyond football. He could also be a total brute who would think nothing of rearranging some guy's face if he said something to irritate the two-time Pro Bowl defensive end. When Alzado retired he held the press conference at the Beverly Hills Hotel. What football player does that? When he died of brain cancer he blamed steroid use for his demise and tried to warn others about the dangers associated with those drugs. Too bad more people didn't listen.

1. Ted Hendricks. "The Mad Stork" was a unique football player in every way. At 6-foot-7, he was consider too tall to play linebacker, but he ultimately made the Hall of Fame as one of the best ever at that position. He also never missed a game in his entire career. That's right—15 years at linebacker without missing a single game. What makes that record even more remarkable was his relentless pursuit of the "good life" off the field. He could match any drinking stories with the likes of Paul Hornung or Bobby Layne. His only promise to his coaches was that he would show up every Sunday and play his heart out. That's exactly what he did and the Raiders could have cared less about everything else.

The 10 Biggest Pro Football Stars Who Played in Los Angeles on Non-NFL Teams

Not every pro football star who played in Los Angeles was a member of a NFL team. There have been several "pro" teams to inhabit the area other than the Rams and the Raiders. Here's a list of players who once called Los Angeles home on teams that weren't a part of the NFL.

10. Cliff Branch. One of the greatest wide receivers in NFL history, Branch played 14 seasons for the Raiders, including four years in Los Angeles. When he "retired" he held the all-time playoff records for career receptions and yards. Branch did not, however, hang up his cleats for good. In 1988, the Los Angeles Cobras became the city's first entry into the Arena Football League. Branch signed on as a wide receiver/defensive back and saw limited action. The team folded after one season and Branch went into permanent retirement.

9. Daryle Lamonica. "The Mad Bomber" electrified football fans as the Raiders' starting quarterback in 1967. That season he was named the AFL's MVP and led the team to their first Super Bowl appearance. Two years later he won his second MVP award while throwing a league-high 34 touchdown passes. When Ken Stabler took Lamonica's starting job in 1972, the former Notre Dame product looked for a new home. He found one with the Southern California Sun of the World Football League in 1975. However, an early season injury ended his pro football career after just a few games.

8. Gary Zimmerman. With his recent induction to the Pro Football Hall of Fame, Zimmerman secured his place with the greatest offensive tackles to ever play the game. In 12 seasons with the Vikings and Broncos, Zimmerman earned seven Pro Bowl berths and a Super Bowl championship. What may be forgotten, however, is that "Zim" started his pro football career with the L.A. Express of the United States Football League. He was a two-year starter with the Express before the USFL folded after the 1985 season.

7. Paul Lowe. Lowe's story is one of the best in local pro football history. After playing college football at Oregon State, Lowe was cut from the 49ers pre-season camp before the 1959 season. He moved to Los Angeles to work in the mailroom for the Carte Blanche Credit Card Corporation owned by the Hilton family. Barron Hilton, the owner of the newly formed Los Angeles Chargers, encouraged Lowe to try out for the team. The free agent responded with 855 yards rushing and instant AFL stardom. He went on to become a legend with the San Diego Chargers.

6. Pat Haden. From his high school days at Bishop Amat High School and his collegiate career at USC, Haden firmly established himself as one of the best quarterback prospects to come from the Los Angeles area. Everyone expected him to take his talents directly to the NFL, but the Rhodes Scholar had different plans. His first paycheck came from the World Football League as a member of the Southern California Sun. He replaced an injured Daryle Lamonica early in the 1975 season and started the rest of the team's games. When the team folded, Haden hooked on the with the Rams for a six-year run in the NFL.

5. Paul Maguire. You may know Maguire as the wise cracking football commentator, but he was also once a pretty good football player. His pro career started in Los Angeles as a linebacker for the AFL Chargers. He was also an excellent coffin-corner punter. In fact, Maguire was the first punting champion of the AFL, averaging 40.6 yards per kick during the 1960 season. He later helped the Chargers to the 1963 AFL title and moved to Buffalo to win two more championships in 1964 and 1965. He was one of just 20 players who played all 10 years the AFL existed.

4. Tommy Maddox. Perhaps no player in pro football history had a stranger journey than former UCLA quarterback Tommy Maddox. He was a first-round pick of the Denver Broncos in 1992 with projections that he would be the next John Elway. That never happened. He bounced around with several teams before finding himself out of the league in 1997. He then went on to sell insurance before hooking up in the Arena Football League in 2000. The next year he signed on with the infamous XFL as a member of the L.A. Xtreme. He went on to lead the team to the championship and earned league MVP honors. When the XFL folded, Maddox signed on with the Pittsburgh Steelers and was named the 2002 NFL Comeback Player of the Year. He retired for good in 2005.

3. Anthony Davis. One of the greatest running backs in college football history, "A.D." was known as the Notre Dame killer at USC, scoring 11 touchdowns in three games against the Irish. His next stop was the WFL's Southern California Sun, where he played before his hometown fans at the Coliseum. Davis did not disappoint. He led the league with 1,200 yards rushing in 1975 and appeared to be on his way to pro football stardom. That all changed when the league folded before season's end and Davis was sent adrift with brief stops in the CFL, NFL, and USFL. A bum knee prevented him from ever approaching the amazing success he enjoyed at USC.

2. Steve Young. Young emerged from the shadow of Joe Montana to become one of pro football's greatest quarterbacks. He led the 49ers to a Super Bowl championship and earned seven Pro Bowl trips during his Hall of Fame career. He also set a standard that no quarterback had ever achieved and few people were there to see it. That's because Young's greatest game occurred in the USFL as a member of the L.A. Express. On April 20, 1984 against Chicago, Young became the first pro quarterback ever to pass for 300 yards and run for 100 yards in the same game. That would prove to be his sole highlight on a team that never paid off his full contract when the league folded in 1985.

1. Jack Kemp. The future Republican vice-presidential candidate and former New York congressman was a former star quarterback in the American Football League. He led the Buffalo Bills to back-to-back championship in 1964 and 1965 and was named the league MVP in the latter season. However, Kemp's pro football career did not exactly start out as planned. Between 1957 and 1959, he was cut by five different teams in the NFL and CFL. Just when it appeared his football career was over, Kemp signed on with the new Los Angeles Chargers and the rest was history. He led the AFL in passing that first season and guided the Chargers to the AFL title game.

When the Rams moved from Cleveland to Los Angeles in 1946 they brought with them a Hall of Fame quarterback in Bob Waterfield. When the Raiders moved from Oakland to Los Angeles in 1982 they brought with them a Super Bowl MVP quarterback in Jim Plunkett. Let's just say that, for the most part, it was all down hill from there.

10. Jay Schroeder. The Raiders traded All-Pro offensive tackle Jim Lachey to the Washington Redskins for a quarterback that had been benched the year before. Schroeder did have one very good year with the Raiders in 1990, leading them to the AFC title, but his completion percentage over five years was less than 50 percent. In his defense, it was amazing he played as well as he did after he spent his college years more focused on minor league baseball.

9. Steve Bartkowski. The Rams fell in love with has-been quarterbacks in the 1970s and 1980s and Bartkowski was a good example of why some guys should retire before embarrassing themselves. After 11 productive years in Atlanta, "Bart" started just six games in his one season with the Rams. He threw two touchdown passes. This was one of many examples of how Georgia Frontiere would fall in love with a good-looking quarterback who played downright ugly on the field.

8. Marc Wilson. Where do I start? Wilson was a quarterback who looked good until he made a mistake during a game. That is when all hell would break loose. Wilson had at least seven games—or so it seemed—where his first pass of the game was picked off. And he never recovered. The Raiders wasted a first-round pick on this guy and compounded that mistake by giving him a huge contract extension. To top if off, his teammates weren't exactly his biggest fans. He was a stiff with an attitude problem.

7. Bill Munson. The Rams selected a quarterback in the first round of the NFL draft three consecutive years. The last of these three was Munson out of Utah State. The Rams benched Roman Gabriel in 1965 to give Munson a chance to start. He proceeded to lose nine of 10 games before Gabriel came back to win three of the final four games. From that point on, Munson was a career backup who apparently was adept at holding clipboards.

6. Todd Marinovich. Has there ever been a greater waste of talent? His was the story of child brought up by an obsessed father trying to mold the perfect quarterback. Al Davis must have bought it because he drafted Marinovich in the first round back in 1991. In his first start, Marinovich threw three touchdown passes to beat the Chiefs. His next start was a playoff loss to the Chiefs. Only seven more games would follow before drug abuse took control of his life. He has had several run-ins with the law for drug and sex crimes since his playing days ended.

5. Bert Jones. Who can forget the cover of *Sports Illustrated* with a smiling Georgia Frontiere and her new man, Bert Jones? It looked as though she had just found a new boy toy, but what she really paid for was a guy who couldn't play quarterback anymore. The Rams traded the fourth overall pick in the draft for Jones despite his slumping numbers in Baltimore. A neck injury ended his Rams run after just four games. Like Bartkowski, Jones' career came to a screeching halt as soon as he put on the Rams' uniform. At least Georgia would always have the *Sports Illustrated* cover.

4. Rusty Hilger. This guy was a con artist from day one. An obscure sixth-round pick out of Oklahoma State, Hilger convinced the Raiders he was the second coming of Joe Namath. He wore that same cage face mask that Namath had with the Jets. He wore Namath's No. 12. The only problem was Hilger had no skill as a quarterback. I was there when Al Davis screamed to drag this bum off the field after just five starts. He later gained some fame as a con artist who stole money from unsuspecting people in a bogus investment management scandal.

3. Dieter Brock. This guy remains a true Rams legend. Brought down from the Canadian Football League, where he was a two-time MVP, Brock played exactly one season for the Rams. His regular season numbers were decent, but his playoff performances were downright wretched. In two post-season games, Brock completed just 16 of 53 passes for 116 yards and no touchdowns. Eric Dickerson still talks about how bad this guy was at quarterback. He would never play another game after his one year with the Rams.

2. Terry Baker. Think about this for a minute: The Rams drafted Roman Gabriel in the first round of the 1962 NFL draft. He had some decent numbers as a rookie and appeared to be the quarterback of the future, which he was. However, the Rams could not resist using the first pick in the 1963 draft to select Heisman Trophy winner Terry Baker out of Oregon State. A run-pass option quarterback in college, Baker had one serious flaw that the Rams apparently missed—he didn't have the arm strength to complete an out-pass from the pocket. The Rams tried to convert him to running back, but it wasn't to be. Baker was one of the biggest busts of all time.

1. Joe Namath. Let's just pretend this never happened. The Rams, desperate to win a Super Bowl, signed a washed-up Namath to lead them to a championship. Instead, Broadway Joe became No Way Joe as he hobbled his way through five games before calling it a career. Like Bert Jones and Steve Bartkowski to follow, Namath was the perfect example of a player who should have known when to call it quits. I also blame the Rams for tarnishing the career of one of the game's greatest legends.

You could be pushing 50 and still be part of the video game craze growing up. I mean, technically "Pong" was a sports themed video game, based on tennis. While I didn't come up in the "Madden" craze, "Tecmo Super Bowl" was big enough that guys in my college dorm would draw teams, make a bracket and have a full on tournament—every day. It's safe to say when the actual games weren't on, it was on!

10. "Golden Tee." Since it was only available at the arcade or in the bar, "Golden Tee" gets knocked down a few spots. But there was never a better use of the trackball as far as I can remember. While it was a bit of a pricey investment—one quarter got you three holes, no matter how well you played—the 18-hole live tournaments connected with other bars is one of the coolest things ever. I mean, who the hell cares who Steven Sobe is? Well, people who play "Golden Tee," that's who.

9. "California Games." I was deciding between this and "Track and Field" and figured what the hell—it's a book of Los Angeles sports lists, I'll give the nod to the half-pipe, surfing a wave, doing countless 360s, and freakin' hacky sack. Never in a million years would I think popping a bean-filled knit ball up in the air and either heading it again or doing a 180 between kicks could be entertaining, but it was one of the most addictive games I ever owned.

8. "Double Dribble." It makes the list for the voiceover and sound effects. The incessant dribbling would make anyone in the room not playing pull their hair out, and the 3-pointer slide whistle followed by white noise that was supposed to be crowd noise was arguably the worst combination of effects ever. But when you got that breakaway and the game cut to the giant still shot of the slam dunk—damn, did you feel special.

7. "FIFA 96." Who would have thought dudes that were into Zelda, Donkey Kong, football and baseball could possibly get interested in international soccer? But thanks to "FIFA '96" being perhaps the best game released that year, it happened. It was the first game with the virtual stadiums, actual names of all the players, and game play better than anything else up to that point. Unfortunately for the rest of the world, the next year's "Madden" game was so good, most of us forgot about "FIFA" after that one glorious year.

6. "Mattel Football." While it's not played on a console or in an arcade, this handheld piece of white plastic with the tiny screen was worth its weight in gold back in the day. Yes, those were dashes situated on three lines, and the only reason you knew you had the ball was because your dash was blinking. But to say it didn't entertain, and to say you didn't get emotionally invested, would be a flat-out lie. I still play mine from time to time, and whenever someone over the age of 35 sees it, they nearly go into shock.

5. "Madden 97." I consider this the most influential and important "Madden" of my life. This was the first edition of "Madden" for the Sony Playstation, a console that happened to come out my junior year of college and had great impact on my life. By great impact, I mean that while most pre-video game dudes were forced to nurse hangovers by watching crappy early morning television, I got over it with "Madden 97." It really was a giant jump from the previous year.

4. "R.B.I. Baseball." I'll always have a soft spot for the rotund players in "R.B.I. Baseball" that looked more like Weeble Woobles than athletes. Your bat looked like the giant red one you used as a kid with the solid wiffle ball that inevitably got dented up after about 10 minutes of play. And the pitching? I mean, you could bend a pitch so hard, so close to the plate that inevitably you had to have a "no curve ball" rule if you wanted to actually get some runs on the board.

3. "Mike Tyson's Punch Out." The Bald Bull's charge, the Sandman's shifty hands, the flash from Mike before the giant right came at you—how many times did you have to play a character before you finally figured out the tells? Don't forget the great one-liners from your enemies, like when King Hippos said, "Do you like my shorts? They're X-X-X large, ha ha ha." I can't think of a worse feeling in a video game than getting Mike Tyson to a point where you were one or two punches from victory and a TKO, only to have the dude connect and knock your ass out so you had to start the damn game over from the start.

2. "NHL 94." Some like "NHL 93" better because of the fighting and the blood on the ice—which is freaking great—but "NHL 94" and the incorporation of the one-timer truly changed sports video games forever as far as I'm concerned. Dudes who didn't give a crap about hockey loved this game and played it religiously. I got so deep that playing with the Kings—The Great One, Lucky, Blake, and McSorely, and Hrudey in goal—got boring. I then adopted the Nucks and started dominating with Pavel Bure, Trevor Linden, and Jeff Courtnall, or played with Verbeek and the freaking Whale. If it weren't for my number one, it would be the best sports video game of all time.

1. "Tecmo Super Bowl." I think this might be a time and place thing. Most dudes my age get a boner when they hear the three words: "Tecmo Super Bowl." It's the same for guys five years younger than me when they hear "Madden." But in "Tecmo," you had Thurman Thomas, Andre Reed, and Jim Kelly—or should I say "QB Bills." You had Christian Okoye's demolition power, the rocket arm and lightening fast running of "QB Eagles," and the one man wrecking crew that was Bo Jackson. No football game will entertain the masses like "Tecmo Bowl" did for us. Plus, eight-play playbooks made things a little more interesting, and if you played it enough you were able to discover the key plays that would make life for your opponent miserable. I was a Chiefs guy since you couldn't tackle Okoye unless you slid into his ankles, and Derek Thomas was a freaking nightmare on D. And I think Nick Lowry might have been the best kicker on the damn thing. Whoever put it together loved them some Chiefs.

Top 10 Reasons Why the David Beckham Experiment Failed

Soccer fanatics hailed the bold move by AEG Group to bring the world's most popular athlete to Southern California, even if it was in the twilight of his career. David Beckham's arrival was so anticipated, the July press conference might have been the most covered sports-related event that calendar year. Kobe Bryant was on a media tour demanding to be traded. The Trojans missed out on a national championship game thanks to a loss at UCLA and settled for the Rose Bowl. And the Dodgers weren't providing the locals much hope. So the spotlight was Beckham's and the Galaxy's to lose. And they did.

10. Made friends with Tom Cruise. Here's all I'm saying: Beckham didn't figure it out until after his inaugural season here, and by then it was too late. Why hang out with a has-been in Tom Cruise, someone whose best days have long past? And why befriend him when Kobe Bryant is a giant fan of yours? Instead of photos all over the local rags of Cruise and Beckham, it could have been sideline shots at Lakers games of high fives with Kobe and every foreign player who rolls in to play.

9. Soccer doesn't play well on TV. Tickets to simply get into his debut were going for $500, which meant many people in town got their first glimpse of Beckham— and the MLS—on the ESPN broadcast. If you're not a fan of the sport to begin with, it's safe to say watching a friendly against Chelsea on TV isn't the best way to sell you on what you've been missing.

8. The $250 million contract. For whatever reason, men have one thing in common: We're convinced other men are making more money than they should be. They're not worth what they're getting paid and therefore somehow negatively affecting our lives. Hearing that the deal that brought Beckham to the U.S. was worth a potential $250 million immediately put him in a hole with the local blue-collar sports fan. They couldn't fathom this guy was worth over twice as much as Kobe Bryant and four times as much as Vlad Guerrero.

7. "Soccer will finally matter" was heard from every rooftop. It's the boy who cried wolf. World Cup at the Rose Bowl, the creation of MLS, Pele's arrival, and AYSO's unmatchable popularity—all were promised to be things that would finally lead to the rise of soccer in America. Yet none of them worked. When presented with that statement there's almost a sense of Schadenfreude as everyone waits once again for soccer's failure.

6. Beckham's on-field style. While there's no denying his name recognition, the style with which Beckham plays the game of soccer isn't apt to draw "ooh's" and "ahh's" from the crowd. Ronaldinho or Cristiano Ronaldo might have done the trick, but casual fans wouldn't have made all that big a deal about their arrival.

5. The Galaxy stink. Whether he was playing with Manchester United, Real Madrid, or his national team, Beckham always had a supporting cast that could do what needed to be done with one of his sweet crossing passes or free kicks. Simply put the Galaxy—or any team in the MLS, for that matter—has a roster with no more than two or three really good players. That's not enough to help Beckham.

4. Who are Victoria and David Beckham? While the world's most popular couple normally couldn't walk an inch outside their door without a gaggle of paparazzi waiting, here they were relegated to B- or maybe even C-List status. Consider David Beckham plays a sport nobody cares much about and his wife was part of a group that hasn't been relevant for over a decade. Their arrival was met with more of a "Who?" than a "Wow!"

3. Injury. It probably didn't help that Beckham arrived with an existing injury and barely played his first season with the team. It's one thing to attend his first tour around the country in an MLS uniform and see what he can do on the pitch. It's slightly less exciting to see him on the sideline in a tailored suit. Every match sold out, but all people got for their money was a Calvin Klein model watching guys play soccer.

2. Those pesky Lakers, Trojans, and Bruins. By the time Beckham returned to action on October 18, Kobe and the Lakers were front-page news with the start of training camp and hourly updates on how Kobe was feeling about the team. The Trojans were making a march toward another NCAA football title. When Beckham announced his return, it was met with a collective feeling of, "They're still playing soccer? It's October!"

1. It's soccer. Sooner or later billionaire Phil Anschutz will discover that the sport simply isn't met with the same level of excitement as it is around the rest of the world. We like fast-paced, up-and-down, high-scoring games filled with crushing hits and at least 10 highlights per game. Soccer is more a sport of nuance—you have to invest yourself for years before being able to totally understand and appreciate what's going on over the course of 90 minutes. Safe to say, the Galaxy won't be getting a very good return on their sizeable investment.

The Rams won just one NFL championship in their nearly 50-year run in Los Angeles/Orange County, but they had plenty of record-setting players. In fact, some of these records continue to stand the test of time. Here's a sampling of the Rams who have set up residence in the NFL record books.

10. Willie Ellison. Few could have imagined a historic day when the Rams played the New Orleans Saints on December 5, 1971. Ellison was a solid back with a largely unspectacular resume, but that all ended on that day at the Los Angeles Memorial Coliseum. He ran for a record 247 yards on 26 carries, breaking two marks in the process. The previous NFL record was 237 yards by the legendary Jim Brown and the pro record was 243 yards by Cookie Gilchrist in the old AFL. Ellison never came close to that kind of game again.

9. Bucky Pope. "The Catawba Claw" was an obscure eighth-round draft pick by the Rams in 1964, but for one season he dominated like few wide receivers in NFL history. His numbers in that 1964 rookie campaign look like a typo: 25 catches for 786 yards and 10 touchdowns. That computes to a mind-boggling 31.4 yards per catch. He had touchdown catches of 95, 70, 68, 65, and 55 yards that season. Unfortunately, he only caught nine more passes in his career after injuring his knee in a 1965 preseason game.

8. Merlin Olsen. A first-round pick for the Rams in 1962 after an All-American career at Utah State, "The Mule" set a record that may never be broken. He was selected to the Pro Bowl after each of his first 14 seasons in the NFL. Only in his final season did he fail to make the squad. Only Hall of Fame offensive line Bruce Matthews has matched Olsen's 14 Pro Bowls, but Matthews' streak didn't start with his rookie season.

7. Deacon Jones. You will not find Deacon's name among the all-time sacks leaders in NFL history because the official records were not kept until 1982. But research has found that Jones was the NFL's all-time sacks leader when he retired in 1974 with 173.5 in 14 seasons. That included three years in which he had more than 20 sacks and a five-year run from 1964 to 1968 when he totaled 102 sacks. Keep in mind that NFL regular seasons were just 14 games before 1978.

6. Tom Fears. On December 3, 1950, Fears set a NFL record with 18 receptions in one game as the Rams beat the Green Bay Packers. Who would have guessed that Fears' pass-catching bonanza would remain atop the record books for 50 years? It wasn't until Terrell Owens caught 20 passes against the Bears in 2000 that Fears was toppled from his lofty perch. By the way, Fears finished the 1950 season with 84 catches in just 12 games. That record remained in the NFL books until 1964.

5. Elroy "Crazy Legs" Hirsch. The Rams of the early 1950s were as potent as any in NFL history. Hirsch's 1951 season was one for the record books. In just 12 games, he caught 66 passes for a record 1,495 yards and a record-tying 17 touchdowns. He also set a record with nine games with more than 100 yards receiving, including a record five-consecutive games over the century mark. To put those numbers in perspective, Hirsch had 659 more receiving yards than any other player in the league.

4. Fred Dryer. Before he became a big television star in *Hunter*, Dryer was one of the most underrated defensive ends in the NFL. Playing of the opposite side of Hall of Famer Jack Youngblood, Dryer had more than 100 unofficial sacks in his career and twice was named to the Pro Bowl. But he did something that no NFL defensive lineman has done before or since. On October 21, 1973, Dryer recorded two safeties in one game against the Green Bay Packers. Keep in mind that no one has had more than two safeties for an entire season. In fact, Dryer's safeties occurred in the same quarter against the Packers. It's safe to say that no one will ever break that record.

3. Norm Van Brocklin. This Hall of Fame quarterback was known for his quick arm and hot temper. He's probably best remembered for leading the Philadelphia Eagles to the 1960 NFL title, but he also did the same thing for the Rams in 1951. In fact, his 73-yard touchdown pass to Tom Fears clinched the championship game against the Cleveland Browns. Van Brocklin also threw for a record 554 yards against the old New York Yanks that season. More than a half-century later that record still stands. The closest anyone has come is a 527-yard day by Warren Moon in 1990. Think of all the great quarterbacks in NFL history and Van Brocklin still sits atop the list. That's amazing.

2. Eric Dickerson. How's this for NFL trivia? Who has held the single-season rushing record for the most years? The answer is the great Eric Dickerson. It has been nearly a quarter-century since he ran for 2,105 yards for the 1984 Rams. That record withstood the challenge of running backs like Emmitt Smith, Barry Sanders, Terrell Davis, and LaDainian Tomlinson. If these guys couldn't break the record, who will? Adrian Peterson was on pace in 2007, but an injury derailed his chance at history. As time goes on, Dickerson's record looks more and more impressive.

1. Dick "Night Train" Lane. Speaking of records, there is one in the books that still amazes a stat-geek like yours truly. Dick "Night Train" Lane was an undrafted free agent defensive back the Rams took a flier on in 1952. That season, as a rookie, he intercepted 14 passes in just 12 games. No one—not even in a 14-game or a 16-game season—has touched that record. That's 55 years and counting through the 2007 season. Also consider that there are twice as many passes thrown in today's game as opposed to the NFL back in 1952. Lane's interception record remains one of the most impressive in NFL history.

Note: Eric Dickerson may be the most underrated running back in NFL history. His single season record of 2,105 yards in 1984 has been on the books for more than 20 years and all challengers have been thwarted. His greatest seasons were with the Los Angeles Rams. He may have become the NFL's all-time career leader had Georgia Frontiere not lost her mind by trading the league's best back in 1987. The four-time NFL rushing leader set down his list of the 10 best running backs he's ever seen.

10. Adrian Peterson. One season is enough to show me that this guy is the closest thing to me I have ever seen. He is the second coming of Eric Dickerson. He's fast, has great feet, and has the power to break tackles. If there is any running back that is going to break my record, it's Peterson.

9. Emmitt Smith. There are a lot of players in the NFL who achieve greatness by being on the right team at the right time. Emmitt was on the perfect team with the best line in the league and a Hall of Fame quarterback. Still, it's impossible to ignore his records and his amazing durability.

8. Terrell Davis. Some people thought Davis was the product of a system, but I haven't seen any other Bronco running back gain more than 2,000 yards in a season. His career was cut short and he may not have done enough to be in the Hall of Fame, but I think he was a great back.

7. Gale Sayers. I never actually saw Sayers play, but I've seen enough film on this guy to tell you that he could have played in any era. There are some running backs that were great back in the day, but Sayers' combination of size and speed, plus the best vision I've ever seen for a running back, convinces me he would be just as dominant today.

6. Marcus Allen. Marcus was not that elusive and he was not that fast, but he was a complete running back. He was the best goal line runner I ever saw, one of the best receiving backs, he could throw the ball, and he could block with the best of them. He also played 16 years in the NFL. That's unbelievable for a running back.

5. Earl Campbell. Growing up in Texas, Campbell was one of my true heroes. He won the Heisman at the University of Texas and then dominated from day one with the Houston Oilers. His "freight train" style ultimately shortened his career, but I have never seen a back strike more fear in a defense. When he was at his peak Earl was almost impossible to stop.

4. Walter Payton. He wasn't that big, but his heart was that of a giant. I loved that he would attack defenders and he was very difficult to bring down. Like Marcus, Payton was a complete back who did everything well. I don't think there was a more admired player in the league when I played. He earned everything he got.

3. LaDainian Tomlinson. He's a Texas guy like me and we've become good friends. He's always telling me that he's going to break my record and some day he might be right. L.T. is very much like Payton, except he's faster in the open field. He plays hurt, which is something most people don't realize because he rarely misses a game. He's got a chance to break Emmitt's career mark if he can just stay healthy for a few more years. I still can't believe he scored 31 touchdowns in one season. Amazing!

2. Barry Sanders. Barry is the only running back that I have ever seen who makes me say, "WOW!" His vision, his speed, and his cutting ability were all second to none. Sometimes it looked like he would split in two. I have to say he had the greatest feet I've ever seen on a running back. He could have broken Payton's all-time record, but he retired at his prime because he just got tired of playing the game. Barry Sanders was a true one-of-a-kind running back.

1. O.J. Simpson. If there was one running back that I tried to copy it was O.J. He was the first running back who combined great size with world-class speed. I remember as a kid watching him run over, run around, and run away from defenses with such class. Whatever else happened to him does not take away from how great he was on the football field. He is still the standard by which all other running backs should be measured.

From the day that Rams owner Carroll Rosenbloom died in 1979, pro football would never be the same in Los Angeles. The perpetrator of the majority of the misery was Rosenbloom's widow, an ex-lounge singer named Georgia. There are few people who were more universally despised—and for good reason. This was a woman who took no prisoners on her mission of total self satisfaction. Here's a list of things that made "Madame Ram" a nightmare for local NFL fans.

8. She killed her husband. Actually there is no proof that Georgia had anything to do with Rosenbloom's death. But the fact that he drowned making his daily ocean swim seemed to raise suspicion, especially after photos of his body showed mysterious marks on his legs. Surely Georgia had nothing to do with his death. So why do so many people think otherwise?

7. Man eater. Rosenbloom's body was barely cold when Georgia went down the aisle with her seventh husband, Dominic Frontiere. Poor sap. He ended up spending time in prison for scalping Super Bowl tickets acquired from his wife. Let's get this straight. He rots in prison and she skates without a scratch? That was the beauty of Georgia.

6. Media harassment. There are so many good stories about Georgia's adversarial relationship with the media, but it may have started with an incident on a team flight. During her first year as owner, Georgia wandered—or staggered, by some accounts—to a media area on the team charter where writers were working on stories. She allegedly plopped on the lap of one writer only to be "accidentally" pushed to the ground. A miffed Georgia banned the writers from ever traveling with the team again.

5. Doctoring photos. This is a personal story worth telling: One year the Rams were late distributing their annual media guide. The league was getting restless and they wanted to know what the wait was all about. At the time, I was working for the Raiders across town and both teams had their media guides printed by the same company. It turns out that the delay was due to Georgia's dissatisfaction with her media guide photo. She had it airbrushed several times to make her face look 40 years younger. She would end up using that same photo for the next decade of media guides.

4. Steve Rosenbloom. It was bad enough that Georgia somehow inherited the Rams, but she really ruffled feathers when she fired Rosenbloom's son Steve, the one groomed to run the franchise. Georgia replaced Rosenbloom with an attorney named John Shaw who basically ran the franchise from that day on. After she married Frontiere it was as if the Rosenbloom name was erased forever from team's history.

3. Cabbage Patch dolls. The absurdity of Georgia as an NFL owner had little to do with her gender, but she always screamed sexism if someone was critical of her handling of the team. After all, how many owners kissed their players on the sidelines—whether their wives cared or not? And how about the time she gave everyone on the team a Cabbage Patch doll? These gestures and several others bordered on sheer lunacy.

2. Bye-bye Eric Dickerson. The Rams had the great fortune of drafting Eric Dickerson with the second pick in the 1983 draft and the former SMU star did not disappoint. In fact, Dickerson set rushing records that still stand to this day, including his single-season 2,105 yards in 1984. Less than three years later, the best running back in the NFL was traded to Indianapolis for a bunch of draft picks. How did this happen? Georgia wouldn't pay her star even close to his market value. How could she when she needed another Gucci purse?

1. She stole the Rams from Los Angeles. Actually, she stole the Rams from Anaheim, but the Los Angeles tag was still in place. There is no question that she had a master scheme to destroy the team so the fans would stop showing up and a move would become possible. She blamed the fans for not supporting the team, but who shows up after five straight losing seasons? The money she heisted from St. Louis was criminal and it was only by chance—Kurt Warner?—that they ever won a Super Bowl. Today, the Rams are every bit as bad in St. Louis as they were those final few years in Anaheim.

Georgia Frontiere died on January 18, 2008. Not a single Los Angeles Rams fan shed a tear.

Let's be clear about some Los Angeles Rams history. The team did not leave town after the 1994 season. Sure, that's when the "Los Angeles" Rams became the St. Louis Rams, but the true move occurred after the 1979 season. That's when they became the "Anaheim" Rams. I grew up a fan of the Rams that played at the Coliseum and when they drifted down the freeway so did my interest in the team. That said, there was an incredible run of seasons for the "true" Los Angeles Rams from 1967 through 1979. During those 13 seasons, the team won nine division titles—and no Super Bowls. Every year seemed to have that one crushing loss that would drive a stake through the heart of all Rams fans. In chronological order, here are the losses this Rams fan will never forget.

10. December 23, 1967, playoff vs. Green Bay. This game was played in Milwaukee's County Stadium. The Rams held the best record in the league, but were forced to play on the road because of some stupid rule that alternated playoff sites. The veteran Packers took full advantage, overcoming an early 7–0 Rams lead with 28 unanswered points. Travis Williams, the Packers one-year wonder, ran for 88 yards and two touchdowns. Quarterback Roman Gabriel was sacked five times as the Packers took revenge for a regular season loss to the Rams.

9. December 8, 1968, regular season vs. Chicago. The Rams were fighting with Baltimore for the division title when the mediocre Bears came to Los Angeles in the penultimate regular season game. The Rams stood at 10–1–1 going into the game, just a half-game back of the Colts with the two teams meeting for what figured to be a showdown the following week. That showdown went down in flames as the Rams lost 17–16 to Chicago. Brian Piccolo—yes, that Brian Piccolo—ran for 105 yards for the Bears, but the big story was a blown call by the officials. The Rams were called for a holding penalty on their final drive. The officials forgot to repeat first down and the Rams got just three downs before turning the ball over. The league later fined the officials for their brain-dead work, but the final score remained the same.

8. December 27, 1969, playoff vs. Minnesota. The Rams seemed on a mission when they started the 1969 season with 11 straight wins. That start clinched the division title and the team then lost the last three regular season games, which were meaningless. The playoff game was set in Minnesota, but the Rams appeared to be in control as they raced off to an early 17–7 lead. But Joe Kapp led Minnesota's comeback and the final nail in the coffin came on Carl Eller's sack of Gabriel for a clinching safety. The Vikings won the game 23–20.

7. December 13, 1971, regular Season vs. Washington. The Rams fired head coach George Allen after the 1970 season and he immediately signed on with the Washington Redskins. The Skins had not made the playoffs since Sammy Baugh was their quarterback, but Allen put together his "Over the Hill Gang" and they came into the Coliseum on a Monday night to play the Rams with the NFC Wild Card spot on the line. The Rams led 7–0, but Washington came back to build a 31–10 lead behind two Billy Kilmer touchdown passes to Roy Jefferson. Los Angeles came back with two touchdowns to make the score 31–24, but the rally ended when Speedy Duncan picked off a Gabriel pass and returned it 46 yards for a touchdown. Allen got his revenge and the Rams missed the playoffs by one game.

6. December 23, 1973, playoff vs. Dallas. The Rams dominated the NFL in 1973, leading the league in both total offense and total defense. Quarterback John Hadl was the NFC Player of the Year and wide receiver Harold Jackson led the league with 13 touchdown receptions. The defense was led by Hall of Famers Merlin Olsen and Jack Youngblood. Everything looked great until they traveled to Dallas for their first playoff game. The Cowboys dominated from start to finish with an easy 27–16 win. This was the first season for coach Chuck Knox and the first of several playoff disappointments that would soil his otherwise great coaching record.

5. December 29, 1974, playoff vs. Minnesota. It was back to the freezing cold of Metropolitan Stadium in Minneapolis, but this time the Rams had something new in their back pocket. The week before the Rams defeated the Redskins for their first post-season victory since 1951. The 1974 NFC title game was a defensive struggle that ultimately was decided by a single play. The Rams were six inches away from a touchdown that would have given them a 10–7 lead, but Hall of Fame guard Tom Mack was called for illegal procedure and a five-yard penalty. The Vikings then intercepted a tipped pass in the end zone and won the game 14–10.

4. January 4, 1976, playoff vs. Dallas. When the Cowboys eliminated the Vikings in the first round of the 1975 playoffs, Rams fans thought this was going to be the year. Dallas was in a rebuilding year and the Rams would get the NFC title game at home. That day at the Coliseum was supposed to be a coronation, but it turned out to be a nightmare. Final score: Dallas 37, Rams 7. The details of the game are still sketchy for me, but I do remember Preston Pearson getting credit for a touchdown reception for a ball that hit the ground. No matter, the game was an embarrassment.

3. December 26, 1976, playoff vs. Minnesota. Another missed opportunity on a blustery day in Minnesota. The Rams had a touchdown called back because the officials blew another call, forcing the team to settle for a field goal attempt and early 3–0 lead. That never happened because the Vikings blocked the kick and ran it back for a touchdown. Minnesota built a 17–0 lead, but the Rams rallied to cut the deficit to four. Quarterback Pat Haden had the team in position for a winning score, but his pass to a wide-open Ron Jessie was late and picked off by safety Bobby Bryant. It was the Rams third straight loss in the NFC title game.

2. December 26, 1977, playoff vs. Minnesota. This time the Rams would not have to play the Vikings in Minnesota. Instead, this playoff game was to set for the sunshine of Los Angeles—or so they thought. The football gods had something else in mind because it poured rain the entire game and the Rams lost in a quagmire, 14–7. Back-up quarterback Bob Lee led the Vikings. He completed only five passes, but did not turn the ball over. Haden threw three picks for the Rams as his smallish hands could not effectively grip the wet ball. What made this loss even more painful was the fact that the Rams had buried the Vikings 35–3 just weeks earlier. Who says it never rains in California?

1. January 20, 1980, Super Bowl vs. Pittsburgh. This was the final game of the "true" Los Angeles Rams and it turned out to be both memorable and painful. The team was not expected to be a factor in the playoffs after winning the division with a mediocre 9–7 record, but road playoff wins in Dallas and Tampa Bay put the Rams in their first Super Bowl. The good news was the game was almost a home game with the action taking place at the Rose Bowl in Pasadena. The bad news was the Steelers were the opponent and looking for a fourth Super Bowl title in six years. Amazingly, the Rams led 19–17 going into the final quarter, but a bomb from Terry Bradshaw to John Stallworth gave Pittsburgh the lead. A late interception by Jack Lambert clinched the victory. It would be another 20 years before the Rams finally got their Super Bowl win, but that team played in St. Louis and no "true" Los Angeles Rams fan gave a damn.

Best Athlete Performances—on the Big and Small Screen

We're in Hollywood, so understandably our athletes have been looked upon to take part is some occasional cameo appearances. On a few occasions the moonlighting turned into a full-time gig. Below are five legitimate acting performances and five others that are so bad they're fantastic.

The Bad

5. Sandy Koufax, Willie Davis, Johnny Roseboro, others. Koufax was soft spoken in real life, so he had no lines during an appearance on *Mr. Ed*. His job was to pitch to the horse standing in the batters box and, with Mr. Ed holding the bat in his mouth, the horse smokes a pitch to the outfield wall. Willie Davis' "I don't believe it" reaction is priceless. But the best moment comes when Davis leaps out the way of a Mr. Ed slide.

4. Wes Parker. Playing himself on the *Brady Bunch*, Wes was dating Greg's hot piece of ass teacher, Miss O'Hara. And true to what most of us felt back in the day, while Greg was smitten with his professor, he was more impressed by being in the presence of a current Dodger. Wes acts all hard while Greg admires him.

3. Don Drysdale. "Big D" did plenty of work in front of the camera, but nothing as great as his telephone conversation in the "Long Distance Call" episode of *Leave it to Beaver*. Talk about patience—he had to dealing with Gilbert, Allen, and the Beav passing the phone back and forth, each one drilling him with countless stupid questions. Don isn't necessarily a stiff in his performance, he's just, well, stiff.

2. Howie Long. Talk about a guy who took a pretty terrible script and film role damn seriously. They way the laid it down in *Broken Arrow*, you'd swear he was convinced he'd be up for an Oscar that year. I would say he was overacting a bit, but that's pretty much standard every Sunday on the Fox set.

1. Shaquille O'Neal. All of his feature films are on equal ground when it comes to futility. Because *Kazaam* is such a dumb name it tends to get all the attention, but *Steel* very well could be one of the worst films ever made. That's not hyperbole—it really might be the worst film ever put into wide release by a Hollywood studio. First of all, who the hell thinks a guy who looks like Shaq would have the name John Henry Irons? Second, he's really going to his uncle's junkyard to use his military weapons background and make weapons to keep up with the government?

Neither Good Nor Bad

O.J. Simpson. We don't want people coming down on us for taking a side on O.J. Simpson. We'll simply point out he was pretty awesome in *The Naked Gun*—and by pretty awesome, we mean it could be one of the best performances by a Hall of Fame athlete in the history of film.

The Best

5. Fred Dryer. While everyone points to the unequaled success of *Hunter*, he'll always be Lt. John LeGarre from *CHiPs* to us. Actually it's a bit fascinating how successful *Hunter* was—Dryer filmed 152 episodes of the cop drama, surpassing any level of success on this list, except for John Wayne. I'm not sure why I watched the show every week—because Hunter was freaking Fred Dryer or Detective Sergeant Dee Dee McCall was hot.

4. John Wayne. Marion Morrison, aka John Wayne, was a former lineman on the late 1920s USC football team. After suffering a body surfing accident, he started working as an extra on a couple sets around town. Before you knew it a legend was born. Take your pick on the best: *True Grit*, *The Quiet Man*, *Rio Bravo*, or a host of others. John Wayne is freaking John Wayne, and you either love him or you're a communist.

3. Merlin Olsen. For four full seasons he played Father Murphy in *Little House on the Prairie* and ended up getting his own spin off. I would venture to guess he was perfect in that role, as many people knew Merlin Olsen more as an actor than as a football player. Plus, who doesn't love his work with FTD?

2. Mark Harmon. The former UCLA quarterback has done everything from the heartbreaking role of Billy Wyatt in *Stealing Home* to arguably his most famous role as heartthrob Dr. Bobby Caldwell on *St. Elsewhere*. But for our money, undoubtedly Harmon's greatest role ever is a no brainer—Mr. Shoop, the P.E. teacher from *Summer School*.

1. Kareem Abdul-Jabbar. As great as he was playing Hakim in *Game of Death* with Bruce Lee, there's no denying the best performance by an athlete in the history of film goes to Kareem for his role as Roger Murdock in *Airplane*. It's one of the greatest conundrums in cinematic history. Was Kareem playing Kareem, or Roger Murdock? And if it was both, as he once told me in an interview, how the hell did he find time to get his commercial pilot's license? When he drops "I've been hearing that crap since I was at UCLA" on little Joey, the rest of the field immediately comes in a distant second.

Top 10 Super Bowl Experience Observations

I've been to eight Super Bowls in my lifetime and watched the rest on TV. I think I actually remember Super Bowl VII while I was in utero. There's no denying the spectacle that is the Super Bowl. What's a book of great lists without a list that chronicles what we remember about the big games we were a part of, either in-person or with a bunch of friends piled on some living room couch? I think Super Bowl parties at my house these days get better attendance than Christmas or Easter.

10. How into it girls are. I'm not sure if it's because there is an actual planning process that goes into the "Super Bowl Party," but damn if it wouldn't' be nice to have the wife so interested in me watching football with a bunch of idiot drunk friends more often.

9. Corporate Guy who's on a free pass. Going to your first Super Bowl can be a bit of a let down because you think of all the players, actors, strippers, and parties that await your arrival. Then you show up, get access to some "VIP" room or invite-only event, and look around at fat dudes in Dockers. Yep, $500–$5,000 tickets are going to limit who's eligible for the Super Bowl weekend experience, and most of the guys aren't people you would hang out with on your most desperate of days.

8. The Lap Dance Ban of Super Bowl XXXV. Tampa, Florida. Giants vs. Ravens. Did we talk about the great defense of Baltimore or the unlikely appearance of a team guided by Kerry Collins? Nope, we talked about how the cops claimed if you went to a strip club and got a lap dance, you would be arrested on the spot. What? Were they not aware Tampa was the lap dance capital of the world? This would be like putting the game in New Orleans and suggesting Bourbon Street is off limits. Well, the scare tactics didn't work, and plenty of fat guys in track pants got their lap dance on, much to the chagrin of the ladies in the clubs themselves.

7. All the different names for the "Super Bowl." Unless a business is an official sponsor of the Super Bowl, they're not allowed to use the term "Super Bowl" and have to come up with alternate names for their contests. So when giving away a trip to "The Big Game" or "The Sunday Spectacular" or "The Football Final" or "The Bowl Brawl" or "Showdown Sunday" or "Kick Ass Party at Dave & Busters"—sorry, it got away from me there for a second. You get the point. I mean, people sit in a room for hours trying to come up with something cool to put on the air or on a countertop stand up, and typically come up way short. Some idiot will say "Buper Sowl" and think he deserves a raise for it.

6. Janet Jackson's weird looking boob. I was in Houston sucking on some lung darts and eating crappy concession stand pizza while mulling about how poorly my prop bets were doing when my Blackberry blew up. Countless friends wanted to know one thing: "Did you see Janet's boob?" No, I didn't. Turns out I wasn't on the right side of the stage, so unless you could tell from the 30th row that it appeared to be a Flintstones' dinosaur egg-shaped boob with a sun pendant secured by a pin through her Flavor Flav clock-sized nipple, I did not see what the people did on TV. News did spread quickly inside the stadium as text tones harmonized and echoed in Reliant Stadium over the next 20 minutes

5. The third stringer just hanging out on Media Day. This guy never has anybody to talk to. Never fails. I guess we enjoy the uncomfortable situation of someone realizing it really wouldn't matter if they were there or not. There are 2,000 media dudes with flash recorders and cameras talking with Tom Brady and Mike Vrabel, but Antwain Spann, if you wouldn't mind, how about snapping a photo of me and ol' Stevie Neal? I love that those guys are like contest winners who have VIP access to everything. Over the course of the week, anytime they make their way into a shot all they're doing is videotaping everything that's happening around them.

4. Patriots and U2 in 2002. New Orleans, five months after 9/11, and to say I wasn't a little on edge would be lying. Flying into The Big Easy and seeing the chain link fence and armed military around the Super Dome was a bit disconcerting. Filing in took about two hours and the typical celebratory Super Bowl mood was replaced by tempered enthusiasm and second-guessing the decision to attend the game. Everyone was wondering if another attack would happen. As for the game, most expected a Rams blowout. The game was the last thing on our minds, until the Rams offense was introduced one-by-one, followed by the announcer simply acknowledging the AFC Champion New England Patriots and the whole team running out together. The Rams looked like they were kicked in the gut for not thinking of it, and everyone who was neutral immediately backed the Pats. We returned to reality temporarily when U2—who, to this day I consider the best halftime show I've ever seen— played "Beautiful Day" and "One" with all the names of those who lost their lives on 9/11 scrolling on giant sheets during the performance.

3. Squares. I think we ought to incorporate the squares method of gambling into everyday life. Zero through 9 across, 0 through 9 down, and not in that order, of course. Depending on how much money your circle of friends is willing to wager, you could be celebrating victories with as much as a grand. Not to mention, after all the squares are full and the numbers are drawn, there's nothing better than getting the 7 and 0 while you're friend is pissed for a good 3 or 4 days because he pulled 5 and 8.

2. The 7:00 hangover. There's nothing worse than looking at the clock, realizing it's 5:30, and discovering you're not only buzzed, but pretty much bombed by halftime. The group of dudes I get together with tap a keg around 10 a.m., and with a kickoff just after 3 p.m., that means eight hours of emptying red Solo cups. It's great—right up until the game is over and you remember you put down about a case of Natty Light yourself and it's freaking Sunday. What a way to start the week.

1. "Super Bowl Shuffle." How could I possible think of anything else? I was 12 at the time and I would go to bed dreaming that Walter Payton was my father, and that the Bears were more important than oxygen. It was one thing to have the 46 defense, another to have the greatest football player of all time, and yet another to have a personality like Mike Ditka as the head coach. But a catchy song like the "Super Bowl Shuffle" took the 1985 Bears from being a loveable team with dynamic personality to a freaking phenomenon. Mike Singletary was my favorite verse and, looking back, Gary Fencik's was the corniest. "I'm Samurai Mike, I stop 'em cold . . ."

I'm not ashamed to admit that YouTube is one of my favorite websites. No longer can we hide from past transgressions and I believe we're a better society for that. This is an infamous top ten list since all the comedy discovered is of the unintentional variety. Most of it comes thanks to music and fashion that couldn't stand up to the test of time. Tread lightly as you'll be confronted with colorful language, awful hair, and some uncomfortable situations should you seek out the selections listed below.

10. Mark Madsen's 2001 Lakers parade speech. There are three parts to this one. It starts with Chick Hearn basically insulting the dude for 40 seconds or so. That's followed by the awkward smile from Mark after he screamed "Yeah!" into the microphone. It really picks up when he follows that with, "Who let the dogs out? WHO? WHO? WHO? WHO?" He then closes strong with a little Spanish for the people.

9. "Tell me how my ass tastes." I believe it was 2006, MLK Jr. Day, when Kobe and Shaq reportedly "buried the hatchet." Those of us close to the situation knew full well it was a giant load, and the two likely would never get along again. Their relationship simply deteriorated to irreparable levels. Shaq got his revenge on Kobe and the Lakers by winning a title in Miami after having been jettisoned by the Lakers, but apparently that still wasn't enough for O'Neal. After his Phoenix Suns were bounced in the first round of the 2007 playoffs, Shaq couldn't lay low and keep quiet. After the Lakers lost to the Celtics in the NBA Finals, he opened his song at a New York City nightclub with "Check it, yo—you know how I be, last week Kobe couldn't do without me."

8. Chan Ho Park kicks Tim Belcher. This is the only video on the list that actually takes place during a game—specifically an Angels/Dodgers game in 1999. Park gave up a grand slam, and then, out of frustration, hit Angels infielder Randy Velarde for the second time. In the bottom of the inning, Park put down a bunt that was fielded by Angels pitcher Tim Belcher, who decided to tag Park himself. Belcher did so rather forcefully and Park was not happy with the move. Park went with a jump kick to Belcher's chest, after which Belcher threw Park to the ground and pummeled him endlessly.

7. Howard Stern on *The Magic Hour*. If you never saw *The Magic Hour*, it's impossible to describe how awful it really was. Somehow a network executive decided Magic Johnson was good enough to host his own late night talk show. For eight weeks, it provided the world with the best unintentional comedy we've ever known. Howard Stern felt the same way and destroyed Magic on his morning radio show from the moment the debut episode aired until Stern's hour-long appearance on the show itself. From leading a band of flatulence wielding dudes to asking Magic to stop trying to "talk like a white man" to his comment "at least you had fun contracting the HIV virus," it was one of the best, most uncomfortable hours on television.

6. Raiders' 1986 "Silver and Black Attack" video. Tom Flores almost steals the show in this music video. His portion of the song is the most sterile, while Mike Haynes' gentlemanly rap comes in a close second. The highlight of the video has to be, once again, the players' dated look. Sure, Matt Millen still rocks that "Cop 'stache," but I can't see Howie Long showing up someplace with a cut at the collar jersey to expose his pecs and chest hair. Todd Christensen's mullet and moustache take the best overall performance award.

5. Bo Jackson's crazy "Tecmo Super Bowl" Run. If you're between the ages of 33 and 42 you know the greatest football video game of all time is "Tecmo Super Bowl." The only problem with "Tecmo" was if you were playing the Raiders, you had no chance of winning. I think I racked up about 15 touchdowns in one game with Bo Jackson, but even that pales in comparison to the effort put on display here.

4. Tommy Lasorda audio stew. This very well could be the best slide show available on YouTube. Most of these Tommy moments were in post-game press conference situations in his manager's office, so only audio exists. But I have to compliment "ruffbizness" on the quality of his choices. There are inanimate objects like oars and baseball cards, and still shots from Lasorda's Sega Genesis video game—the slide show manages to keep our attention for nearly six minutes of Tommy rants.

3. Just Say No, by the Lakers. It's not synched up, which is a bit of a bummer, but the tank top and swim trunk combo most of the guys are wearing in this PSA do a good job of keeping your attention away from the players' mouths. Where is Kareem? Why is he sitting in a studio for his verse while the rest of the team, coach Pat Riley included, is dancing together in a line? Kurt Rambis trades his horn-rimmed glasses for what look to be senior citizen wrap-arounds in a nice shade of rose. You might need to use your pause button, but check out Magic Johnson's antiperspirant caked up in his pit hair. Couldn't a production assistant have helped him out with that one?

2. "Ram It." These guys are freaking good. Limousine Willie, Herc, Big Daddy Hill—I mean, the Los Angeles Rams can dance, sing, and actually keep a beat when they're rapping. Jackie Slater looks like he knows how to play the sax and the cheerleaders are hot in a 1985 sort of way. Best performance goes to the "Hollywood handsome, Dodger city tough" Nolan Cromwell, who, while sporting feathered hair and a neatly trimmed beard, delivers the line: "I like to Ram it, as you can see nobody likes ramming any more than me."

1. "Baseball Boogie." The 1986 video starring a number of Dodgers is so far ahead of the rest we could have made it numbers 1 through 10. Talk about having it all—the pastel yellow, purple, blue, and pink satin jackets, the Jheri curl hair on Duncan and Howell, Orel Hershiser's chicken-wing, knee-knocking dance, and Pedro Guerrero's helmet head. You can watch it over and over and over again and never tire of the sheer lunacy behind thinking this was a great idea. Pay especially close attention at the beginning to Rick Honeycutt's 360 spin at the start of the video—easily my favorite move.

This wasn't an easy list to put together, so lets go over the rules. First up, *The Hustler* and *Rounders* aren't sports movies. Last time I checked it's a tough enough argument to suggest racing and golf are sports. So while these two probably could have made the top 10, I'll file them under "guy movies" as opposed to "sports films." Second, I'm not a *Raging Bull* guy, and here's why: It's one hell of a film, almost perfect actually. But I never find myself longing to watch it. Each of the 10 films on the list below make their way into my rotation from time to time, for some reason that doesn't hold for the Jake La Motta story. Maybe it's because it's so damn depressing. Finally, we're all a product of our environment. Films that might not have any sort of impact on those 10 years older or 10 years younger than me could be in the list below, but if you're in my same age group chances are we're on the same page.

10. *Chariots of Fire.* Couple reasons why this makes the cut for me when so many others list it in their honorable mention category. While I love Kenny Loggins "I'm Alright," "Chariots of Fire" by Vangelis is, next to the *Rocky* theme, the most recognizable sports movie theme of all time. It helps that the video played incessantly on VH-1 for a good three months, and starts with the bearded Vangelis sucking on a lung dart while dudes are running a marathon in the background. As for the film itself, religious themes prevail. Harold overcomes anti-Semitism and has quite possibly the best scene in the movie when he rips around the Great Trinity court before the clock strikes 12. Eric, the Scottish missionary, has a dilemma of whether or not to race in his Olympic event on Sunday, weighing the decision to stay faithful to either his country or his religion. It won Best Picture at the 1982 Oscars, which rarely happens with sports flicks.

9. *Brian's Song.* I'm not sure a made for TV movie belongs on the list. But thanks to its immense popularity after debuting on ABC, the film eventually found its way into theatres. I'm not an emotional man—that's been well chronicled—but *Brian's Song* just so happens to be the one film that makes soulless fools like me weep like a child. Caan and Billy Dee are perfect in their roles as Brian Piccolo and Gale Sayers, and the true bonus of the film is actual footage of the real Sayers running the ball for the Chicago Bears. It's a racial commentary, it's a buddy flick, and it's a sports movie that's about the relationships sports forces you to create.

8. *The Bad News Bears.* Any top 10 sports movie list that ignores this triumph of a film should be disregarded immediately. Who can't relate to Kelly Leak joining the team and playing seven positions at the same time while hitting .950 on the season? Didn't all our Little League coaches show up drunk with a sixer of tall boys in one hand and a fungo in the other? The best thing about the film is the collection of players on the team: racists, twins that don't speak English, a girl, and a piece of white trash. It pretty much looked like every Little League team I played on—with the exception of the Chico Bail Bonds sponsorship. I had "Solan's Funeral Home" on the back of my jersey.

7. *The Karate Kid.* What, karate isn't a sport? It's the quintessential childhood film of my generation. It passes the "When the movie's over, you're in the parking lot practicing some move you saw on the big screen" test with flying colors. Who didn't try the "crane kick" and get the crap kicked out of them by their school's Johnny Lawrence? Elisabeth Shue was the hottest girl in America for a good six months after the film was released, and when she took it off in *Leaving Las Vegas* many of us finally had closure dating back to the day we first saw this film in 1984. Add to it Joe Esposito's "You're the Best" theme during the All Valley Karate Tournament montage and you have an all-time classic on your hands.

6. *Breaking Away.* I can hear you already: "Cycling, really? Come on." If Rocky climbing the Philadelphia Art Museum stairs is the best training scene in the history of sports movies, then Dave Stoller riding from Indy to Bloomington at 60 MPH with a truck driver as his drafting aid has to be a close second. *Rocky* has the trumpet, *Breaking Away* has Mendelssohn's "Italian" symphony as its soundtrack. I love the "Cutters" against the students at Indiana University storyline because it was/is every bit as tense as the film portrays it. Dennis Quaid is stellar and Jackie Earl Haley perfect, but the star of the film is Mr. Stoller, played by Paul Dooley. Any kid who ever had a pipe dream of playing professional sports past the age of 10 probably heard some of the same quotes Dooley delivered with grace: "No, I don't feel lucky to be alive. I feel lucky I'm not dead. There's a difference."

5. *Slap Shot.* I remember my parent's conundrum when I was a wee lad watching this film for the first time. The language and storyline were so filthy they couldn't possibly allow me to watch along with them, but the film was so engrossing and the characters so rich they didn't want to flip off the TV and miss it themselves. Luckily the latter won out and I was about 9 or 10 the first time I saw this Paul Newman classic. Speaking of Newman, the performance he turned in as Reggie Dunlop might trump his Fast Eddie Felsen in *The Hustler*. The Hanson brothers might be the best supporting role in the history of cinema. I think they had a total of 10 minutes of screen time, and every second of it is legendary.

4. *Bull Durham.* This is probably the finest acting effort put forth by Kevin Costner. Without beating around the bush, it's the best baseball movie of all time. People that don't agree haven't been exposed to minor league baseball and can't understand the ridiculousness that transpires in the film is, for better or worse, historically accurate. There is a "Nuke" in every town, there is a "Crash" in every town, "Annie" may be a bit unique, but "Millie" sure isn't. There are about 50 "Millie's" no matter what Class A park you're visiting. What makes this movie a true rarity in the sports genre is that it works on a baseball level, but the dialogue away from the game is even more compelling.

3. *Rocky.* The end of Rocky is what solidifies its place in the pantheon of sports movies. The idea of a washed-up fighter actually hanging with a heavyweight champion is ridiculous and to actually have Rocky win at the end would have been too much. Instead, we weren't so overwhelmed with an endorphin rush, which allows us to process the characters and the journey more effectively. Rocky was pretty worthless as a human being at the start of the film. As someone who grew up in a neighborhood similar to Balboa's, I know guys like Rocky. For some, it was high school football, others it was minor league baseball or Chicago Golden Gloves. Every one of them was an amateur that was never good at much else, but not good enough at sports to be a professional. This film was the reason why they all ended up at the same local bar, reliving past glories they're not quite ready to let go of. That same trumpet is still playing the same theme song in their head.

2. *Hoosiers.* It's the only gusty underdog story with an unthinkable win at the end that isn't cheesy. It helps that it's based on a true story, and helps even more Gene Hackman plays coach Norman Dale. While certain scenes stand out—"Shooter," played by Dennis Hopper, pulling off the picket fence—there are two reasons this film rises to toward the top of this list. First, the believability of Jimmy Chitwood as a star basketball player, with actor Maris Valainis demonstrating one of the best looking shots the screen has ever seen. Second, Hackman's monologue while measuring the court when the team reaches the state finals is one of the best "I just got chills" scenes, no matter the genre of film.

1. *Caddyshack.* This wasn't a hard choice. Most people put *Caddyshack* on their list because they think they can sneak a comedy into their top 10. It's not really a sports movie, but a gold thread runs through the entire story. While the most memorable scenes involve puppets and a greens keeper, the best dialogue is saved for the golf course: "No, that guy was Mitch Cumstein, my roommate . . . good guy." Or at least stories relating to golf: "Big Hitter, the Lama." Point is, it's close enough to being a sports movie to make any best sports movie list. Spaulding's snot, Lacy's tops, Judge Smails' speeches, Ty's sarcasm, and anything Carl and Al Czervik said or did while on screen—it's not only the best sports movie of all time, it's the best film of all time. So it has that going for it, which is nice.

L.A. Athletes One Celebrity Cousin/Comedy Writer/ Undefeated Professional Wrestler Thinks He Can Best in a Fight :: Cousin Sal from *Jimmy Kimmel Live*

Note: Did you know that Cousin Sal is an undefeated professional wrestler? 'Nuf said.

10. Earl Boykins. He's simply the most adorable thing ever to hit the hardwood floor. Not sure if I could bring myself to it.

9. David Eckstein. I'm half as Jewish and have three inches on him. Enough said.

8. Pee Wee Reese. The fact that he hailed from the mean streets of Brooklyn is completely overshadowed by his unfortunate nickname.

7. Any woman ever to play for the L.A. Sparks. Except for maybe Zheng Haixia—6-foot-8 is 6-foot-8.

6. Brett Butler. I might even let him use his bat. That's how confident I am.

5. The Angels' Rally Monkey. Why pick on a harmless monkey? Because it deserves a beating for the boatful of loot it cost me in the fall of 2002—that's why.

4. Kurt Rambis. I would never hit a man with glasses . . . unless I absolutely had to fill out a stupid list like this one.

3. Rod Carew. Such a great hitter. Such a frail physique. Such a sucker for my patented Boston Crab.

2. O.J. Simpson. On paper it doesn't look good for me—but I swear on the rings under Marcia Clark's eyes I would do whatever possible to win this one.

1. Fernando Valenzuela. Taquitos and margaritas have ravaged his body over the years. But I think I could still take him.

Established with the 1967 expansion, the Kings have just one Stanley Cup Finals appearance and zero championships on their resume. It's not a storied franchise, but damn do people love them some Kings hockey in this town. Thankfully, there have been some moments worth reliving, the best of which is arguably the greatest period of hockey in NHL history.

10. 1967 Expansion. Considering our NFL problem, it's safe to say we understand teams are not guaranteed to us here in Los Angeles. The Great Expansion of 1967 was not as easy a process as some might think. This was no ordinary expansion, but instead a doubling in the size of the league from six teams to 12. There were a number of things that had to fall into place for us to have our beloved Los Angeles Kings. First, Jack Kent Cooke had to beat out four other competing bids. Second, both St. Louis and Vancouver were far more competitive markets, but the Original Six had issues with placing franchises in those cities, allowing Los Angeles to come into play. Finally, the Western Hockey League was making inroads and seen as a threat, thus the Kings were created to temper the enthusiasm surrounding the Los Angeles Blades.

9. December 1, 1988. Wayne Gretzky had done it twice and Mario Lemieux had done it once (he would go on to do it two more times in his career), but on this date Bernie Nichols joined the "8 points in one game" coterie with his 2 goals and 6 assists against the Toronto Maple Leafs.

8. February 10, 1981. The first NHL All-Star Game on the west coast was played in Los Angeles at the Forum. There's no better way to host this type of exhibition than by having the hometown guys be the stars of the show. The Triple Crown Line of Dionne, Taylor, and Simmer were introduced as the starting forwards, but that would be the last highlight. Mike Luit, a goalie from St. Louis, played 31 minutes of shutout hockey.

7. April 23, 2001. The Kings rallied in a decisive Game 6 against the Detroit Red Wings in the first round of the playoffs. The series started with the Kings losing the first two games and almost falling to 3–1 (see No. 3 below). But after winning three straight, the Kings looked to make it four in a row with a win at home. Trailing 2–1 midway through the third period, Adam Deadmarsh knotted things up at 2. That score would hold until just over four minutes into overtime when "Deader" scored the game and series winner, knocking the Wings out of the playoffs in the first round for the first time since 1994.

6. April 10, 1990. In the signature game of the series, the Kings defeated the defending Stanley Cup champion Calgary Flames by a score of 12–4. While Wayne Gretzky was experiencing the worst post-season of his career thanks to a lower back injury, Dave Taylor, Tomas Sandstrom, and Tony Granato carried the Kings. Each had a hat trick—in fact, the three players scored nine goals on their first nine shots. The Kings went on to beat the Flames in six games before being swept by the Edmonton Oilers.

5. Triple Crown Line. Marcel Dionne, Charlie Simmer, and Dave Taylor came close to accomplishing an NHL first in the 1979–1980 season, but Taylor's 90 points were just short of matching Dionne's 137 and Simmer's 101. The next season they would not be denied. Once again Dionne led the way with 135 points, Taylor bettered his point total from the previous season by 22, finishing with 112, and Simmer reached 105, making the trio the first to include three players above the century mark. How good were they? The line contributed at least a point in 56 consecutive games over the course of two separate seasons.

4. April 22, 1976. The Kings were down 3–1 at the start of the third period against Boston in Game 6 of this quarterfinals series, one game removed from a humiliating 7–1 defeat in Game 5. A Mike Corrigan goal cut the deficit to 3–2, and with just over two minutes to play Corrigan was involved with one of the craziest goals you'll ever see. He caught Bruins goalie Gerry Cheevers going after a loose puck in the corner and beat him to the puck. Cheevers tripped Corrigan, but no penalty was called. While sliding on his stomach, Corrigan got a stick on the loose puck and deflected it off Cheevers' stick for the tying goal. Butch Goring scored the game winner in overtime, and was carried off the ice by his teammates. Boston went on to win in seven games.

3. April 18, 2001. The Stunner at Staples. Down 2–1 in the series against the heavily favored Detroit Red Wings, the Kings found themselves trailing 3-0 at the start of the third period. It's one thing to come back over the course of 20 minutes, and something completely different when your first goal comes at the 5:14 mark. That's what little known Scott Thomas did when he made the score 3–1. Head coach Andy Murray pulled his goalie, Felix Potvin, with just over three minutes left and was rewarded when Josef Stumpel scored a power play goal with 2:27 left. Again, Murray pulled Potvin and again was rewarded when Bryan Smolinski tied the game with a scorcher past Chris Osgood. Just 2:36 into overtime Eric Belanger got his first playoff goal to give the Kings the overtime victory and even the series up at 2 games.

2. May 29, 1993. I think it's safe to say a performance Wayne Gretzky has called "the best NHL game of his career" is worthy of a slot this high on the list. Gretzky had been heavily criticized in the media for not playing better in the Conference Finals against Toronto. As the story goes, the Kings' captain told his teammates he needed their help. If they won Game 6, he'd take care of Game 7 in Toronto. "The Great One" made good on his promise, tallying 4 points and scoring a hat trick, which hasn't been accomplished in a Game 7 since. The 5–4 victory advanced the Kings to their first NHL Stanley Cup Final.

1. April 10, 1982. Known as "The Miracle on Manchester," and to call it a miracle might be an understatement. The Kings were facing the impressive Edmonton Oilers in the division semifinals, a team that came into the post season with 111 points. Conversely, the Kings backed into the playoffs with 63 points. The Oilers roster included Gretzky, Messier, Fuhr, Coffey, and a host of other All-Stars. The Kings countered with young players like Daryl Evans and Bernie Nicholls, along with the Triple Crown Line, although Charlie Simmer had missed a considerable portion of the season with a broken leg. Trailing 5–0 at the start of the third period, the Kings scored two early goals to cut the deficit to three. A busted play caused a strange third goal when Grant Fuhr was knocked back into his goal by his own defenseman and brought the puck across the goal line. Now the crowd was into it. When Oilers defenseman Gary Under took a major penalty for high sticking, the Forum was delirious. The Kings' Dave Lewis was then hit with two minutes for roughing, creating a 4-on-4 for two more minutes of play. During that stretch, defenseman Mark Hardy was able to put a wrister from just inside the blue line past Fuhr. The final three minutes of the game was played with the Kings a man up and with just 10 seconds remaining, Wayne Gretzky missed a chance to clear the puck. Hardy took a shot on goal, but Fuhr made the stop. The rebound ended up on the stick of rookie Steve Bozek and he scored, sending the game into overtime and the Forum crowd into a frenzy. The game winner came on a face-off in the Oilers zone, with Evans taking a one-timer to complete the greatest comeback in NHL playoff history. The Kings' 6-5 win propelled them to a 3–2 series upset.

While the Kings have never won a Stanley Cup, there's no denying they've had plenty of talent walk over the years. The greatest player in the history of the game was a King and one of the great goal scorers hung up his skates a couple seasons ago. The majority of this list is admittedly comprised of scoring forwards, as defenseman and goalies have long been the organization's shortfall.

10. Kelly Hrudey. In his seven-plus seasons with the Los Angeles Kings, Hrudey was in net for the only squad to make the Stanley Cup Finals, in 1993. He was always solid, but not spectacular, posting just three more shutouts over the course of his career with the Kings than Rogie Vachon had in his best single season.

9. Butch Goring. Goring was considered one of the league's most complete players. He excelled at face-offs and on the penalty kill, was a solid passer, great on breakaways, and could put the puck in the net. He scored more than 25 goals seven times during his 10 seasons with the Kings, which concluded after 1979-1980. While Goring is best known as an Islander after winning the Conn Smythe and four consecutive Stanley Cup titles, he will be remembered as one of the all-time great Kings greats for his all-around contributions.

8. Bernie Nicholls. After joining the Kings for the final 22 games of the 1981-1982 seasons, Nicholls scored 14 goals and amassed 32 points in just 22 games. His encore was even more spectacular, scoring four goals in the team's first round upset of the Edmonton Oilers. He is one of just eight players to score 70 or more goals in a single season, which he accomplished in 1988-1989.

7. Charlie Simmer. Arrived with great fanfare after being promoted halfway through the 1978-1979 season and scoring 21 goals in just 37 games. As the left winger on the Triple Crown Line, Simmer topped the century mark in back-to-back seasons and was named a first team All-Star after both. His 32.75 shooting percentage in 1980-1981 is still the best single season mark in league history.

6. Rob Blake. Blake was one of the best defensemen in the league while playing parts of 12 seasons with the Kings. His hip check is so devastating they write folk songs about it in his home province of Ontario. Adding to his physical prowess is his ability to score. He posted 46 points his rookie season and 59 the year the Kings made their only Stanley Cup appearance.

5. Dave Taylor. No King has played more games for the franchise than Taylor's 1,111. He played right wing on the famed Triple Crown Line in 1980-1981, and posted totals of 47 goals and 112 points. While he'd never reach those highs again, Taylor was an invaluable part of the Kings teams of the late 1970s through the early 1990s. His grinding style of play made him a physical presence on a talented line of scorers and he became a respected two-way player.

4. Rogie Vachon. Already a legend from winning the Vezina in Montreal, Vachon arrived in Los Angeles just in time to help the struggling franchise. He was hockey royalty, and you could argue no player was more valuable to their team at the time than Vachon was to the Kings. He finished second in MVP voting to Bobby Clarke in 1975. The 1974-1975 season was Rogie's best statistically as he won 27 games, lost 14, and posted a career best 2.24 GAA with 6 shutouts. He recorded 32 shutouts during his entire Kings tenure.

3. Marcel Dionne. If it weren't for the lack of post-season success Dionne would be at the top of this list. You can make the case that no player is more under appreciated in his or her respective sport than Dionne. He's considered the greatest player to have never won a Stanley Cup. Not only did he never win a title, he never even made the finals. While he was with the Kings, his teams only made it out of the first round three times. In just under 12 seasons with the Kings, Dionne, who centered the famed Triple Crown Line, won the Art Ross Trophy and the Lady Bing in 1980. He topped the century mark six times with the Kings and had 94 points on two separate occasions. Not only is he is the Kings' all-time leader in goals and points leader, but also fourth in the NHL in career goals and fifth in career points.

2. Wayne Gretzky. In his nearly eight seasons with the Kings, "The Great One" was still plenty great. He led the Kings to their only Stanley Cup Finals berth in 1993, ironically enough in a season where he played in just 45 games. He returned for the post-season and scored 40 points, 15 more than the team's second best player. His regular season numbers were typical, jaw-dropping Gretzky. He averaged 115 points per season for L.A., but that includes three seasons of playing just 45, 48, and 62 games. He also led the league in assists five times, points three times, and points per game twice while wearing the silver and black.

1. Luc Robitaille. He played 14 of his 19 seasons for the Los Angeles Kings, and there's no doubt when you think of Kings hockey he's the first player that comes to mind. The eight-time All-Star won the Calder Trophy—he's the only King to do so—in 1987 after putting together one of the best rookie seasons in Kings history with 45 goals and 84 points. When he retired, he was the all-time leading left winger in goals (668) and points (1394) in league history. He also tops this list because of his personality and contributions off the ice. You'd be hard pressed to meet a more kind and generous person, never mind a Hall of Fame athlete, who is so humble and genuinely considerate to others.

Luc Robitaille's "Lucky Goals"

Instead of putting this into list form, I found the conversation I had with Luc so compelling I wanted to transcribe it for you in the hopes you would get the same feeling I had in the moment he and I were talking. Robitaille is one of the greatest players we've ever had in Los Angeles, but because the Kings never won a Stanley Cup—and because we are a Lakers and Dodgers town first—he's often overlooked, and that's not cool. He's the most affable superstar I've ever been around, and it's about time we start to celebrate what he achieved more than we have in the past. Below is a summary, in his words, of our conversation about his most memorable goals over the course of a hall of fame career.

October 9, 1986. I'll never forget my first game. I was so nervous that I was shaking on the bench. It took about four minutes before I actually got my first shift in. I'll never forget stepping on the ice, going right to the front of the net, the net being empty, Marcel Dionne over in the corner with the puck, and me yelling at him in French "Marcel . . . Marcel. . . ." He passed it to me, and I tipped it in. At that moment I just knew there was this something, something remarkable there. The first time on the ice in my NHL career, the first time I touch the puck, and what does it do but go in the net.

March 1987. Down by two to Calgary, Marcel gave me a pass, and I think it was Al McInnis who tripped me, and I scored while I was on my stomach sliding toward the goal. When I see the replay I still say to myself, I have no idea how I did that. I'm on my stomach and I manage to get my stick out to hit the puck. I do remember knowing where I wanted the puck to go, and it found that little hole behind Mike Vernon to get in the net. It's a cool goal because it's always on the highlight films.

May 27 and 29, 1993. Game 6 and Game 7 against Toronto in the 1993 Conference finals. I scored the game-tying goal earlier in Game 6, and I gave it to Wayne in overtime for the game winner. Once we got that win, in front of our home crowd, we knew we were going to win in Toronto in Game 7. Wayne just owned that game, scoring three goals, and we were on to the Stanley Cup Finals.

June 1, 1993. After getting that Game 7 win against the Leafs (a game Wayne Gretzky has called the best performance of his career) we went to my hometown, Montreal, for the Stanley Cup Finals. Here I am playing in the place were I grew up for the Stanley Cup. We won Game 1, 4-1, and I had two goals, the first two of the game, and I still remember how high I felt after that game. It was like a childhood dream come true; this was the place I had all these images of things happening when I was a kid, and it actually played out that way.

January 7, 1999. My 500th goal was a bit surreal, because when I got into the league it wasn't something I set out to do. I just wanted to play in the NHL. All I wanted to do was make it and stick around for a bit. Then it seemed like all of a sudden, one day, I have 500 goals. And in that moment it just hit me, it hit me how special things were.

Passing the "Rocket." I'll never forget doing an interview in the middle of the season, and this guy said to me, "So how do you feel?" And I said, "About what?" And he replied, "Your next goal is going to tie Rocket Richard's career total." It was goals 543 to tie and 544 to pass him. I'll never forget almost freezing at that moment, because the "Rocket" Richard was *the guy* where I grew up. He was just like Babe Ruth is in the United States. Most of you have never seen him play, but you know all the stories—he was the player you always heard about. That's the Rocket Richard for me. I felt very humbled. I said to myself, I didn't know if I should pass him. I didn't know if that was the right thing to do. Safe to say the next two goals were very special to me.

The 2001 playoffs against the Red Wings. Down 3-0 against Detroit in a playoff game, and having a part in two of the three goals scored before Adam Deadmarsh scored the game-winner in overtime, was a great thrill. That was one of the great comebacks I took part in.

November 10, 2001. I think of myself as a King, of course, but when I was on the Red Wings I had a few special goals. One was my 600th goal. That was a big deal; it's a very special mark that only a few players have reached. I also remember scoring a big goal in Game 7 of the conference finals that helped us get to the Stanley Cup finals against Carolina, where I won my first and only Stanley Cup.

January 19, 2006. I scored three goals in a game against the Thrashers to break Marcel Dionne's record as the all-time goals leader in Kings history (550). I'll never forget after the game, coming in the room and the guys gave me a standing ovation. You know as a player you never get that, and that's some good memories, something I'll keep forever.

Everyone knows that Wayne Gretzky was the greatest hockey player of all time, right? After all his number "99" is retired throughout the entire league. So why does this Kings fan have an empty feeling when I think about "The Great One"? Here are some reasons why Gretzky was not all that when he skated in Los Angeles.

9. Coach Killer. Gretzky's first season with the Kings resulted in the franchise's third best record. So why was coach Robbie Ftorek fired? When you had Gretzky you had to play by his rules. Both Tom Webster and Barry Melrose would suffer similar fates during the Gretzky era.

8. Uniforms. The Lakers and the Kings shared more than a home at the "Fabulous" Forum. They also shared owners Jack Kent Cooke and Jerry Buss, and sported similar color schemes for their uniforms. The purple and gold was as synonymous with Kings hockey as it was for the Lakers. That went out the window when the Gretzky arrived and the Kings changed to silver and black. When did Al Davis take over the team? Those were some bad uniforms with mediocre results.

7. Bad Trade with St. Louis. Gretzky had enough of the Kings by his eighth season with the team. In essence, he forced the team to trade him to St. Louis because of his wife's ties to the city. The Kings got little in the trade outside of journeyman Craig Johnson and, to make matters worse, Gretzky bolted from St. Louis after the season. His entire career with the Blues amounted to just 13 games. So much for his "need" to be in St. Louis.

6. Rewriting Team History. Believe it or not the Kings had a history before Gretzky arrived. In fact, the most entertaining teams in franchise history came before Gretzky with the fabled Triple Crown Line of Marcel Dionne, Charlie Simmer, and Dave Taylor. Dionne especially was hurt by the presence of Gretzky. It's as if the NHL's fifth all-time leading scorer never existed. True Kings fans will tell you that either Dionne or Luc Robitaille were the best in team history.

5. Recycled Edmonton Oilers. In an effort to make Gretzky more "comfortable" with his surroundings, the Kings did everything in their power to reassemble his old Edmonton teams. Jari Kurri, Paul Coffey, Charlie Huddy, and others joined Gretzky and Marty McSorley (who came in the Gretzky trade from Edmonton), but to no avail. Whatever happened during the heyday of the Oilers was not repeated in L.A.

4. Bandwagon Fans. This is typical of most cities, but Los Angeles actually had a true base of hockey fans that loved the Kings. It wasn't long after Gretzky's arrival, however, that many of those fans lost their place in line. The Hollywood elite, who never gave a crap about hockey, suddenly showed up at games just because Gretzky was on the ice. The atmosphere was never the same at the Forum. Of course, once Gretzky left, so did the bandwagon fans—never to be seen at another hockey game.

3. Bruce McNall. This was the fraud that pulled off the Gretzky deal that "changed" hockey forever in Los Angeles. In reality, McNall was living a lie and he had Gretzky covering his back. McNall put the Kings in financial ruins while bilking six banks for the tune of $236 million. Amazingly, Gretzky was a frequent visitor of McNall's while he served several years in prison for bank fraud. While Gretzky continued to celebrate McNall's existence, the Kings were forced into bankruptcy.

2. Championships. Let's get this straight. The Kings acquired the best player in hockey at the prime of his career and they won exactly zero championships in eight seasons with the "Great One." Actually, it gets worse. Everyone talks about their one run to the Stanley Cup Finals in 1993, but how about the four losing seasons during his eight-year skate? Or how about not even making the playoffs his last three years with the team? To make matters worse, Edmonton won the Stanley Cup just two years after Gretzky left town. So who got the better of that deal?

1. A Failed Franchise. The Kings were a franchise that made the playoffs 12 times before Gretzky arrived. Since that miracle run in 1993, the Kings have been in the playoffs just four times in 15 seasons. Answer this question: Are the Kings a better franchise because Gretzky played for the team? The answer is clear to any true hockey fan. The Kings have become a laughing stock in the NHL and Gretzky has no further ties with the team. Thanks for the memories "Great One"!

I'm not afraid to admit I'm a hockey nut. I love me the puck. From the time I was a wee lad and had my Uncle Frank pick me up in his red Caddy to attend various sporting events, I always left and still leave the hockey arena wishing the game wasn't over more than any other sport. This is why it crushes my very being to have the team I cheer for be in such disarray. I wish I didn't have to put together the following list, but reality is exactly that, and here we are.

10. Fans. You're too good to the team. Average attendance has no business being that high. Creating actual sellouts on multiple occasions—not just Red Wings games—for arguably the worst team in the league? Spending hundreds of thousands of dollars on merchandise every single season? Why kiss the salary cap when you don't have to? Even Donald Sterling had to suck it up and start paying players when things got too bad for the Clippers and people quit paying attention.

9. Versus. The television deal the NHL agreed to post-strike isn't doing anyone any favors. In a competitive market like Los Angeles, not having a legitimate hockey outlet is crushing. Do you think a sports fan is going to watch the Lakers on a national telecast or seek out the Vs. channel so he can see some Kings-Thrashers action? That means less team revenue, and in turn less money for payroll.

8. The Miracle on Manchester. It was too good a game, maybe the greatest in the history of the sport. It's number one on our list of greatest Kings moments, so I won't go too far into detail. But I wonder if the sports gods decided that it was so good, we can't give them anything else that could possibly rival it, so why bother trying.

7. Manhattan Beach. It's too good to these players. When you're living in Detroit, Ottawa, Buffalo, or Calgary there's plenty to be pissed off about. The weather, the fact your every move is chronicled by every local news outlet, and fans actually know who you are and hold you accountable is motivation. Not here. Dudes roll the streets anonymously and everyone lives in the posh beach/party community of Manhattan Beach. Good break, good food, good-looking women, and great bars. "Who cares if we lost 6-1 tonight, I'll see you later at Sharkeez!"

6. No Soul. Every player who's been the guts of the team has been traded away at some point. Butch Goring, Rogie, Bernie, Blake, Dionne—when you look at the list it's borderline lunacy. They traded Wayne Gretzky for a couple guys named Vopat and Patrice, for god's sake. As bad as that was, sending Luc Robitaille to the Penguins was terrible. Seeing him win a cup with the Red Wings still gets my gag reflex going.

5. The Ducks. While the fans are dedicated and fill Staples Center far more often than they should, too many casual hockey fans will focus on the Ducks because it's a superior product. Two Stanley Cup Finals and one championship this decade. That's better than the Kings' 40-plus years of existence. It doesn't help that most kids who play hockey are in Orange County, which happens to be Duck Country.

4. Youth Movement. The second you hear youth movement you know you're toast. Columbus and Nashville are places for the marketing campaign "The Kids Are Alright," not Los Angeles. While the Ducks are scrambling to get under the cap with all their big-time talent, the Kings are scrambling to hit the minimum team salary thanks to so many kids that belong in Manchester actually playing in the NHL.

3. Goalies. Rogie Vachon left in 1978, and we've yet to meet a great goalie since. Sure, Kelly Hrudey helped the Kings to the Stanley Cup Finals in 1993, but his GAA and save percentage were a bit pedestrian. Since Hrudey left, tell me if these names strike fear into opponents: Fiset, Storr, Potvin (off the scrap heap), Cechmanek (off the scrap heap), Cloutier, Huet, and Garon. What's that you say? Huet and Garon aren't so bad? When they wanted more cash, they were allowed to leave.

2. Tim Lieweke. When you live in the greater Los Angeles area and the president and CEO of the Kings uses terms like "Cost Certainty," "Level Playing Field," and "Reckless Spending," you know you have issues. After the strike was resolved, Lieweke told Kings fans we now have a deal in place that will allow a Stanley Cup title to come to LA—and it did, for the Ducks. In the meantime, the Kings have become one of the worst franchises in all of hockey.

1. Phil Anschutz. The man who owns the team loves soccer. The Kings are simply a vehicle to be part of Staples Center and the Los Angeles sports scene. Consider he invested more in one player on the L.A. Galaxy—the freaking L.A. Galaxy—than the combined payrolls of the previous five Kings teams.

The 10 Most "Interesting" Looking Athletes in Los Angeles History

We can do this list because we're ugly. If you forgot or didn't know, just take a look at the cover and try to hold your lunch down. If there were a list of radio personalities that weren't easy on the eyes, we'd be on it and we're totally cool with that. So, that having been said, here are 10 dudes that are, well you know.

10. Tyronn Lue. I mean he looks like Jar Jar Binks. Literally, I'm not kidding. Get a photo of Lue and Jar Jar, put them next to one another and tell me I'm wrong. Plus, I think Jar Jar was less annoying.

9. Randy Johnson. Remember he played his college ball at USC. Johnson has the ugly trifecta going: beak of a nose, bad skin, and the worst haircut of all time with that mullet. At least he's all awkward with that 6-foot-10 frame walking around. I'd feel guilty for being so harsh, but by all accounts he's one of the least friendly guys you'll ever meet.

8. Bill Walton. Red hair, 7-feet tall, neck beard, giant teeth, deep guttural voice, and one of the worst hippie wardrobes in his day—it was like your curtains were attacking you.

7. Jim Plunkett. The Raiders QB might be all right looking in photos or on television. But when you got up close you couldn't help but feel like his face was squishing out of his helmet. It was so scary linebackers didn't want to blitz him.

6. Nick Van Exel. I'm not sure if it was the bug eyes or the perfectly round head, but Nick looked like he was wearing a Halloween mask every day. When he had the weeklong growth on his upper lip, I found him especially unattractive.

5. Chris Kaman. I'm not sure if Kaman falls into the ugly category or the really, really weird looking one. It helped a bit when he cut his hair, but he's still got the deep-set eyes and giant nose to go with his narrow mouth and that pasty white skin.

4. Ian Laperriere. I guess when your nose is situated in the middle of your right cheek you have a bit of a problem. Seemed like after every game Lappy came into the locker room with an "Awww shucks, I broke my nose again" story.

3. Keith Closs. I mean, wow. Where do you start? The freckles, the crooked afro, the gangly body? The best attribute was his "F*** The World" tattoo across his back. Priceless.

2. Gary Gaetti. The Rat King. I want to write something else, but the former Angel was actually a pretty nice guy, and if I keep going this is going to get a bit harsh. What a nose and teeth combo, though. I mean, dude looks like Splinter guiding the Teenage Mutant Ninja Turtles.

1. Sam Cassell. If this list exists in every city where Cassell played ball he'd tops across the board. It's not that he's the ugliest person to ever walk the earth, he just happens to look like a sketch of an alien, which I'm guessing isn't attractive in most towns across the country.

A good five generations of people waited for their beloved Kings to be the first team on the West Coast to hoist the Stanley Cup and officially become part of the NHL instead of "some team that plays in California." But it didn't work out that way, instead, new ownership, a shrewd general manager, and a collection of players that truly were in it for "team" put together a magical season, and a wild playoff ride that people in Orange County paid attention to just long enough to sort of remember what happened.

10. February 25, 2005. Henry Samueli purchases the Mighty Ducks from The Walt Disney Co. for somewhere in the neighborhood of what they paid for it in expansion fees back in 1993—$50 million. Samueli was very similar to Arte Moreno, the new owner of the Angels at the time: independently wealthy, successful in his field, and eager to win.

9. June 20, 2005. Brian Burke was hired to run the front office. Burke brought instant credibility and a slice of grit to a franchise that at the time was best known as the team named after a kids' movie starring Emilio Estevez who wore purple and teal uniforms.

8. Rob Niedermayer. The 2003 trade that brought Rob to Anaheim from Calgary would turn out to be a huge move in the summer of 2005, but it nearly paid instant dividends as the Ducks made it to the Stanley Cup Finals in 2003. Rob piled up 10 points over the 21 games as a defensive forward, and of course his presence on the team is what led older brother Scott to shun the only NHL team he'd ever known (New Jersey) in free agency for a chance to play with family.

7. November 15, 2005. The previous regime had thought it made the biggest splash in the 2003 free agency period when it signed Sergei Federov to a 5-year, $40 million deal, instead it turned out to be disaster. Under contract at $8 million per season through 2008, Brian Burke took care of the egregious error by doing a salary dump with the Columbus Blue Jackets in return getting a young player named Francois Beauchemin. The move would put them in place.

6. Lost to Edmonton in 2006. Conference Finals of the 2006 Stanley Cup playoffs the Ducks' hopes came to a grinding halt when they ran into a white hot Edmonton Oilers club. Losing to that particular team worked out for both the Ducks and Chris Pronger. After that 2005–2006 season, Pronger wanted out of Edmonton, and the Ducks wanted Pronger. Chris knew how close Anaheim was to winning the cup, and the Ducks knew how valuable he was to the series they had just lost, and fortunately for both parties there was a deal to be made.

5. Ilya Bryzgalov. As a back up to Gigeure, Bryzgalov was one of the best goalies in the league over the course of the regular season, boasting an impressive 2.47 GAA and .909 save percentage. While winning 10 games for the Ducks over the 82 played prior to the playoffs is a bonus, when he was called upon in the post-season because of a family emergency for Giggy, the Ducks' quarterfinals hopes rested on his stick and glove. He allowed just 4 goals in his first 3 games, the Ducks winning every contest to take a commanding 3–0 lead in the best of 7 series. Gigeure came back in Game 5 to close it out, and remained the Ducks net minder for the remainder of the post-season.

4. Teemu Selanne. At the age of 35 Teemu Selanne decided to rejoin the Anaheim Ducks after rehabbing his knee during the lockout season in Finland. All he did in his first season back in Southern California is lead the team in scoring, totaling 90 points with 40 goals. The following season he would better that number by 4, giving him his highest point total in nearly a decade. In the post-season he added another 5 goals and 15 points.

3. Giant Pads. Brett Hull and the Ottawa Senators can complain all they want, but all Jean Sebastian Gigeure keeps doing is winning. Already owner of the most prestigious individual award in the NHL, the Conn Smythe Trophy, Giggy nearly lost his job with the Ducks thanks to the spectacular play of back up Ilya Bryzgalov. But he would get first crack at the gig in October 2006 and simply went undefeated that month, posting his best regular season numbers: 36 wins, 4 shutouts and a 2.26 GAA. He improved on those numbers in the post-season, going 13 and 4 with a 1.97 GAA.

2. Checking Line. Maybe I like my hockey a little more nasty than most, but anytime you tell me to choose between a checking line or high powered offense, I'm going with the grinders. In the Stanley Cup Finals some wondered if the Ducks would be able to keep up with the Daniel Alfredsson, Dany Heatly and Jason Spezza line that had piled up 23 goals and a ridiculous 58 points heading into the Stanley Cup Finals. The trio of Rob Niedermayer, Sammy Pahlsson and Travis Moen not only held the top 3 to just 5 goals over the 5 games, but match that total with 5 goals themselves, including the only goal scored in the 1-0 Ducks victory in game 2. Some suspected the Conn Smythe might go to one (Pahlsson) or all of them.

1. Scott Niedermayer. There's no question without his decision to leave the Devils and join his brother Rob in the summer of 2005 none of this would have been possible. By signing Niedermayer the Ducks not only landed the premiere free agent post lockout, but signaled to the team and the rest of the league they were a legitimate title threat. The team took on his personality, a punch the clock and get it done work ethic, and thanks to the biggest star on the team having no ego, not one other player was allowed to be the least bit selfish. The addition of Chris Pronger in the 2006 off-season meant for nearly every minute of every game the Ducks had either Scott or Chris on the ice, and each is considered one of the greatest defensemen of his generation.

There are a few conditions to this here list. Number one, I'm going on the assumption that 3 percent of the people in this country have enough cash to belong to Riviera, Bel-Air, LACC, and the like. So big-time privates are out. I'm excluding San Diego County because if you really care about this list you're smart enough to know that's a trip in itself with another 10 courses. This is California, so aesthetics play a big part. You should know you're playing here, not in the Midwest. Most of the spots are a bit pricey, but last time I checked acres of land on the Pacific Ocean weren't exactly cheap, so pony up that cash.

10. Rancho Park. Consider this an honorable mention at 10. I'm not sure if it still rings true, but at one point this was the busiest golf course in the world. There is a tremendous amount of history at this Municipal tract including an 18th hole where Arnold Palmer shot a 7 over and a plaque commemorates his tough go in a championship round. It's well taken care of, but because it's relatively inexpensive and in the middle of the city, it's hard to get on, and takes 6 hours to get around.

9. Heartwell. Why am I including an 18-hole, 2,143-yard, par-54 course on the list? If you're in Southern California you might as well run the tract Tiger grew up on. Yes, 18 holes, all par 3's, fully lighted by the way, and just $14.00 during the week, $16.00 on the weekend. You head to the restroom and what's that stuck on the wall, a scorecard from 1980 with Tiger's name on it commemorating the day he logged his first birdie on the 91 yard 3rd hole. Again in 1980, *at the age of 4*, he shot 70 for a 16-over.

8. Robinson Ranch. Probably the one course I included that caused people to scratch their head. There are a hundred of these courses in the 805/661 area codes. Canyon setting, tremendous risk/reward and thanks to fairways sculpted into the sides of mountains, low handicappers only. So what separates Robinson Ranch from Lost Canyons, Moorpark, and Tierra Rejada? Those damn greens. You find me more challenging, or for that matter, better greens in the Los Angeles area and I'll pay for your round. I've actually 5 putted at Robinson Ranch Before. They can't even measure it on the Stimpmeter it's so fast. I recommend the Valley course, and the 15th hole might be my favorite.

7. Oak Quarry. I'm not crazy about golf in the 909, which is why the USGA course, despite being a tremendous spot, didn't make the cut, but Oak Quarry is so unique I couldn't leave it off. Carved into an actual rock quarry, I say with great certainty there's no place like it—unless teeing off over a 200-foot chasm onto a fairway that's 20 feet above you is normal. You always hear the Grand Canyon makes you realize how brief your time might be on our planet. Oak Quarry provides that same effect when you're on the par-3 14th staring at the giant limestone wall encompassing the green.

6. Ojai Valley. George C. Thomas Jr. design—if the name doesn't ring a bell, he happened to be the dude who put together the aforementioned LACC, Riviera and Bel-Air. Tremendous history having been built in 1923 and part of the Ojai Valley Inn and Spa which is north of Los Angeles and off the beaten path a bit. Make a weekend out of it, stay at the Inn, swim in the pool, eat on campus and of course play a whole lot of golf. I love the first hole, which has you tee off above the tree line whipping in the wind below.

5. Sandpiper. One of two courses you have to hit up when you roll north to the Santa Barbara area. Completely different from Ojai which I mentioned earlier, as that's the Valley and this is the ocean. Some call it, "A Poor Man's Pebble Beach," which comes thanks to the ocean views, but it's nothing like Pebble. When you check in and see the clubhouse, you'll say it's "a homeless man's Pebble Beach." Don't worry about a pre- and post-game drink or meal, all the cash this place makes is put back into the course. Just buy a sixer to take with you and eat at Super Rica before your round. It's a toss up between the 10th and 11th for signature hole, so I'll punt.

4 and 3. Pelican Hill North/South. Since they were reopened I'll say both courses are worthy of mention. They're both beautiful, each has countless Pacific Ocean views from the course, and they're both ridiculously expensive. But like a bottle of fine wine, you can worry about the price tag later, because in the moment it's easy to understand why you dropped that mess of cash. Two Tom Fazio designs, and if you can't play 36 go with the north—the finishing hole is worth it. You'll need a giant drive over a canyon to hit the fairway, followed by a shot over another canyon to land on the green. Once the resort portion of Pelican is finished I'd be surprised to not see this become one of the premiere golf vacation destinations in the world.

2. PGA West. There's a six pack of courses at PGA West all of which are worthy, my favorite simply happens to be the Norman. Maybe It's because I've rented houses in the past on the fairways, stumbled out of the pool, thrown a polo on and had mouth agape at the spectacular surroundings. The Terra Cotta Mountains in the background, the vibrant wildflowers, and the lush emerald fairways make it the most beautiful course in the desert. There are two types of courses in Southern California worth playing—ocean view and desert beauty. This tops the desert portion. Pay attention on the 15th hole with all the bunkers scattered throughout every part of the fairway.

1. Monarch Beach. Not hard to guess why Monarch tops my list (remember that aesthetic comment at the top?). It's only located in the most desirable place to live in Southern California—Dana Point. The par-4 3rd hole, which runs parallel to the Pacific, might be the most beautiful I've ever played. Panoramic views of the ocean, excellent conditions, challenging course, and a number of locations to hit up after the round for a drink and some eye candy (Surf and Sand or The Montage).

Mascots rule. I have no qualms saying it. Now don't get me wrong: there have been times I wish I had been smart enough to have attended Stanford so I could hit up games for the sole purpose of worshiping the Stanford Tree. But here in Southern California we have some pretty good representatives when it comes to the ridiculous mascot that only an alumnus or alumna could love.

10. Joe and Josie Bruin, UCLA. Why so low? Having a couple as your mascot is beyond lame, especially when Josephine gets Joe all dressed up in those tourist shorts and tropical shirts to match her outfit. When they come together on the sideline you want to punch yourself in the junk because it's so uncomfortable.

9. Traveler and Tommy Trojan, USC. Not one, but two mammals grace the USC sidelines. While they may be majestic creatures, a fit human combined with a beautiful Arabian horse aren't the result of some student dressed up in felt. Besides, who wants their mascot relieving him or herself in front of everyone during the game?

8. The Golden Eagle of Cal State. Typically I think of two types of mascots when it comes to the Eagles. A regal representation of a bird that's come to be a somewhat symbol of our country, and San the Eagle, one of my favorite Muppets that happens to look an awful lot like Phil Jackson. Point is, the Cal State L.A. Golden Eagle is neither. It's almost a penguin. I think we gotta hit 'em up for a redesign.

7. Willie the Wave, Pepperdine University. Could have been top had they not gone for the molded wave head with ridiculous sunglasses. Back in my day you got the feeling the athletic department looked around and said, "How do we make a mascot that's a wave?" And Willie was what came out, a giant blue nothing with a white Mohawk. Beloved by those who went to Pepperdine, disgusting to the many who didn't. Often voted the worst mascot in all of college athletics, which as far as we we're concerned is pretty cool. Now, it looks like something out of a Nestea commercial.

6. Peter the Anteater, University of California Irvine. Almost made the top spot. The neck—that's what it's all about. Peter has a good 2-foot-tall neck before getting to that angled head of his with the giant black racing stripe on the side of it. I'm not sure why this is, but others agree with me, there's something reminiscent of Space Ghost in the design. I think it's the narrow and intimidating eyes.

5. Prospector Pete, Cal State University Long Beach. Much like Willie the Wave, I liked the original, less mobile incarnation of Pete, but the newly introduced prospector from 2000 isn't too bad. I mean, they did keep the giant chin that's at least twice as wide as the top of his head, and even added a pretty cool pickax to the costume. Plus he's got a pretty gnarly underbite to boot.

4. Tuffy Titan, California State University Fullerton. I'm a sucker for anything with a trunk, and damn does Tuffy have that covered. While Tuffy is your typical anthropomorphic mascot, the head portion of the costume is traditional elephant. No wacky giant eyes, no smile in place of the tusks, just a plain elephant head with regular sized floppy ears, he looks a bit depressed too.

3. Cecil Sagehen, Pomona College. Nothing like a mascot outfit that leaves one exposed from the knee down. But from the knee up you got a blue fuzzy outfit that looks rather ridiculous. Best part of Cecil is, according to the Pomona College website, the sagehen, when being attacked and in danger, defends itself by doing what? Running around in circles. Word is, Cecil mimics this approach while rallying his teams on from certain defeat.

2. Johnny Poet, Whittier College. Just hit up that website and prepare to be intimidated to the nth degree. Nothing strikes fear into opponents like a scribe with his quill. What? You think I mock? How dare you? Johnny Poet is a hero to all here in Southern California, especially considering the real John Whittier was a fireside poet and abolitionist with one heck of a neck beard.

1. Cal State Northridge Matador. The beautiful cleft chin, the plastic smile and the empty gaze that adorns the Northridge Matador is a thing of beauty. Add in the traditional headgear and this tanned man of Euro descent clad in deep maroon is a marvel to behold. I think he might be cross-eyed.

With all of their success in football it's hard to think of USC as dominant in any other sport. The fact is the Trojans have won more national championships in baseball than they have in football. USC has won 12 NCAA titles in baseball; that is double the total of any other school in the country. Rod Dedeaux was the legendary coach who guided the school to 11 of those championships including five in a row from 1970 through 1974. Here is a list of the best baseball players to ever play for Troy.

10. Steve Busby. Injuries limited his major league career to just three full seasons but they were impressive to say the least. Pitching with the Kansas City Royals from 1973 to 1975, Busby won 56 games, was named to two All-Star teams and did something no other pitcher has done in the history of major league baseball – throw no-hitters in each of his first two big league seasons. The first came in only his tenth major start and the second a little more than a year later. Arm injuries derailed what could have been a Hall of Fame career.

9. Bill "Spaceman" Lee. This quirky lefty was one of the great characters in the history of the game. He was also a better than average pitcher. Lee won 119 games in 14 major league seasons with the Red Sox and Expos including three consecutive 17-win seasons with Boston from 1973 to 1975. He also started two games in the 1975 World Series. Lee talked openly about smoking marijuana and he even ran for President of the United States in 1988 on the Canadian Political Rhinoceros Party ticket. His slogan during that campaign said it all – "No guns. No butter. Both can kill."

8. Ron Fairly. Not many major league players have lasted 21 seasons but former Trojan Ron Fairly made that exclusive list. He spent most of his career with the Dodgers and Expos recording 1913 hits, 215 home runs, and a pair of All-Star game appearances. The highlight of his career occurred in the 1965 World Series for the Dodgers when he hit .379 in seven games with 11 hits and two home runs. He concluded his career with the Angels in 1978.

7. Dave Kingman. "Kong" was one of the most devastating long ball hitters in the history of the game. He was also one of the greatest whiff artists of all time. Kingman was a pitcher for part of his time at USC but his power stroke intrigued big league scouts. His career numbers are some of the most peculiar in major league history. He hit 442 home runs in just 16 seasons including 48 for the Cubs in 1979. However, his career batting average was just .236 and his on-base percentage was a lowly .302. In 1982 he led the National League with 37 home runs but his .204 batting average was lower than that of Steve Carlton who won that year's Cy Young Award. Kingman was a true one-of-a-kind.

6. Barry Zito. Zito's career is still a work in process but it's clear that he would rate with the greatest USC baseball players of all time. Through the 2007 season he had a career record of 113-76 making him one of the best left-handed pitchers in baseball. In 2002 he had a fabulous season going 23-5 for Oakland and earning the American League Cy Young Award. He also was chosen for the first of his three All-Star game appearances. Zito has been amazingly durable and he stands a chance to win more than 200 games before his career is over.

5. Bret Boone. While rumors of possible steroid use has raised some questions about his sudden surge of power the latter part of his career, Boone still has to rate as one of the great Trojans in big league history. His 2001 season alone was one for the books. That year he hit 37 home runs with a staggering 141 RBI and a .331 average. He would also top the 100 RBI mark the next two seasons. He was also an excellent glove at second base winning four Gold Glove awards. His brother Aaron, another USC product, was also a major league All-Star.

4. Fred Lynn. No rookie in baseball history was showered with more honors than Fred Lynn in 1975. That season he led the Red Sox to their first pennant in eight years while earning both Rookie-of-the-Year and MVP honors. He is still one of just two rookies to be named a league MVP. His career numbers included 306 home runs, four Gold Gloves and the 1979 American League batting title. He was also named to nine straight All-Star teams with both the Red Sox and the Angels. Only a series of injuries prevented him from attaining Hall of Fame status.

3. Mark McGwire. Whether McGwire reaches the Hall of Fame is only a question of did he or didn't he. The first man to hit 70 home runs in one season has become one of the poster boys for steroid use even though he was never tested during his career. His numbers are certainly worthy of inclusion in Cooperstown. His 583 home runs ranked eighth all-time entering the 2008 season. His 10.6 at bats per home run are No. 1 in the history of the game. He was also named to 12 All-Star teams and he won a Gold Glove for his slick work at first base. His will be a career under review for many years to come.

2. Randy Johnson. One of the most devastating pitchers in major league history, "The Big Unit" entered the 2008 season with an outside chance of reaching 300 career victories. His 284-150 career record is truly remarkable as is his 4,616 strikeouts – second all-time to Nolan Ryan. Johnson has won five Cy Young Awards including four straight from 1999 through 2002. Mix in nine strikeout titles and ten All-Star game selections and you have a sure fire first ballot Hall of Famer when he becomes eligible.

1. Tom Seaver. "Tom Terrific" is the greatest Trojan of them all and perhaps the most respected pitcher of all time. Consider that he still holds the record for the highest percentage of votes for any player elected to the Hall of Fame. In all, he recorded 311 victories with 3640 strikeouts and a 2.86 ERA. In 1969 he led the amazing Mets to a World Championship winning 25 games and the first of his three Cy Young Awards. He was also named to 12 All-Star teams. When it comes to great USC players, Seaver is still the standard by which all others are compared.

The 10 Best USC Running Backs Who Did Not Win the Heisman

No college has had a greater running back tradition than USC. The Trojans have had five running backs win the Heisman – Mike Garrett, O.J. Simpson, Charles White, Marcus Allen, and Reggie Bush. Here's the best of the rest since the Heisman was introduced in 1935.

10. C.R. Roberts. Before Syracuse's Ernie Davis won the Heisman in 1961, few African-Americans got even a sniff of the prized award. Just ask Jim Brown. Roberts was not even an All-American despite some incredible games during the 1956 season. He led the Trojans in rushing that season despite splitting time early on with Jon Arnett. The highlight was his school-record 251 yards against Texas on just 12 carries. Not even O.J. could top that mark.

9. Chad Morton. "Little Chad" was the lead back for some of the worst teams in USC history yet he came within 15 yards of posting back-to-back 1000-yard seasons. Despite his diminutive size (he was just 5-8 and 191 pounds), no runner in school history ran with a greater degree of toughness. He still ranks amongst the top ten career rushers in school history.

8. Ricky Ervins. Between Marcus Allen's 1981 Heisman season and Reggie Bush's 2005 Heisman season no USC running back gained more yards in a single year than Ervins in 1989. His 1395 yards as a junior included nine games with 100 or more yards – five of which came consecutively. He wrapped up the season by being named the MVP of the Rose Bowl gaining 126 yards on 30 carries. His hopes for a Heisman the following season were derailed by an ankle injury.

7. Clarence Davis. Imagine trying to be the running back to replace O.J. Simpson. That was the task for Clarence Davis in 1969. All he did was finish fifth in the nation in rushing while leading the Trojans to an undefeated season. In fact, he was leading the nation in rushing yards for most of that year. Davis suffered through some injuries the following year but he went on to Super Bowl glory as a member of the 1976 Oakland Raiders. His 137 yards rushing led the Silver and Black to their first Super Bowl win.

6. Frank Gifford. Long before his Hall of Fame career with the New York Giants and eternal fame as the longest serving member of the *Monday Night Football* crew, Gifford was a one-year wonder running back at USC. His first two varsity seasons saw him play mainly on defense before his switch to feature back in 1951. That season he ran for 841 yards while PASSING for an additional 303 yards. He also kicked 26 extra points and two field goals. All that and he didn't finish in the top 12 Heisman finishers. His moment in the spotlight would come further down the road.

5. Sam Cunningham. If the Heisman were based on social significance, Sam "Bam" Cunningham would have secured the hardware. During his sophomore season in 1970, Cunningham and the Trojans traveled to Alabama to take on Bear Bryant's all-white team. Cunningham gained 135 yards on just 12 carries in a performance that Bryant said changed South football forever. Sam "Bam" would finish his USC career with a four-touchdown Rose Bowl MVP showcase against Woody Hayes and his Ohio State Buckeyes.

4. Jon Arnett. Arnett should have won the Heisman Trophy in 1956. Unfortunately, a school violation cost him half the season. Arnett was coming off an All-American junior season with the hopes of becoming USC's first Heisman winner. Through his first five games in 1956, he had already rushed for 625 yards which was tops in the nation. That's where his season ended because of alleged payouts to players including Arnett. Paul Hornung won the Heisman that season with a 2-8 Notre Dame team. There is not doubt Arnett was a better player that year.

3. Lendale White. Had it not been for Reggie Bush, White could have easily won the Heisman Trophy in 2005. Consider that he earned third-team All-American honors while SHARING time with Bush. He also is USC's all-time touchdown scorer despite opting out of his senior season to play in the NFL. As a sophomore, White gained 118 yards on just 15 carries with two touchdowns as the Trojans demolished Oklahoma in the BCS title game. The following year he had 124 yards in the BCS showdown with Texas. He was a true big game player.

2. Ricky Bell. The late great Ricky Bell is largely forgotten these days but he was an incredible running back at USC. After playing linebacker and fullback his first two years, Bell took over the tailback duties in 1975 and promptly led the nation in rushing. His first start was a record-setting 256-yard performance against Duke. The next season was highlighted by a still school record 347 yard game against Washington State on an amazing 51 carries. An injury cost him the Heisman and he would not live to see his 30th birthday succumbing to a rare muscle disease in 1984.

1. Anthony Davis. There are still people who think "A.D." did win the Heisman Trophy in 1974. He should have won the honor but too many votes were already in when he led USC to that incredible 55-24 comeback win over Notre Dame. He scored four touchdowns that day after scoring SIX touchdowns against the Irish two years earlier. As a USC running back you are measured by what you do in the rivalry games like Notre Dame and UCLA. No Trojan running back grabbed the spotlight to those games like "A.D." Anthony Davis.

No school has more players in the Pro Football Hall of Fame than USC. A total of 11 former Trojans have gained the game's greatest honor. That said, not all USC players have been successes at the next level. All of the following players were first round draft picks and none of them will enter the Canton shrine without a ticket.

10. Mike Hull, 1968. Hull was probably best known as a blocking back for O.J. Simpson on USC's 1967 national championship team but the Chicago Bears thought he would be much more when they selected him with the 16th pick in the 1968 draft. They could have not have been more wrong. Hull hung on for seven years in the NFL with the Bears and the Redskins and gained a total of 207 yards rushing. That's just under 30 yards per season.

9. Chris Claiborne, 1999. The Butkus award winner as the nation's top linebacker, Claiborne was selected ninth overall by the Detroit Lions. Injuries derailed his career that is still on hold at the start of the 2008 season. After four years with the Lions, Claiborne bounced around with the Vikings, Rams, and Giants without any success. Just to add to the Lions misery is the fact 16 players selected after Claiborne have been selected to at least one Pro Bowl. Claiborne was chosen for none.

8. Al Cowlings, 1970. "A.C." is best known as O.J. Simpson's best friend who took his buddy on a ride in a white Bronco but he was also an All-American defensive end during his days at USC. The Buffalo Bills chose him the fifth overall pick in the 1970 draft thus reuniting him with Simpson who he had known since their high school days in San Francisco. While O.J. was flying through parking lots to become a media superstar, Cowlings played on five teams in ten years without gaining any notoriety. That is until that day in the Bronco.

7. Tody Smith, 1971. The little brother of Bubba Smith, Tody was considered a "steal" when he fell to the Cowboys with the 25th overall pick in 1971. His career in Dallas would last all of two seasons. Houston and Buffalo gave him a brief look over the next few years but he never lived up to the hype. He died in his sleep in 1999 at the age of 50. His son is currently a high school student who has already committed to USC. Dakota Castillo-Smith stands 6-8 and could someday make good on the promise his father failed to realize.

6. Mike Taylor, 1968. The Pittsburgh Steelers built their dynasty of the 1970s with brilliant drafting. Unfortunately, Chuck Noll was not with the Steelers when they got ready for the 1968 draft. That was the year that FIVE Trojans were selected in the first round including offensive tackle Mike Taylor. Unlike his college teammate Ron Yary who was selected first overall in the same draft, Taylor was a colossal bust for the Steelers. The tenth pick overall did not even last two years in Pittsburgh before shuffling around three other teams over the next few years. Noll became the Steelers coach in 1969 and promptly picked Joe Greene in the first round. Now that's a draft pick.

5. Dave Cadigan, 1988. No school has had more offensive linemen selected in the first round of the NFL draft than USC. Some of those chosen went on to great careers like Hall of Famers Ron Yary and Anthony Munoz. Dave Cadigan was supposed to follow in their footsteps when the Jets picked him with the eighth choice in the 1988 draft. Five years later he was in the unemployment line. Oh by the way, the Vikings also went offensive line with their first round pick that year. Picking 19th overall, Minnesota picked up Randall McDaniel who went on to start 12 straight Pro Bowls.

4. Todd Marinovich, 1991. He was the "chosen one" or so his father thought when Marinovich was a young boy. Marv Marinovich was a former USC football player who had a brief taste of pro football but he expected much more from his young son. Todd was put on a strict diet and rigorous training program with the plan to someday be one of the greatest quarterbacks in the history of the game. It looked good when he set national high school records and led USC to a Rose Bowl win his freshman season but then the wheels fell off. The Raiders picked him 24th overall after he had been all out exiled at USC and he played just two years with the Silver and Black. Drug problems and frequent arrests have been Marinovich's story ever since.

3. R. Jay Soward, 2000. Soward burst onto the national college football scene when he scored four touchdowns against UCLA as a freshman. He was a wide receiver with all the tools to be a superstar but his personal demons cut short his road to success. He admitted that he smoked pot every day at USC but the Jacksonville Jaguars could not pass up on his amazing talent. They selected Soward with the 29th pick in the 2000 draft and they've regretted it ever since. From day one Soward was a nightmare for the Jags often skipping practice for "other" activities. Coach Tom Coughlin even resorted to sending a limousine to pick Soward up for practice. His NFL career lasted one year.

2. Mike Williams, 2005. To be fair, Williams is still a work in process but considering his collegiate success his NFL career has been a disaster. How good was Mike Williams at USC? Some thought he was as good as any college receiver ever. In just two seasons he caught 30 touchdown passes and he was a unanimous All-American as just a sophomore. Williams was so good that he decided to challenge the NFL rule that prohibited players to enter the league unless they were three years removed from high school. He lost his case and had to sit out the season. The Lions picked him with the tenth pick in the 2005 draft and he was scored just TWO touchdowns in three NFL seasons with three different teams.

1. Darrell Russell, 1997. Unlike the other players on this list, Russell was a STAR in the NFL. By his second season, Russell had already been named to the Pro Bowl and he would add All-Pro honors the following year. There was not a better defensive tackle in the league that the affable kid from Pensacola, Florida. He was the complete package. That's is until drugs took over his life. Russell was suspended for four games in 2001 and then banned for the entire 2002 season for persistent failed drug tests. He played just eight NFL games after that. Ultimately, a good life gone bad ended in a fatal car crash in 2005. Russell was just 29 years old.

The series started with a 76–0 thrashing by USC back in 1929 but since then there have been some incredible gridiron match-ups between these inner-city rivals. These are the biggest upsets between the schools over the past 50 years.

10. 1984. Rose Bowl bound USC (8-1; ranked No. 7) was coming off a victory over No. 1 ranked Washington to clinch a Rose Bowl bid but they came up flat against UCLA (7-3; unranked) losing 29-10. USC quarterback Tim Green predicted the Trojans would put a whipping on UCLA but it was Green who got whupped completing just 18 of 39 passes with three interceptions. John Lee kicked five field goals for the Bruins.

9. 1971. It had been a disappointing season for USC (6-4; unranked) but they came into the UCLA game on a four game winning streak. The Bruins (2-7; unranked) were a flat-out disaster on their way to one of the worst seasons in school history. The game was perhaps the worst ever played between the two rivals ending in a 7-7 snore fest. It's hard to believe that the next season these teams would have a combined 17-2 record going into the big showdown.

8. 1995. The Trojans (8-1-1; ranked No. 11) were led by All-American wide receiver Keyshawn Johnson while the Bruins (6-4; unranked) were without their star running back Kareem Abdul-Jabbar. The result was a stunning 24-20 victory for the Bruins. Quarterback Cade McNown keyed an early 21-0 lead for UCLA and the Bruins held on from there. USC still went to the Rose Bowl while McNown earned the first of his four straight victories as the Bruins starting quarterback against the Trojans.

7. 1987. UCLA (9-1; ranked No. 5) looked unbeatable going into this game with a Rose Bowl bid on the line. The Bruins had won six straight games with Troy Aikman at quarterback. Meanwhile, USC (7-3; unranked) were considered easy pickings despite the play of quarterback Rodney Peete. Ultimately the Trojans won 17-13 on a controversial touchdown reception by Eric Affholter. Aikman and the Bruins also lost the following year to the Trojans making the future NFL Hall of Famer 0-2 against his most bitter college rival.

6. 1960. John McKay was one of the greatest coaches in college football history leading USC to four national championships. However, his first season was almost his last as the Trojans (3-5; unranked) played UCLA (5-1-1; ranked No. 11) at the Coliseum. The Bruins were led by All-American single-wing back Billy Kilmer but it was USC quarterback Bill Nelsen who stole the day leading the Trojans to a 17-6 win. McKay's job was saved and two years later he led USC to an undefeated season and his first national championship.

5. 1992. The most unlikely hero in the history of the series led UCLA (5-5; unranked) to a stunning 38-37 victory over USC (6-2-1; ranked No. 15). Quarterback John Barnes, a fifth-string walk-on, threw for 385 yards including 204 in the fourth quarter alone. Receiver J.J. Stokes caught six passes for an amazing 263 yards including a 90-yard touchdown that proved to be the difference. Barnes remains the greatest one-game wonder in UCLA football history.

4. 1989. Not all upsets are victories. Some upsets end up with no winner. That was the case when USC (8-2; ranked No. 8) hosted UCLA (3-7; unranked) at the Coliseum. The Trojans were heading for a third straight Rose Bowl appearance led by freshman quarterback Todd Marinovich. UCLA came into the game with a five-game losing streak in what turned out to be the worst season in Terry Donahue's 20-year tenure in Westwood. The Bruins had a chance to win the game but Alfredo Velasco's 54-yard field goal attempt hit the crossbar as time expired.

3. 1985. The Bruins (8-1-1; ranked No. 8) were on a roll having won three straight games against the Trojans (4-5; unranked) and this game figured to be a Rose Bowl clincher for UCLA. Someone forgot to tell USC because they won the game 17-13. Ryan Knight led the Trojans with 147 yards rushing but it was Eric Ball's goal line fumble late in the fourth quarter that doomed the Bruins. The good news for UCLA came later that night when Arizona State lost to Arizona giving the Bruins a backdoor entry into the Rose Bowl.

2. 1959. USC (8-0; ranked No. 4) had dreams of a national championship when they took the field against UCLA (3-3-1; unranked) at the Coliseum. The Trojans had the most feared twins in college football – Marlin and Mike McKeever but these two wrecking balls could not stop UCLA's Billy Kilmer when the game was on the line. Kilmer led the Bruins to a fourth quarter rally in a 10-3 victory. USC's quarterback, Willie Wood, would go on to star as a safety with Vince Lombardi's legendary Packers.

1. 2006. It's always great to upset your rival but to knock them out of the national championship game is beyond your wildest dreams. USC (10-1; ranked No. 2) was one win away from a trip to the BCS championship game. All that stood in their way was a UCLA team (6-5; unranked) that had lost seven straight games to the Trojans including a 66-19 shellacking the previous season. What happened that day at the Rose Bowl defies all logic. UCLA's defense dominated and quarterback Patrick Cowan made just enough plays to pull out a 13-9 victory. No other upset comes close.

To say that UCLA is a basketball school is not telling the whole story. After all, only 11 of UCLA's 100 NCAA championships occurred on the hardwood. The Bruins have also had a rich tradition in football with scores of All-Americans and several players who have gone on to great success in the NFL. Here's the best of the best when it comes to UCLA flavor in pro football.

10. Dave Dalby. It's not often that a center makes an impact on the football field but Dalby was a central figure on three Super Bowl championship teams with the Raiders. In fact, he is the only center to start on three Super Bowl champions (Mike Webster started just two of the four Super Bowls he won in Pittsburgh). Dalby was a fixture for the Raiders in his 14-year career taking over as the starter when Hall of Famer Jim Otto retired. He was named to just one Pro Bowl but his teammates were the ones who knew his true value.

9. Randy Cross. To begin this list with two offensive linemen may seem strange but Randy Cross, a former UCLA teammate of Dalby, also had the distinction of starting for three Super Bowl champion teams. Cross spent his entire 13-year career with the San Francisco 49ers playing both guard and center. He was named to three Pro Bowls and had the rare privilege of going out a winner as the 49ers beat the Bengals in Super Bowl XXIII. It was Cross and the offensive line that made all the key blocks to allow Joe Montana to drive the team to a historic victory.

8. Freeman McNeil. One of the most underrated running backs in NFL history, McNeil shares a record with the fabled Barry Sanders. They are the only running backs in NFL history to average at least four yards per carry in every year of their career for those who played at least ten seasons. McNeil was a model of consistency with three Pro Bowl selections in his 12-year career all with the New York Jets. He led the NFL in rushing during the strike-shortened 1982 season and he averaged an amazing 5.9 yards per carry at age 32.

7. Carnell Lake. Lake was a question mark coming out of UCLA. He was considered too small to play his collegiate position at linebacker but the Pittsburgh Steelers came up with the answer. After selecting Lake in the second round of the 1989 draft, the Steelers moved him to strong safety where he started from game one of his rookie season. In ten years in Pittsburgh, Lake was named to five Pro Bowls and he scored five defensive touchdowns. He also started for the 1999 Jacksonville Jaguars that posted a 14-2 record, the best in the NFL.

6. Kenny Easley. One of the greatest defensive backs in college football history, Easley was a three-time All-American who made the transition to the NFL without missing a beat. He was named to five Pro Bowls during his seven-year career with the Seattle Seahawks while earning All-NFL recognition from 1983 through 1985. In 1984 he was named the NFL's Defensive Player of the Year, one of only four safeties ever so honored. The only thing that prevented him from a place in the Pro Football Hall of Fame was a kidney ailment that shortened his career.

5. Tom Fears. In an era when most teams ran the ball three our of four plays, the Los Angeles Rams, under Coach Clark Shaughnessy, decided that the best way to win was through the air. Fears was a star in the innovative offense from day one, leading the NFL in receiving in each of his first three seasons. In 1950, Fears had a season that rates with the best in NFL history. He caught a then-record 84 passes for a league-high 1,116 yards and seven touchdowns. His 84 receptions were 32 more than any other receiver in the league. The following season he caught a 73-yard touchdown pass for the winning score as the Rams won their only NFL title. He was named to the Hall of Fame in 1970.

4. Jimmy Johnson. Johnson was best known at UCLA as Rafer's little brother. Rafer Johnson was the legendary decathlete who won Olympic gold in 1960. Jimmy Johnson would go on to earn his own taste of immortality as one of the greatest cornerbacks in NFL history. During his 16-year career with the San Francisco 49ers, Johnson played in four Pro Bowls and was named All-NFL from 1969 through 1972. He intercepted at least one pass in 14 consecutive seasons. He also earned a spot in the Hall of Fame in 1994.

3. Troy Aikman. Aikman's career at UCLA was bittersweet because he couldn't beat USC – in other words he was a quarterback who couldn't win the big one. Few could have imagined that Super Bowl glory would be in his future when the Cowboys made him the first overall pick in the 1989 draft. As a rookie, Aikman was pounded during a 1-15 season but just three years later he was named Super Bowl MVP. The Cowboys won three Super Bowls with Aikman at the helm and he would earn six Pro Bowl bids along the way. In 2006, Aikman joined the great quarterbacks of his era with his selection to the Pro Football Hall of Fame.

2. Jonathan Ogden. Speaking of the Hall of Fame, they may as well get Ogden's bust ready even though he is still very much active as a member of the Baltimore Ravens. The huge offensive tackle won an Outland Trophy at UCLA as the nation's top lineman but his exploits in the NFL have been even greater. During his 12-year career, Ogden has been named to 11 Pro Bowls. He has also earned All-NFL status in four seasons and he led the Ravens to their only Super Bowl title in 2000. He has hinted about retirement going into 2008 if only to pursue his other passion – as a NFL commentator. Who's going to say no to a man that stands 6-8 and weighs 340 pounds?

1. Bob Waterfield. It may seem strange to select a quarterback who played more than 50 years ago as the greatest Bruin ever to play in the NFL but Waterfield was THAT special. He started his career with the Cleveland Rams in 1945 and promptly led the team to the NFL championship while earning league MVP honors. He also guided the Rams to a second championship in 1951 after their move to Los Angeles. To put things in perspective, Waterfield was not only the team's quarterback but also the team's punter and place-kicker. He also played defensive back during his first four seasons intercepting 20 passes during that span. Few NFL players could match Waterfield's limitless skills.

UCLA stands alone with 100 NCAA championships. The school's Athletic Hall of fame is like a who's who of sports. But which athletes stand in the front of the line? With all due respect to Bruins like Troy Aikman, Evelyn Ashford, Cobi Jones, and Lisa Fernandez, here is my list for the greatest UCLA athletes of all time. Find any school to match this list.

10. Jimmy Connors. This one is a bit of a cheat because Connors only attended UCLA for one year but he did win the NCAA tennis championship in 1971. Just three years later, Connors was on top of the tennis world winning both Wimbledon and the US Open in convincing fashion. All told, Connors won eight grand slam tournaments and earned a spot in the Tennis Hall of Fame.

9. Florence Griffith-Joyner. Controversy followed her remarkable performance at the 1988 Summer Olympic Games but Flo-Jo remains the standard for all female sprinters a full decade after her untimely death. She still holds the world records for both the 100 m and the 200 m. Was it steroids that catapulted her to the top of the track world age the age of 28? We may never know the whole truth but her sense of style and flash helped put her center stage in the world of sports.

8. Bill Walton. The big man out of Helix High School in San Diego may well have been the most dominant college basketball player of all time. His amazing 1973 NCAA title game performance is without question the best of all time. In UCLA's victory over Memphis State, Walton scored 44 points on 21 of 22 shooting. He was a three-time college basketball player of the year and only the second basketball player to win the coveted Sullivan Award as the nation's top amateur athlete.

7. Karch Kiraly. Kiraly is the greatest volleyball player of all time. He is the only person to have won Olympic gold medals in both indoor and outdoor volleyball. His domination on the sand continued well into his 40s which is truly a remarkable feat considering the necessity to keep his legs fresh. The "Thunderball in Volleyball" is to his sport what Tiger Woods and Wayne Gretzky are to their sports.

6. Ann Meyers. The first four-time All-American in women's basketball history, Meyers was a true pioneer in a sport that needed a star to get to the next level. Meyers led UCLA to their only women's basketball national title in 1978 and was a member of the first USA women's Olympic team in 1976. She was also the first woman to sign a NBA contract participating in a three-day tryout with the Indiana Pacers. Meyers was the first woman inducted into the UCLA Athletic Hall of Fame and she is also a member of the Basketball Hall of Fame.

5. Arthur Ashe. Some athletes extend their influence well beyond the playing field. Ashe was such an individual. Although his life was cut short by AIDS which he contracted from a tainted blood transfusion, Ashe became a true civil rights leader after becoming the first African-American to win Wimbledon in 1975. Ashe was also the NCAA champion in 1965 and the first ever US Open champ in 1968. The US Open tennis facility is named in his honor.

4. Rafer Johnson. Johnson was not only the greatest decathlete of his day but also a fine basketball player and student body president. His greatest moment came during the 1960 Olympic Games in Rome where he beat out fellow Bruin Yang Chuan-Kwang for the gold medal in the decathlon. He later became a close friend of the Kennedy family and a key contributor to the Special Olympics. Johnson was also the one chosen to carry the Olympic torch on its final leg at the 1984 games in Los Angeles.

3. Kareem Abdul-Jabbar. There is no question that the former Lew Alcindor had the greatest career in college basketball history. He not only led UCLA to three consecutive championships but he was also the tournament's MVP three times. With Alcindor in the middle, the Bruins record was 88-2 with both losses coming by just two points. As Kareem Abdul-Jabbar, the New York product played 20 seasons in the NBA winning six MVP awards and six NBA titles. He is also the all-time leading scorer in NBA history.

2. Jackie Joyner-Kersee. Joyner-Kersee was arguably the greatest female athlete of all time. She won six medals in the heptathlon and long jump competing in four different Olympic Games. Her gold medals in the heptathlon in 1988 and 1992 cemented her standing as the greatest female athlete of her time. She also played basketball during her time at UCLA scoring more than 1000 points in her career. She stills holds the world record in the heptathlon.

1. Jackie Robinson. The man who broke the color barrier in major league baseball was also the first athlete to earn letters in four different sports at UCLA. Robinson excelled in track as a long jumper, as a forward in basketball, and as a running back in football. His worst sport at UCLA was, ironically, baseball. In fact he hit just .091 in his only season on the UCLA baseball team. You can make the argument that Jackie Robinson was the greatest athlete of all time. There was certainly no athlete more important.

The 10 Greatest College Hoops Players Who Didn't Go to UCLA

When it comes to college hoops in LA, some think it all starts and ends with UCLA. To some degree that's true but there have been some great local basketball talents from other Southland schools. Here's a list of great basketball players based on their college careers and not necessarily what they did in the NBA.

10. John Rudometkin. The Reckless Russian was a two-time All-American at USC in the early 60's. He played much bigger than his 6-6 stature leading the team and scoring in three straight seasons. In 1961, Rudo led the Trojans to a conference championship and a No. 7 national ranking averaging 24 points and 12 rebounds per game. His NBA career was cut short due to a cancer scare that he would eventually survive.

9. Leon Wood. A complete point guard, Wood started his collegiate career at Arizona but transferred to Cal State Fullerton for his final three seasons. As a junior he averaged 18 points and 11 assists. This next season he raised his scoring average to 24 points per game. Wood would go to on earn a gold medal for the 1984 Olympic team. After six mediocre seasons in the NBA, Wood changed jerseys to become a NBA official.

8. Raymond Lewis. If you have never heard of Raymond Lewis, you know nothing about basketball. Lewis was without a doubt the greatest basketball player never to play in the NBA. A high school and schoolyard legend from Watts, Lewis played just one varsity season of college basketball at Cal State Los Angeles and finished second in the nation in scoring. That season he put up 53 on third-ranked Cal State Long Beach. A contract dispute with the Philadelphia 76ers ended his NBA career before it started. The rest of his story can be found elsewhere in this book.

7. Gus Williams. Unlike other players on this list, Williams is better known for his pro career than his college career. The fact is Williams was a great player from the get go. As a senior at USC, Williams averaged better than 21 points per game to earn second-team All-American honors. As a junior he led the Trojans to within one game of dethroning Bill Walton's UCLA Bruins for a conference championship. Unfortunately in those days second place teams did not earn a spot in the NCAA tournament. That spot was always reserved for UCLA.

6. William "Bird" Averitt. The player who beat out Raymond Lewis for the 1973 NCAA scoring title was William "Bird" Averitt of Pepperdine. He averaged 33.9 points that season including 11 games with 40 or more points. His two-year scoring average was 31.5 points per game. He left a year early to play in the ABA where he embarked on a rather unremarkable pro career. Averitt was the first Los Angeles area college player to lead the nation in scoring.

5. Paul Westphal. Westphal was the one that got away from John Wooden and UCLA. After a great prep career at Aviation High School, Westphal was expected to join Wooden's machine in Westwood but he decided to go cross-town to USC. He led the Trojans to a memorable 24-2 season as a junior with both losses coming to UCLA. He earned second-team All-American honors that season and third-team honors the following year when injuries cut short his senior season. Of course Westphal would go on to become a NBA all-star and successful NBA coach.

4. Bill Sharman. Before he became a Boston Celtic legend, Sharman was an All-American at USC long before UCLA was cranking out national championships. As a senior he averaged nearly 19 points per game when that actually meant something. What set Sharman apart from his peers was his adept shooting touch. Most players of his era were still shooting two-handed set shots. Sharman would become one of the first great jump shooters in the NBA and he would join John Wooden and Lenny Wilkens as the only people inducted into the Basketball Hall of Fame as both a player and coach.

3. Harold Minor. "Baby Jordan" was an incredible talent and the only USC player to ever be a unanimous first-team All-American. He averaged better than 20 points in each of his three seasons at Troy including a career-high 26.3 mark as a junior. There was no doubt about his future greatness in the NBA until he actually played in the NBA. He did win two Slam Dunk Championships but his total game fell far short of his moniker. No player has ever been referred to as "Baby Jordan" again.

2. Ed Ratleff. Ratleff was the only non-UCLA player from the Los Angeles area to be a two-time consensus first-team All-American. He played for Jerry Tarkanian at Cal State Long Beach and led the 49ers to a No. 3 national ranking in 1973. Can you imagine Cal State Long Beach was once ranked that high? His game was complete with a smooth style similar to UCLA's Keith "Jamaal" Wilkes. Ratleff was also a member of the infamous 1972 Olympic team that was robbed of the gold by some corrupt officials. Like his fellow teammates on that team, Ratleff will never claim his silver medal.

1. Hank Gathers and Bo Kimble (tie). Their names will forever be linked as teammates on those explosive Loyola Marymount teams from 1987 through 1990. Gathers led the nation in scoring as a junior while Kimble was tops in the country as a senior. They both started their collegiate careers at USC but transferred to the Paul Westhead coached Loyola team that would break all college basketball scoring records. In the end, however, their legacy was the sudden death of Gathers and Kimble's left-handed free throw tribute in the ensuing NCAA tournament. Believe me no two players ever captivated the city of Los Angeles to the level of these lifelong friends.

Through the 2007-08 season, it has been 33 years since John Wooden retired from his lofty perch as the greatest college basketball coach of all time. He won 10 NCAA championships in his final 12 seasons and appeared in a record 12 Final Fours. That was the legacy that eight coaches have tried to follow over the past 33 years. Some have done better than others but overall the results are pretty good. In those 33 seasons, UCLA has appeared in 26 NCAA Tournaments while winning 13 Pac-10 championships. They have also played in six Final Fours. But, the only number that counts is national championships and the Bruins have won just one since Wooden left the bench. Here's rating the UCLA coaches that have followed the Wizard of Westwood.

8. Larry Farmer, 1981–1984. Farmer was a valuable member of three UCLA national championship teams when he played for Wooden in the early 1970s. He subsequently served as an assistant coach at UCLA for six years before becoming the first African-American Head Coach in school history. Farmer was well liked by everyone but his three-year run with the Bruins resulted in the first firing of a head coach since the Wooden era. Overall his record was 61-23 but his post-season ledger consisted of just one game, an upset loss to Utah in the second round of the 1983 NCAA tournament. Farmer's recruiting was also sub par as subsequent coaches found out.

7. Walt Hazzard, 1984–1988. Hazzard was the catalyst of Wooden's first national championship team in 1964. He is also one of just six players to have their jerseys retired at UCLA. That all seemed good when the Bruins hired Hazzard following Farmer's dismissal but the four years that followed were perhaps the weakest in the post-Wooden era. Hazzard's first team won the 1985 NIT title that meant nothing at a school like UCLA. The following year they lost in the FIRST ROUND of the NIT at home to UC Irvine. Hazzard did lead the Bruins to a Pac-10 title in 1987 but they lost in the second round of the NCAA tournament. A 16-14 record sealed his fate in 1988. Hazzard's final record was 77-47.

6. Gary Cunningham, 1977–1979. How can a coach with a record of 50-8 in two seasons rank near the bottom of this list? Consider the circumstances that led to Cunningham's hiring in the first place. Cunningham had been the top assistant for the final four years of Wooden's coaching run at UCLA and everyone thought he was the heir apparent for the job. Cunningham, though, had other ideas. He left coaching for two years to run the recreation center at UCLA. When Gene Bartow quit before the 1977-78 season, Cunningham reluctantly accepted the job knowing full well he would leave as soon as possible. He had a team that should have gone to two straight Final Fours but they fell short both years in the NCAA tournament. He did little recruiting and left the program in worse shape than when he arrived.

5. Steve Lavin, 1996–2003. The accidental coach had quite the roller coaster ride during his seven-year run as the UCLA basketball coach. He had been an obscure assistant on Jim Harrick's staff in 1995 when the Bruins won the national championship but the defection of top assistants Mark Gottfried and Lorenzo Romar coupled with the sudden firing of Harrick put Lavin on the hot seat. He won just one conference championship during his tenure but he also made five runs to the Sweet Sixteen over a six-year period. Only one other coach could match that tournament success during the same period and that was Duke's Hall of Famer Mike Krzyzewski. Lavin was an outstanding recruiter but a less than polished game coach. His final team posted the first losing season in 55 years at UCLA but their final win that year came in the Pac-10 tournament against # 1 ranked Arizona. That one game typified the entire Lavin era.

4. Gene Bartow, 1975–1977. What coach is his right mind would accept the UCLA job immediately after the retirement of John Wooden? Bartow at least looked the part. He wore glasses like Wooden and seemed to be cut from the same Midwest mold. He had led Memphis State to the 1973 NCAA championship game where he lost to UCLA on a day that Bill Walton scored 44 points on 21-22 shooting. Bartow soon found out that anything less than a championship was deemed a total failure in Westwood. His first team made the Final Four only to get blasted by the undefeated Indiana team. The next year was a flat out disaster as the Bruins were ambushed by Idaho State in the Sweet Sixteen. Bartow appeared on a radio show shortly thereafter and was destroyed by upset callers. The next thing you know, he left town to start a basketball program at Alabama-Birmingham. No one shed a tear when he left.

3. Larry Brown, 1979–1981. Brown is the only coach on this list who has earned a place in the Basketball Hall of Fame. He is probably most famous for being the one coach who can turn around the fortunes of a team from day one. It didn't exactly turn out that way at UCLA. His first team finished fourth in the Pac-10 ending a run of 13 consecutive conference championships. Many were surprised that UCLA even got an invite to the NCAA tournament that year but the Bruins made the most of their opportunity and Brown was the catalyst. With a lineup that included four freshmen amongst the top seven players, UCLA stunned # 1 ranked DePaul in the second round and followed with upset wins against Ohio State and Clemson to get to the Final Four. Purdue fell in the semi-finals leaving UCLA to play Louisville for the title. They came up short that day but Brown's legacy from that one tournament cemented his place in school history.

2. Jim Harrick, 1988–1996. Harrick is best remembered for two things at UCLA. First and most important was his championship run in 1995. It remains to date the only national championship at UCLA since Coach Wooden left. Harrick is also remembered for being fired just one year after winning that championship for "lying" to school officials about an illegal recruiting infraction. The truth be told, Harrick was fired because Athletic Director Pete Dalis was not his biggest fan. It was an unfortunate finish to an eight-year run that saw UCLA re-establish itself as one of the best basketball programs in the country. The only thing that knocks Harrick out of the top spot on this list is some ugly losses in the NCAA tournament. The worst was his final game losing to Ivy League champ Princeton. Still, he is the only UCLA coach other than Wooden to have an NCAA championship banner hanging in Pauley Pavilion.

1. Ben Howland, 2003–present. In just five years, Howland has clearly established himself as one of the best college basketball coaches in America. Consider what he has done at UCLA after replacing Steve Lavin. Just three years after inheriting a 10-19 team, Howland had UCLA in the NCAA championship game for the first time since 1995. He followed that with two more Final Four appearances making UCLA must the tenth team ever to make three straight Final Fours. The future looks bright as UCLA will welcome the top-ranked recruiting class in the nation for the 2008-09 season. Howland is the perfect combination of a coach who can recruit the top players in the country while maximizing their skills once they arrive on campus. He is also one of Coach Wooden's biggest fans. Unlike some of his predecessors who tried to get out of Wooden's shadow, Howland understands the benefits of the Coach's legacy. He may not win ten championships but Ben Howland is sure to go down as the best thing to happen at UCLA since the Wooden era.

The 10 Worst NCAA Basketball Tournament Losses for UCLA

No school has a greater basketball tradition than UCLA. Their 11 national championships are the most ever as is their 18 appearances in the Final Four. However, there have been stumbles along the way. Even John Wooden felt the pain of some unforeseen losses. Here's a list of the most embarrassing tournament defeats in Bruins history.

10. Arizona State, 1963 Regional Semifinal. This was a UCLA team that featured players like Walt Hazzard, Gail Goodrich and Keith Erickson but they had not yet reached championship status. That would have to wait another year when the 1964 team went undefeated for the school's first national title. In 1963, UCLA won a one-game playoff to secure the conference title and then they were matched up against an Arizona State squad featuring Jumpin Joe Caldwell. This was a blowout from the outset with the Bruins trailing 62-31 at the half. Hazzard, Goodrich and Erickson combined for 5 of 25 shooting to seal UCLA's fate. Arizona State coasted to a 93-79 win.

9. Tulsa, 1994 First Round. The outcome of this game at the subsequent success of the Bruins mirrored the previous game mentioned from 1963. UCLA was the fifth seed in the Midwest Region playing No. 11 Tulsa. Despite the efforts of Ed O'Bannon and Tyus Edney, the Bruins got rocked early, trailing 46-17 at one point and 63-38 at the half. The final score of 112-102 was not reflective of the magnitude of this blowout. The only positive was the motivation provided for the following season that saw UCLA go on to win their first national championship in 20 years.

8. Utah, 1983 Second Round. The Bruins won the Pac-Ten championship with a veteran team that featured Rod Foster, Darren Daye and Kenny Fields. They were the second seed in the West Region with a first round bye. There opponent was 10-seed Wyoming coming off an upset first round win against Illinois. The Bruins held a two-point lead at the half but fell apart down the stretch losing 67-61. The anonymous trio of Pace Mannion, Angelo Robinson and Peter Williams led the way for the Utes with 18 points each. This would be the one and only NCAA tournament game for Coach Larry Farmer giving him the distinction of being the only post-Wooden coach to go winless in the tournament.

7. Brigham Young, 1981 Second Round. Larry Brown made quite a debut as the UCLA coach in 1980 leading the Bruins to the national title game after finishing just fourth in the conference. The following season saw UCLA improve on their regular season record only to get blasted by BYU in their first tournament game. The Bruins were a third seed but had to travel to Providence, Rhode Island – the first time they had ever played in a region other than the West. BYU was led by Danny Ainge who torched the Bruins for 37 points. Brown was so despondent he took the New Jersey Nets job after the season.

6. Penn State, 1991 First Round. Don MacLean still cries about this defeat. The Bruins were the fourth seed in the Easy playing No. 13 Penn State. The Nittany Lions had no basketball tradition and figured to be easy prey for a Bruin team featuring MacLean (UCLA's all-time leading scorer) and Tracy Murray, the highest scoring forward tandem in the country. It wasn't meant to be. Penn State won 74-69 as MacLean got into early foul trouble after a hot-shooting first half. MacLean blasted the officials for putting him on the bench for some bogus calls. This was Jim Harrick's first ugly loss in the tournament as UCLA coach. There would be more.

5. DePaul, 1979 Regional Final. Everything was in place for the Bruins to make a serious run at a national championship. The team was led by three seniors – David Greenwood, Roy Hamilton and Brad Holland. All three players were first-team All-Pac 10 selections. There was also a hot shooting junior forward named Kiki Vandeweghe. All that stood in their way of a Final Four appearance was a DePaul team that UCLA had dominated earlier that season. Another thing in the Bruins favor was DePaul's lack of a bench. Their five starters played all but two minutes in this game. Nonetheless, the Bruins came out flat and trailed 51-34 at halftime. A late rally brought the final score to 95-91 DePaul as their legendary coach Ray Meyer made his first trip to a Final Four in 36 years.

4. North Carolina State, 1974 National Semifinal. Losing to the No. 1 ranked team in the country would not qualify as an upset under normal circumstances but that was not the case as the Bruins coughed up their chance of an eighth straight national championship. It had been a strange season for a Bruin team led by All-Americans Bill Walton and Keith Wilkes. Their record 88-game losing streak had been snapped by Notre Dame. UCLA also lost consecutive road games against Oregon and Oregon State. Still, they were favored to beat a NC State team that was ranked No. 1 but had lost to UCLA earlier that season by 18 points. The Bruins led by 11 points in the second half and by seven in the second overtime only to lose 80-77. Walton still says this loss put an unforgivable stain on his legendary UCLA career.

3. Idaho State, 1977 Regional Semifinal. UCLA's success in the NCAA tournament was so over-the-top that everyone assumed the Final Four was part of their schedule. Going into the 1976-77 season, the Bruins had played in TEN consecutive Final Fours and no one expected that streak to end anytime soon. The 1977 team was led by Marques Johnson, the unanimous choice as national player of the year. They were ranked No. 2 in the country going into the tournament with the prospect of a much-anticipated match-up against UNLV looming in the West Regional final. All that stood in their way was Idaho State. Final Score – Idaho State 76, UCLA 75. Steve Hayes scored 27 points for Idaho State and the Bruins Final Four run was over. So was Gene Bartow's coaching career at UCLA. He quit under the pressure of following in Wooden's footsteps despite a two-year record of 52-9.

2. Indiana, 1992 Regional Final. With the previous year's first round loss to Penn State in their rear-view mirror, the 1992 Bruins won the Pac-10 championship to secure a No. 1 seed for the first time in 13 years. Don MacLean, Tracy Murray, Mitchell Butler and several other Bruins on that team would eventually find a roster spot in the NBA. They raced to the regional final where Bob Knight and Indiana were waiting. The Hoosiers did not appear to be a tough opponent although forwards Calbert Cheaney and Alan Henderson were fine players. What happened next could only be described as UCLA's worst nightmare. The Bruins lost 106-79, the biggest margin of defeat in the school's tournament history. Coach Jim Harrick was speechless after the game although he did say something about Indiana's superior talent. Nice try Coach. This was a flat out choke by a team that should have punched its ticket to the Final Four.

1. Princeton, 1996 First Round. Pete Carril had been coaching at Princeton for 30 years and although he had won several Ivy League championships, he had never won a game in the NCAA Tournament against a ranked opponent. That all changed in 1996 when Princeton faced the defending NCAA champion Bruins in the first round of the Southeast Regional. UCLA was upset that they had been sent packing even though they had won the Pac-10 championship. Still, a first round game against a team without a single scholarship player appeared to be a gift. It was not. UCLA led most of the way including a seven-point margin with just minutes left but the Tigers pulled in out in the end by the score of 43-41. The victory propelled Carril into retirement and a spot in the Hall of Fame. The loss proved fatal for Jim Harrick as he was fired by UCLA for "recruitment" violations. More accurately, losing to an Ivy League school is not good for job security.

No school has played in more Final Four games than UCLA. It makes sense that the Bruins have also had some of the greatest individual performances in Final Four history. My list does not include any player twice or any two players from the same season.

10. Kiki Vandeweghe, 1980 semifinal vs. Purdue. The Bruins started the tournament as a No. 8 seed but a victory over No. 1 ranked DePaul keyed their run to the Final Four. In the semis, UCLA faced a Purdue team with 7-1 All-American center Joe Barry Carroll but the biggest player on the court was Vandeweghe. His 24 points keyed the victory but it was his slam-dunk in the face of Carroll that broke Purdue's spirit.

9. Lucius Allen, 1968 semifinal vs. Houston. This was the revenge game as the Bruins took on undefeated Houston at the Final Four. Earlier that season, the Cougars had snapped UCLA's 47-game winning streak and Elvin Hayes went off for 39 points. The rematch wasn't close as the Bruins won 101-69 having led by as many as 44 points. Allen came closer than any UCLA player ever to have a triple-double in a Final Four game. His line read 19 points, nine rebounds and 12 assists.

8. Kenny Washington, 1964 final vs. Duke. Washington had been a valuable bench player for UCLA on their undefeated run to a first-ever national championship. But no one could believe what he did in the title game against Duke. Washington scored 26 points and grabbed 12 rebounds as the Bruins completed a 30-0 season. Amazingly, Washington was NOT named to the all-tournament team.

7. Steve Patterson, 1971 final vs. Villanova. Patterson was largely overlooked during his UCLA career playing second fiddle to the likes of Sidney Wicks and Curtis Rowe. But he saved the best for last with a 29-point, eight-rebound performance in the title game against Villanova. Ironically, the player who never got his due was slighted once again as he lost the Most Outstanding Player award to Villanova's Howard Porter. Porter was later stripped of the honor for having signed a pro contract before the tournament.

6. Richard Washington, 1975 final vs. Kentucky. Washington is probably the least appreciated All-American in UCLA history. His performance at the 1975 Final Four rates with the best in school history. First he hit the game-winning shot against Louisville in the semis and then he scored 28 points and pulled down 12 rebounds as the Bruins gave John Wooden his tenth and final national championship.

5. Ed O'Bannon, 1995 final vs. Arkansas. The Bruins finally won their 11th national championship 20 years after Wooden's retirement. Playing against the defending national champions, UCLA won going away led by O'Bannon's 30-point, 17-rebound virtuoso performance. The Wooden Award winner completed an amazing career comeback from a devastating knee injury suffered as a freshman. He also got the opportunity to share the victory with his brother Charles, UCLA's other starting forward that season.

4. Sidney Wicks, 1970 final vs. Jacksonville. UCLA was not supposed to win another national championship after the graduation of Lew Alcindor but they stunned everyone by beating a Jacksonville team led by 7-2 Artis Gilmore. Early in the title game, Gilmore dominated the smaller Bruins inside but Wicks convinced Coach Wooden that he could do some defensive damage playing behind the much taller center. He was right. UCLA won by 11 as Wicks had 17 points, 18 rebounds and, most amazingly, five blocks, four of which came at Gilmore's expense.

3. Lew Alcindor, 1969 final vs. Purdue. There is no question that Lew Alcindor (Kareem Abdul-Jabbar) was the greatest college player of all time. He led UCLA to three consecutive championships and an 88-2 record. He was also the only player to earn three Most Outstanding Player awards capped off by his final collegiate game against Big Ten champion Purdue. The Bruins won 92-72 as Alcindor scored 37 points and secured 20 rebounds. To be honest, I could have used any one of his final four games on this list.

2. Gail Goodrich, 1965 final vs. Michigan. At 6-foot-1 and perhaps 165 pounds, Goodrich hardly looked the part of a giant killer but the Hall of Fame guard did just that as UCLA beat No. 1 ranked Michigan in the 1965 national title game. Goodrich scored what was then a championship record 42 points including 18 of 20 free throw attempts. His ability to penetrate the larger Wolverines front-line showed the fearless nature of his game. He remains, in my opinion, the greatest UCLA guard of all time.

1. Bill Walton, 1973 final vs. Memphis State. It may be the greatest individual college basketball performance EVER. Capping off a second consecutive perfect season, UCLA dismantled Memphis State 87-66 as Walton broke Goodrich's scoring record with 44 points. Even more amazing was his 21-22 shooting. Just ONE missed shot for an entire game! He added 13 rebounds for good measure. One negative note: Walton missed three of five free-throw attempts. Okay, he wasn't perfect but Walton came as close to perfection as any college player in history.

When your roster of alumni includes the likes of Hall of Fame players like Kareem Abdul-Jabbar and Bill Walton you might assume that success at UCLA translates into success in the NBA. Actually there have been some Bruins that have exceeded expectations in the NBA while others have been down right busts.

Surprises

5. Jack Haley. Alright, he was never much of a player at UCLA or in the NBA but the fact that he ever played a single game of pro ball is a downright miracle. Haley came to UCLA as a walk-on when the program had hit rock bottom. By his senior year he was the starting center on a Pac-10 championship team but the NBA barely noticed making him a fourth round pick (79th overall) in 1987. Amazingly he lasted ten years in the NBA with four different teams. He even earned a championship ring serving as Dennis Rodman's best friend.

4. Kiki Vandeweghe. It's hard to believe now but Vandeweghe basically begged for a scholarship to go to UCLA. He improved his game each year and led the Bruins to the national title game as a senior. Selected 11th overall in the 1980 NBA draft, Vandeweghe was picked AFTER the likes of James Riley, Mike O'Koren, and Michael Brooks. He went on to become a two-time all-star and averaged 20 points per game over his 13-year career. Three times he exceeded 2000 points.

3. Swen Nater. Here's a trivia question that stumps even the most ardent pro basketball fans. Who is the only player to lead both the ABA and the NBA in rebounding? The answer is Bill Walton's back-up center at UCLA. Nater did not start a single game in two years as a Bruin but he went on to become a very solid pro averaging nearly 12 rebounds per game over his 11-year career. He was a two-time ABA All-Star and the rookie-of-the-year in 1974.

2. Reggie Miller. When the Indiana Pacers drafted Miller with the 11th overall pick in the 1987 draft the groans could be heard from one side of the state to the other side. EVERYONE wanted the Pacers to choose local boy Steve Alford who had just led Indiana to the national championship. Obviously they made the right choice. Miller, who was drafted behind Dennis Hopson and Reggie Williams (who?), went on to become the greatest Pacer of all-time and his place in the Hall of Fame is a forgone conclusion.

1. Mark Eaton. Who knew? Eaton was an ex auto mechanic who was discovered by a local junior college. He played two years at Cypress Community College and then transferred to UCLA where he sat on the bench for two years. The Utah Jazz selected him in the fourth round (72nd overall) based on one thing – his height. At 7-foot-4, Eaton was worth a look and he exceeded all expectations by becoming one of the defensive forces in the league. He made first or second team All-Defense five times and twice was named the NBA Defensive Player of the Year. He led the league in blocked shots four times and is still the NBA leader with 3.5 blocks per game for a career.

Busts

5. Don MacLean. Through the 2008 season, MacLean is still the all-time leading scorer not only in UCLA history but Pac-10 history as well. Injuries curtailed his NBA career after Washington selected him in the first round in 1992. He won the NBA's Most Improved Player award as a sophomore but after that it was all down hill. He ended up playing for seven different teams in nine NBA seasons playing just 50 games his last four years.

4. Kenny Fields. Even when he was at UCLA, Fields never seemed to live up to the hype. Larry Brown even kicked him off the team for part of his freshman season. He went on to become the Pac-10 player of the year and the Milwaukee Bucks made him a first round selection in the 1984 draft, a decision they would soon regret. His entire NBA career consisted of just four seasons averaging six points and less than three rebounds per game.

3. Roy Hamilton. To this day Dick Vitale will tell you the reason he was fired as the Detroit Pistons coach was the drafting of Roy Hamilton. A three-year starter at UCLA, Hamilton was supposed to be the prototypical NBA point guard but such was not the case. Hamilton's NBA career lasted one year in Detroit and one GAME in Portland. The good news was Hamilton's post-NBA career as he became a prominent sports television producer.

2. Richard Washington. After being the Most Outstanding Player in leading UCLA to the 1975 national championship and a consensus All-American the following year, Washington became the first Bruin to leave school early for the NBA draft. He was selected 3rd overall by the Kansas City Kings ahead of Adrian Dantley and Robert Parish. Five years later his career was over having twice finished fifth in the NBA in personal fouls. You can look it up.

1. Ed O'Bannon. O'Bannon was one of the greatest high school players ever to come out of southern California and then he went on to UCLA leading the Bruins to the national championship in 1995. That year, O'Bannon was named the Wooden award winner as the nation's top player. The New Jersey Nets used their ninth pick to select O'Bannon and then watched his skills deteriorate on the bench. His final NBA numbers are stunning. He played just two seasons averaging five points while shooting less than 40%. What did he expect playing for the Nets?

You know how this list goes. We start with the number one, then figure out a top 10, which grows to 25, and before you know it we're at 250 and have to cut it in half and then some. We get it—there are some damn good athletes that didn't make the list. But try to tell us the ones we included aren't worthy and you're in for an argument. When putting the list together we figured, once an Angelino, always an Angelino. So both post- and pre-Los Angeles statistics hold (as you'll see with our number 100). That said, we present the greatest athletes in the history of the city.

100. David Beckham. While he might not have done it here, there's no denying his soccer prowess on the international stage, where he won championships with both Manchester United and Real Madrid.

99. Cobi Jones. Jones was a four-year star on the UCLA soccer team. He leads all U.S. players with 164 caps and is the L.A. Galaxy's all-time leading scorer with 66 goals and 86 assists. He was also named an MLS All-Star in his first seven seasons.

98. Fred Dryer. The underrated defensive end is still the only player to have ever recorded two safeties in a single game. That's great and all, but his true fame is on the small screen, where he's likely the most successful athlete turned actor thanks to his starring role in *Hunter*.

97. Lisa Fernandez. While at UCLA, Fernandez was a three-time softball Player of the Year. She won three gold medals for the U.S. and holds an Olympic record for 25 strikeouts in a single game.

96. Craig Stadler. Stadler was a four-time All-American at USC, where he won the U.S. Amateur Championship. In the PGA, he won 13 events, including the 1982 Masters. "The Walrus" was a member of two Ryder Cup teams.

95. Mike Haynes. Haynes spent half of his 14-year Hall of Fame career as a member of the Los Angeles Raiders. He's widely considered one of the best cornerbacks in the history of the league. He earned nine trips to the Pro Bowl and was an All-NFL pick with the Raiders in 1984 and 1985.

94. Fred Lynn. He won three national championships at USC while playing under legendary coach Rod Dedeaux. Lynn was the first rookie to win a Most Valuable Player award in 1975 with the Red Sox, and while an Angel in 1983 became the only player to hit a Grand Slam in an All-Star Game.

93. Elton Brand. There has to be at least one Clipper on this list, and Brand is the best to ever wear the uniform. Over seven seasons he averaged 20 and 10 and led the Clippers to the franchise's only playoff series victory in 2006 over the Nuggets.

92. Tom Fears. After a stellar career at UCLA, Fears led the NFL in receiving in each of his first three seasons with the Los Angeles Rams. He had a record 84 receptions in 1950 and his 18 catches in one game that year was an NFL record that stood for 50 years until Terrell Owens broke it in 2000 while playing with the 49ers.

91. Tim Salmon. The Angels' all-time leading home run hitter (299) was the 1993 Rookie of the Year. In 2002, he helped the Angels to their first World Series title, hitting .346 with two home runs in the World Series.

90. Eric Karros. The Los Angeles Dodgers' all-time leading home run hitter (270) was the 1992 Rookie of the Year. Karros played his college ball at UCLA.

89. Jerry Robinson. Robinson was one of the greatest linebackers in college football history. In 1978 he became UCLA's first three-time All-American and the first consensus three-time All-American since SMU's Doak Walker did it 30 years earlier. Robinson enjoyed a successful NFL career, including a run with the Los Angeles Raiders.

88. Ed O'Bannon. He led the UCLA Bruins to the 1995 NCAA Championship, scoring 30 points and grabbing 17 rebounds in the title game against Arkansas. O'Bannon won the Wooden Award that season and is one of only six men to have their number raised to the rafters at Pauley Pavilion.

87. Stan Smith. An All-American tennis payer at USC, Smith became the top ranked player in the world in 1972. While a Trojan, he was a three-time All-American. As a professional, he won the 1971 U.S. Open and Wimbledon in 1972.

86. Ricky Bell. One of the greatest running backs in USC history, Bell led the nation in rushing in 1975 with 1,875 yards (bowl game not included). Bell was the runner-up for the 1976 Heisman Trophy and became the first-ever pick of the Tampa Bay Buccaneers. He would pass away and the age of 29 from a rare heart disease after completing a successful NFL career.

85. Garret Anderson. Anderson is the Angels' all-time leader in a multitude of categories, including games played, runs, hits, total bases, and RBIs. He was named MVP of the 2003 All-Star Game and played an integral role in the team's 2002 World Series title.

84. Teemu Selanne. The Ducks' all-time leading scorer made his biggest impact on his second stint with the team. While he led the NHL in goals in both 1998 and 1999, it was his 94-point 2007 season that helped the Ducks to their first Stanley Cup title. In the post-season, he scored five goals and piled up 15 points.

83. Roman Gabriel. The Rams first-round pick in 1962 was a mainstay at quarterback for the team for 11 seasons. In 1969, he was named the NFL's Most Valuable Player as the Rams started the season 11–0. He would also appear on *Gilligan's Island*.

82. Lindsay Davenport. Out of Palos Verdes, Davenport was the top ranked women's tennis player in the world in 1998. Winner of three Grand Slam titles— 1998 U.S. Open, 1999 Wimbledon, and 2000 Australian—Davenport also won the gold medal in singles tennis at the 1996 Olympics. At 6-foot-2 she's the tallest woman to win a Grand Slam, and over the course of her career won more than $21 million.

81. Don Sutton. The all-time winningest pitcher in Dodgers' history (233) holds countless career records with the team, including strikeouts (2,696). Ironically, Sutton won his 300th career game with the other team in town, the Angels, in 1986.

80. Michael Cooper. Other than Kareem Abdul-Jabbar and Magic Johnson, he's the only player to be part of all five of the "Showtime Lakers" championships. He was the NBA's Defensive Player of the Year in 1987. He also coached the L.A. Sparks to two WNBA championships in his post-playing career.

79. Corey Pavin. Pavin played his college golf as an All-American at UCLA. He's won 27 tournaments worldwide, including 15 on the PGA tour and capped by the 1995 U.S. Open. He was also a member of three separate Ryder Cup teams.

78. Norm Van Brocklin. He won three NFL passing titles as a member of the Los Angeles Rams. His 73-yard touchdown pass to Tom Fears was the winning score in the Rams' only NFL title, in 1951. He would later add another championship as quarterback of the Eagles in 1960.

77. Lynn Swann. Swann earned All-American honors in 1973 as a wide receiver/punt returner at USC. He helped the Trojans to a National Championship in 1972 and later earned four Super Bowl rings, a Super Bowl MVP award, and a spot in the Hall of Fame as a member of the Pittsburgh Steelers.

76. Reggie Jackson. Mr. October spent five seasons with the California Angels, leading them to two division championships. He led the American League in home runs in 1982, made three All-Star appearances, and hit his 500th career home run as an Angel in 1984.

75. Cynthia Cooper. A product of South Central Los Angeles, Cooper played alongside Cheryl Miller and helped lead USC to back-to-back championships in 1983 and 1984. She won a gold medal in 1988 and was the WNBA's first MVP in 1997 and again in 1998. She also led the Houston Comets to four consecutive WNBA championships.

74. Sinjin Smith. After a spectacular college career at UCLA that ended with two National Championships, Smith put beach volleyball on the map by competing in more beach volleyball tournaments than any other player in the history of the sport. Plus, he looked pretty hard when he was on *Magnum P.I.*

73. Gary Beban. UCLA's only Heisman Trophy winner (1967), Beban had many memorable games, including the Bruins' shocking upset over top-ranked Michigan State in the 1966 Rose Bowl. He also performed heroically with 301 yards passing in a 21–20 loss to O.J. Simpson's USC team—a performance that resulted in a loss, but clinched college football's greatest individual honor.

72. Mark McGwire. A teammate of Randy Johnson's at USC, McGwire set a major league record with 49 home runs as a rookie in 1987. He also became the first major leaguer to hit 70 home runs in a season in 1998. He retired with 583 home runs and 11 All-Star appearances.

71. Carson Palmer. The Pac-10 leader in career passing yards (11,621), total offense (11,818), and touchdown passes in a single season (33), Palmer holds every significant career passing record in USC history. He was the first USC quarterback to win the Heisman trophy (2002).

70. Walt Hazzard. Before Hazzard arrived at UCLA, John Wooden had never won a National Championship. That changed in 1964 when Hazzard earned All-American honors while guiding UCLA to a perfect 30–0 season. Hazzard was the MOP of the tournament, and earned an Olympic gold medal later that year.

69. Kirk Gibson. Gibson was responsible for the most memorable single moment in Los Angles sports history when his game winning pinch-hit home run cleared the right field wall in Game 1 of the 1988 World Series. Gibson also earned regular season MVP honors that year.

68. Jackie Slater. He played in more games than any other offensive lineman in NFL history during a 20-year run with the Rams, 19 of which were in L.A. A first-ballot Hall of Famer, Slater played in seven Pro Bowls and led Eric Dickerson to a record 2,105-yard season in 1984.

67. Howie Long. One of the most versatile defensive lineman in NFL history, Long spent 12 seasons with the Los Angeles Raiders, earning eight Pro Bowl selections and winning a Super Bowl on his way to induction into the Pro Football Hall of Fame. After his on-field career, Long won an Emmy Award for his work as a football analyst.

66. Reggie Miller. Miller emerged from his sister's shadow to become one of the leading scorers in UCLA history. He won the 1985 NIT MVP and went on to great success with the Indiana Pacers, connecting on more 3-pointers than any player in league history.

65. Bill Sharman. USC's first basketball All-American, Sharman became one of the best shooters of his generation while helping the Boston Celtics to four NBA titles. He later coached the Lakers to their first NBA championship in 1972. He is one of just three people to be in the Basketball Hall of Fame as both a coach and a player.

64. Jack Youngblood. Youngblood was second all-time in sacks (unofficially) when he retired from the Rams in 1984. Over the course of 14 seasons with the Rams, he played in seven Pro Bowls. Youngblood was one of the toughest players to ever hit the field, playing in the 1980 Super Bowl with a broken leg.

63. Tracy Austin. Injuries cut short a career that could have paralleled the greatest in tennis history. Austin, out of Palos Verdes, beat Chris Evert to win the 1979 U.S. Open at age 16 and then two years later defeated Martina Navratilova for a second U.S. Open title. To this day, Austin is still the youngest ever U.S. Open champion.

62. Anthony Davis. Davis is best known as "The Notre Dame Killer" after scoring 11 touchdowns in three games against the Fighting Irish. His second half kickoff return for a touchdown in 1974, keyed the Trojans' infamous 55-point run in just 17 minutes against Notre Dame.

61. Marques Johnson. Johnson helped lead UCLA to the 1975 National Championship, and was the first winner of the John Wooden Award in 1977. Johnson would go on to play in four All-Star Games over an 11-year NBA career that included a stint with the Los Angeles Clippers.

60. Bob Seagren. The 1968 gold medalist in the pole vault was a product of USC. He went on to even greater recognition by winning the inaugural "Superstars Competition" in 1973 and the "World Superstars" competition in 1977.

59. Elroy "Crazy Legs" Hirsch. Hirsch was one of the first superstar wide receivers in NFL history, leading the Rams to the 1951 NFL Championship. He posted a record 1,495 yards receiving and 17 touchdowns in just 12 games that season. Hirsch was elected to the Pro Football Hall of Fame in 1968.

58. Evelyn Ashford. A member of five Olympic teams following a stellar college career at UCLA, Ashford is one of only four women to have won four gold medals in track and field. She won the 100-meters in 1984 and took silver in 1988.

57. Charles White. The all-time leading rusher in USC history, White won the 1979 Heisman, two Rose Bowl MVP awards, and went on to lead the NFL in rushing in 1987 as a member of the Los Angeles Rams.

56. Bobby Grich. The first inductee into the Angels Hall of Fame, Grich led the Halos to three division titles in 10 seasons with the club. He led the AL in home runs and slugging percentage in 1981. One of the most underrated second basemen of all time.

55. Marcel Dionne. Not arguably, but *the* most underrated player in NHL history, Dionne centered the Kings' Triple Crown Line. He tallied more than 130 points in three consecutive seasons (1979–1981) and ranks fifth in career points and fourth in career goals among all NHL players. He tops all Kings in career points.

54. Frank Gifford. The NFL's first "Golden Boy," Gifford was a converted defensive back at USC before an All-American senior season as a running back put him in the national spotlight. Gifford went on to a Hall of Fame career with the New York Giants, and infamy on *Monday Night Football*.

53. Mike Piazza. Arguably the greatest hitting catcher of all time, Piazza was the National League Rookie of the Year in 1993. He set a record for catchers with a .362 batting average in 1997 and his career numbers are unrivaled for backstops with 427 home runs and a .308 average. The Dodgers still haven't recovered from his trade to Florida in 1998.

52. Jamaal Wilkes. Teamed with Bill Walton to lead UCLA to two National Championships as a two-time All-American. In the NBA, Wilkes won a title with Golden State (1975) prior to his arrival in Los Angeles, where he won three more with the Lakers (1980, 1982, 1985).

51. Kenny Easley. One of only two three-time All-Americans in UCLA history, Easley went on to a stellar seven-year NFL career with the Seattle Seahawks. He was named the NFL's Defensive Player of the Year in 1984, but his career was cut short due to kidney problems.

50. Vladimir Guerrero. One of only two Angels to win an MVP award, Guerrero led the Angels to four division titles in his five years with the team. He averaged 31 home runs and 110 RBIs per season.

49. Lisa Leslie. A true Los Angeles star, Leslie spent her college years at USC and her WNBA career with the Sparks. She is the all-time leading scorer in WNBA history, and the winner of four Olympic gold medals, the last coming one year after the birth of her daughter.

48. Randy Johnson. Perhaps the most feared Left-Handed pitcher of all time. Johnson had a stellar career at USC before becoming a 5-time Cy Young award winner (4 consecutive from 1999-2002). Johnson is second to only Nolan Ryan on the All-Time strikeout list.

47. Mike Garrett. USC's first Heisman Trophy winner. Garrett led the nation in rushing in 1965 and set an all-time colligate record with 3,221 yards in his career. Later became the first NFL running back to have a 1,000-yard season with two separate teams (Chiefs and Chargers).

46. Gail Goodrich. Led UCLA to two National Championships. His 42-point performance in the 1965 NCAA title game set a record for most points by an individual player. He would later be the Lakers leading scorer on their 1972 title team.

45. Troy Aikman. After transferring to UCLA from Oklahoma, Aikman finished third in the 1988 Heisman voting and went on to lead the Dallas Cowboys to three Super Bowl titles and earn a spot in the Pro Football Hall of Fame.

44. Bob Waterfield. The first pro sports super-star in Los Angeles history. After his college career at UCLA while leading the Bruins to their first ever Rose Bowl appearance, Waterfield returned when the Rams moved to Los Angeles from Cleveland in 1949. Waterfield was the NFL's most complete player as a quarterback, safety and kicker. He led the Rams to their only NFL Championship in 1951.

43. Steve Garvey. Garvey helped the Dodgers win four National League pennants, won the MVP in 1974, and set a National League record for 1,207 consecutive games. One of only two players to be voted a starter in the All-Star Game as a write-in candidate.

42. Florence Griffith-Joyner. Her performance at the 1988 Olympic Games is still in the record books. That year she set world records in both the 100 and 200 meters, the 100 meter record still stands.

41. Ronnie Lott. One of the most devastating hitters in football history. This 10-time Pro-Bowler first earned notice during his all American career at USC. Lott would go on to win four Super Bowl rings as a member of the San Francisco 49ers, and as a member of the Los Angeles Raiders would put together an All-Pro season in 1990

40. James Worthy. One of the greatest clutch players in NBA history, Worthy's 36-point, 16-rebound, 10-assist performance in Game 7 of the 1988 NBA Finals earned him the Finals MVP. Worthy is a member of the Basketball Hall of Fame.

39. Jimmy Connors. Played just one season at UCLA and won the NCAA Championship. Would go on to win seven Grand Slam titles, and became the only player to win the U.S. Open on three different surfaces (grass, clay, hard court).

38. Anthony Muñoz. Perhaps the greatest offensive tackle in pro football history. Injuries marred his All-American career at USC, but he would go on to be an 11-time Pro-Bowler in 13 seasons with the Cincinnati Bengals.

37. Fernando Valenzuela. The only pitcher ever to win Rookie of the Year and Cy Young honors in the same season. "Fernandomania" in 1981 culminated with the Dodgers' first world championship in 16 years. He played in six All-Star Games and threw a no-hitter in 1990.

36. Jean Sebastien Giguere. "Giggy" led the Ducks to not only their first Stanley Cup championship, but the first to be won by a team that played on the West coast. Prior to the 2007 title, Giguere was awarded the Conn Smythe playing for the losing Ducks in the 2003 Stanley Cup Finals, only the fifth player in Stanley Cup history to win the award while losing the championship.

35. Ann Meyers. Meyers was the first four-time All-American in women's basketball history. She led UCLA to the National Championship in 1978 and became the first woman ever to sign an NBA contract.

34. Karch Kiraly. Arguably the greatest volleyball player of all time, he is the only player to win gold medals in both indoor and outdoor volleyball. He was a four-time All-American at UCLA, as the Bruins won three national championships during his four seasons.

33. Reggie Bush. While at USC, the winner of the 2005 Heisman electrified the college football world. Bush led the nation with 2,011 all-purpose yards that season and helped USC to the National Championship game, where they came up just short of a third national title. In his three seasons at USC the Trojans lost just two games.

32. Pancho Gonzales. In the pre-open era (pre-1968) Pancho dominated the world of professional tennis. He was ranked No. 1 for eight consecutive years, and legend has it he got his start on public courts near Exposition Park using a 51-cent racket.

31. Maury Wills. As a 27-year-old rookie, he helped the Dodgers win the 1959 World Series, and just three years later he was named the league MVP. Wills was the first player ever to steal more than 100 bases in a single season.

30. Cheryl Miller. After a dominating high school basketball career at Riverside Poly, where she scored 105 points in one game, Miller became a four-time All-American at USC, wining back-to-back national championships in 1983 and 1984. While injuries prevented her from having a professional career, she is often cited as the all-time greatest female basketball player, and perhaps the best in her own family.

29. Luc Robataille. "Lucky" is the all time leader in career points (1395) and goals (668) for an NHL left winger, his 577 goals with the Kings is a franchise record. Despite having been jettisoned two separate times, Luc will forever be considered the face of the Los Angeles Kings. His rookie season Luc put up 45 goals and 84 points, making him the Kings' only Calder Trophy winner in franchise history.

28. Bo Jackson. His run with the Los Angeles Raiders included just parts of four seasons, but his impact was unforgettable. His Monday night performance in Seattle against the Seahawks, with 221 yards, including a 91-yard touchdown run (exited the tunnel), will forever raise the question "What if?"

27. Rafer Johnson. One of the greatest decathletes of all time, Johnson defeated fellow Bruin C.K. Yang to win the 1960 Olympic gold in Rome. He also became a pioneer for the Special Olympics.

26. Merlin Olsen. During his 15 years with the L.A. Rams, he played in a record 14 Pro Bowls. Teamed with fellow Hall of Famer Deacon Jones as the most devastating defensive line tandem in NFL history.

25. Tom Seaver. After playing his college ball at USC, he went on to become one of baseball's most successful pitchers with 311 career wins, and three Cy Young awards. Led the Amazin' Mets to their improbable World Series run in 1969.

24. Matt Leinart. Arguably the greatest college football quarterback of all time, Leinart led the Trojans to 34 consecutive victories, two National Championships, and won the 2004 Heisman.

23. Oscar De La Hoya. Announced his arrival on the boxing scene by winning gold at the 1992 Summer Olympics. De La Hoya has won world titles in six different weight classes. In his post fight career De La Hoya has not only become a successful promoter, but a fixture in the Los Angeles business community.

22. Don Drysdale. Attended Van Nuys High School and teamed with Sandy Koufax to form the most devastating pitching duo of the 1960s. Won the 1962 Cy Young award, led the league in strikeouts three seasons, and set all-time records with six straight shutouts and 58.2 consecutive scoreless innings.

21. Shaquille O'Neal. In delivering the Lakers three NBA championships during the 2000s, Shaq won all three NBA Finals MVPs with some staggering numbers: He averaged 30 points and 15 rebounds per game. Over his eight seasons with the Lakers, Shaq led the NBA in field goal percentage six times and was named the league's MVP in 2000. The only thing keeping his this far down on the list was his unceremonious departure.

20. Wilt Chamberlain. In his five years with the Lakers Wilt continued the dominance he was known for throughout his unprecedented NBA career. In 1972 Chamberlain earned the NBA Finals MVP honors in leading the Lakers to their first ever championship. In his 80 career playoff games with the Lakers Wilt would average 22.3 rebounds per game, and countless blocked shots, a statistic that wasn't kept as an official statistic. In his final season he set the record that still stands for best field goal percentage over the course of a regular season, converting 72.7 percent of his shot attempts.

19. Venus Williams. Venus would precede her younger sister on the world stage making a run at the 1997 US Open title only to lose in the final. Since then she has won seven Grand Slam titles, five of them at Wimbledon, including back-to-back championships in 2007 and 2008.

18. Serena Williams. There is the Serena Slam, where she won all four Grand Slam tournaments consecutively, but not in the same calendar year. She became just the fourth women's player in the open area to win the four consecutive grand slam tournaments. Her 2008 U.S. Open victory gave her nine career titles and also signaled her comeback as the world's best player.

17. Eric Dickerson. Still the single-season rushing leader in NFL history, his 2,105 yards in 1984 has been approached but never surpassed. The only thing that prevented him from retiring as the NFL's all time leading rusher was that ill-fated trade on Halloween night 1987. Sent to the Indianapolis Colts for eight players, Dickerson joined a brutal Colts team that couldn't best take advantage of his talents, while the Rams never recovered either, moving to St. Louis in 1995.

16. Elgin Baylor. When the Lakers moved from Minnesota to Los Angeles in 1960, Elgin Baylor averaged 34.8, 38.3 and 34.0 points per game during the team's first three years in Los Angeles. In fact, that first season in Los Angeles, he also averaged 20 rebounds per game and five assists. Baylor was Dr. J, before Dr. J. His hang time was the stuff campfire stories were made of. While he never won a championship—he retired nine games into the 1972 season—he's still considered one of the greatest to have ever played the game.

15. Jackie Joyner-Kersee. Arguably the greatest female athlete of all time spent her college years at UCLA where she was a stand out basketball player having been voted one of the 15 best in school history. She won the Heptathlon in consecutive Olympics (1988 and 1992) after winning the silver in 1984. In 1988 along with the heptathlon she won gold in the long jump. *Sports Illustrated* voted Joyner-Kersee the greatest female athlete of all time ahead of Babe Didrikson.

14. Deacon Jones. The man that defined the term "sack" in pro football, as in literally created the name for tackling the quarterback in the backfield. The Secretary of Defense during his 11 years with the Rams had an unofficial total of 180 sacks, including three years of more than 20 at a time when they played just 14 games. He was the most feared defensive player by quarterbacks of all-time.

13. Kobe Bryant. Perhaps the most polarizing sports figure in L.A. sports history. As talented a player that's ever laced 'em up. He scored 81 points in a game against the Toronto Raptors, won the NBA regular season MVP in 2008 and two consecutive scoring titles. A 10-time NBA All-Star who has won three championships and compiled staggering playoff statistics overshadowed by the dominance of Shaquille O'Neal. By the end of his career, it's likely he could be at the top of this list.

12. Nolan Ryan. When the Angels acquired Nolan Ryan from the New York Mets, nobody had the slightest idea how dominant he would become. In 1973 with the Halos, he set a still record, 383 strikeouts (with a DH, by the way) and threw two no hitters in the same season. All told, Ryan struck out 5,714 batters in an unprecedented 27-year major league career (no other player has played as long) with a staggering seven no-hitters, records that will never be touched.

11. Bill Walton. Injuries marred Walton taking his rightful place alongside the greatest centers in the history of basketball. That being said, there's no denying what he did in college. The man won his first 73 games played, and won consecutive National Championships. He was a three-time college player of the year, and a two-time Final Four MOP. His 21–22, 44-point game in the 1973 championship against Memphis State will likely stand the test of time as the best tournament performance ever.

10. O.J. Simpson. While reading the name may make one squeamish, there's no denying what he accomplished on the field of play. He is arguably the greatest running back in the history of college football. In two years at USC he rushed for 3,423 yards in just 21 collegiate games. He won a National Championship, won one Heisman and came close to winning a second. His future success in the NFL cemented his place in football lore.

9. Jerry West. Mr. Los Angeles Lakers. As a player, West is the only player from a losing team to win the NBA Finals MVP. Years of frustration ended when he brought the L.A. Lakers their first title in 1972. After his retirement, he headed to the front office and became the architect of the "Showtime Lakers" (five titles) and the Shaq-Kobe Lakers (three titles).

8. Marcus Allen. Allen accomplished as much as any player possibly could. While attending USC he won the Heisman, became the first colligate player to rush for 2,000 yards in a single season, and led his team to a National Championship. After graduating, he became a Super Bowl MVP, a regular season MVP after leading the NFL in rushing in 1985, and he is a member of both the College and Pro Football Halls of Fame.

7. Wayne Gretzky. Although he never brought a Stanley Cup to Los Angeles, he literally brought hockey to Los Angeles 21 years after it officially arrived in the Expansion of 1967. He re-wrote the NHL's record book, including career statistics for goals and points, which were realized while he was a King.

6. Pete Sampras. Out of Rolling Hills, Sampras has won more Grand Slam titles (14) than any player in history. His first title made him the youngest ever U.S. Open Champion at age 19. He won seven Wimbledons in eight years, and retired with a victory in his final match, the 2002 U.S. Open.

5. Sandy Koufax. His time in the spotlight was brief, but his dominance was unmatched in the history of baseball. Willie Stargell put it best when he said, "Trying to hit Koufax's curve ball was like trying to eat soup with a fork." Winner of three Cy Young awards, led the league in ERA five consecutive years, threw a no-hitter in four consecutive years, and helped the Dodgers to four World Series titles (3 in L.A.). He retired at age 30.

4. Jackie Robinson. Before he became the man who broke the color barrier in professional sports, Jackie Robinson was perhaps the greatest all-around athlete in Southern California history. While at UCLA and Pasadena City College he was a four-sport star, and his weakest sport was baseball. That all changed with his 10 years of service with the Brooklyn Dodgers. He is the only player to have his number retired by an entire league.

3. Tiger Woods. He was born and raised in Cypress, CA. By age 30, he was already the greatest to have ever played his sport. Not only has he won 14 majors—and counting—through 2008, but he also revolutionized golf. He also very well could be the most recognizable athlete in the world. The only thing that keeps him from the top of our list, is his inability to win the L.A. Open.

2. Earvin "Magic" Johnson. The most important piece of the "Showtime Lakers," Magic brought an entertaining style to sports in the entertainment capital of the world. He would be elected mayor of Los Angeles if he ran today, more than a decade after having played his last game with the Lakers. The numbers: Three NBA MVPs, three Finals MVPs, two All-Star MVPs, and five NBA titles. And all of this in a career that was cut short.

1. Kareem Abdul-Jabbar. The numbers do it more justice and any words we could attach: Three National Championships at UCLA and a three-time Final Four MOP. During his tenure with the Lakers, he won five NBA titles, earned three NBA regular season MVP awards, and one Finals MVP award.

Index